Brazil's Living Museum

Brazil's Living Museum

Race, Reform, and Tradition in Bahia

ANADELIA A. ROMO

THE UNIVERSITY OF NORTH CAROLINA PRESS • CHAPEL HILL

© 2010 THE UNIVERSITY OF NORTH CAROLINA PRESS

All rights reserved / Manufactured in the United States of America

Set in Arnhem and TheSans

The paper in this book meets the guidelines for permanence and durability of the Committee on Production Guidelines for Book Longevity of the Council on Library Resources.

The University of North Carolina Press has been a member of the Green Press Initiative since 2003.

Library of Congress Cataloging-in-Publication Data

Romo, Anadelia A.

 Brazil's living museum : race, reform, and tradition in Bahia / Anadelia A. Romo.

 p. cm.

 Includes bibliographical references and index.

 ISBN 978-0-8078-3382-7 (cloth : alk. paper)
 ISBN 978-0-8078-7115-7 (pbk. : alk. paper)

 1. Bahia (Brazil : State)—History. 2. Bahia (Brazil : State)—Race relations. 3. Blacks—Brazil—Bahia (State)—Government relations. 4. Blacks—Race identity—Brazil—Bahia (State)—History. 5. Bahia (Brazil : State)—Civilization—African influences. 6. Politics and culture—Brazil—Bahia (State)—History. I. Title.

 F2551.R65 2010

 981'.42—dc22   2009039479

cloth   14 13 12 11 10   5 4 3 2 1
paper   14 13 12 11 10   5 4 3 2 1

for Tim

CONTENTS

ACKNOWLEDGMENTS

After many years of work on this manuscript, it is a pleasure to finally be able to acknowledge, in print, the many colleagues and friends who have helped along the way. For their valuable comments and careful readings, I thank many generous souls, including Patrick Barr-Melej, Dain Borges, John Coatsworth, João José Reis, Julia Rodriguez, and John Womack. Carrie Endries, Carlos Romo, Allison Tirres, and Teresa Van Hoy were especially diligent in providing feedback on multiple drafts. A special thanks also goes to Jane Mangan, who read the entire manuscript at an early point and provided critical support and advice throughout the project.

In addition to these colleagues at various institutions, I have been remarkably lucky to land in a most supportive and collegial department, where many have provided comments on the work at various stages. Mary Brennan, Lynn Denton, Paul Hart, Ken Margerison, Jimmy McWilliams, Margaret Menninger, Angela Murphy, and Dwight Watson all helped improve the manuscript and offered generous and unflagging support more generally. At Texas State I have also been the recipient of two Research Enhancement Grants that have allowed me the time and resources for research. I thank the History Department, in addition, for course releases that made the final work on this project possible. At the University of North Carolina Press, Elaine Maisner has been a patient advocate. I thank her for her hard work and early support of this manuscript. Anonymous reviewers provided careful readings and helpful comments that improved the work as a whole. Meticulous copyediting by Alex Martin further enhanced the text. A portion of chapter 2 was published previously in "Rethinking Race and Culture in Brazil's First Afro-Brazilian Congress of 1934," *Journal of Latin American Studies* 39, no. 1 (2007): 31–54, and a section of chapter 3 has been published recently in "O que é que a Bahia representa? O Museu do Estado da Bahia e as disputas em torno da definição da cultura baiana," *Afro-Ásia* (2010). I am grateful to both for granting permission to reprint the material here.

I have also received crucial assistance on various technical aspects of the book. C. Scott Walker rapidly and expertly created the map of Brazil for this work. Teri Andrews used her graphic design skills to improve the image of *Bahia tradicional e moderna* included here. Special acknowledgment goes to Michelle R. Williams in the Interlibrary Loan department at Texas State University. She has borne my countless loan requests with speedy efficiency and a constant smile, and my research would not have been possible without her. I also thank the staff at the Nettie Lee Benson Library (especially Jorge), for their general goodwill and their assistance in letting me use their collection over the last few years.

Critical guidance has come from librarians and archivists across the United States and Brazil. While they are too numerous to list here individually, I should make special mention of Janet Olson at the Melville J. Herskovits Collection and the archivists at the Museu Nacional and CPDOC who have always been particularly helpful. I am also grateful to the State Archive of Bahia for letting me look at some of their collections while they were still being cataloged. Bibliographer Peter Johnson had nothing to do with this project, but his wit and his rigorous expectations helped me decide to study Latin America to begin with.

In Brazil, scholars Olívia Maria Gomes da Cunha and Gilberto Hochman have been most generous with their time in showing a foreign scholar around Rio and providing critical archival advice. I am most indebted, however, to João José Reis for first introducing me to Brazilian history in a course I took with him as an undergraduate. At the end of the semester he wrote his contact information on the chalkboard and invited us all to call him if we were ever in Bahia. I think I must be one of the few who took him up on that offer. I owe much thanks to his patient and generous guidance during my various trips to Bahia and also to his careful reading of a portion of this manuscript. In Bahia, my research was made much more enjoyable by my friendships with two remarkable women, Carla Cruz and Cicinha Moreira. Both opened up their homes to me and made me sorry to live so very far away. My time there would not have been the same without their warmth, generosity, and humor. I thank also Licia do Prado Valladares, who took the time to talk with me about her father, José do Prado Valladares; I appreciate her openness and her insights.

Finally, I am very grateful to my friends who have supported me throughout this process and celebrated each deadline along with me (even as they thought there couldn't possibly be another one). More important, they have helped me forget about the book and simply enjoy life. My long-time friends are now scattered, but their ability to make me laugh always makes them seem close. Special thanks go to Carrie Endries, Justine Heilner, Magda Hinojosa, Jessica McCannon, Susan McDonough, and Stephanie Saulmon for always staying in touch. Locally, Kelly Lyons, Teresa Van Hoy, Melissa Zellers, and the wider Trinity crew has kept me happy and well fed. My extended family has also played a critical role in encouraging this work and in supporting me more generally. I thank my parents Ricardo and Harriett Romo, my brother, Carlos, and his wife, Lynsey, for their constant encouragement; Carlos took a special interest in this work for which I am grateful. The extended O'Sullivan clan has been understanding of this project but, more important, has accepted me as one of their own. Thank you to Rose and Michael, Jennifer, Michelle, Pamela, and Courtney. Most central in this effort, and in all of my efforts for the past sixteen years, has been my soulmate, Timothy O'Sullivan. Tim has read and edited the entire manuscript, but he has also taken on a significant burden in taking care of the details of our daily lives throughout this process. This book would have been very difficult without his support; my life would seem empty without it.

Brazil's Living Museum

North Atlantic Ocean

Boa Vista

RORAIMA

AMAPÁ
Macapá

Manaus

Belém

AMAZONAS

PARÁ

São Luís
MARANHÃO

Fortaleza

CEARÁ

Teresina

RIO GRANDE
DO NORTE

Natal

ACRE

Rio Branco

Porto Velho

PIAUÍ

João Pessoa

PARAÍBA

RONDÔNIA

TOCANTINS

PERNAMBUCO

Recife

MATO GROSSO

Palmas

ALAGOAS

SERGIPE

Maceió

BAHIA

Aracaju

Cuiabá

GOIÁS

Salvador

Brasília

DISTRITO
FEDERAL

Goiânia

MINAS GERAIS

MATO GROSSO
DO SUL

Belo Horizonte

ESPÍRITO
SANTO

Campo
Grande

SÃO PAULO

Vitória

RIO DE JANEIRO

South
Pacific
Ocean

PARANÁ

São Paulo

Rio de Janeiro

Curitiba

SANTA CATARINA

Florianópolis

South Atlantic Ocean

RIO GRANDE
DO SUL

Porto Alegre

500

Miles

Brazil

Between Africa and Athens: Bahia's Search for Identity

The northeastern state of Bahia occupies a critical position in Brazil's imagination and in its history. Alternately romanticized and denigrated, it has served both as a cradle of Brazilian national identity and as an embarrassing symbol of Brazil's backwardness. More recently, Bahia has played a central role in representing Brazil's African roots, both for Brazilians and for the millions of tourists who travel to Salvador, the state capital. It has become universally accepted that Afro-Bahians—whose ancestors were brought forcibly with the Atlantic slave trade, and who still today represent the vast majority of the population—have maintained a cultural autonomy that has guarded their traditions from the modernizing tendencies of Brazil's South. It is tribute to the power of this vision, and to the vibrancy of Afro-Bahian culture itself, that this latest role for Bahia now seems natural. Yet to see Bahia as inherently, essentially rooted in Africa ignores a creative and important process of cultural crafting that has been at work over the course of the twentieth century. To see Bahia as a cultural preserve is to see it as static, whereas Bahian culture has been anything but.

Bahia's story in many ways parallels that of Brazil, a nation that during the twentieth century reinvented its culture and came to embrace African heritage as central to its national identity, whether in the rhythms of samba or in the very essence of its cuisine. While the general outline of this story may be clear, however, it is still riddled with ambiguities, and much of its historical evolution is still muddy.[1] This is even more true for Bahia, which witnessed the most dramatic incarnation of this cultural transformation. But because Bahia hosts the greatest black majority of any state in Brazil, many have viewed the process there as an inevitable outcome. Yet demography is not destiny; it still remains unclear how and when Bahia came to reinvent itself in the midst of a turbulent century that overturned much of the accepted knowledge about race, culture, and the nature of African heritage. This book gives Brazil's larger question of national identity a regional answer, paying close attention to how Bahia has struggled to redefine itself over the twentieth century. As I show, such a transformation was in no way natural or inevitable; rather, it resulted from sustained, and often controversial, efforts.

These efforts took place in a rapidly changing landscape of racial ideology. Though race in Bahia was discussed at the beginning of the twentieth century in the realm of medicine, the discourse moved by the 1930s to the social sciences and, finally, by the 1950s, to anthropology. This book traces ideas of race across the disciplines and thus follows debates about race where and when they proved most pivotal. Bahia proves a particularly interesting setting to examine racial ideology, as Afro-Bahians have played a powerful role in shaping these debates. Leaders in the Afro-Brazilian religion of Candomblé were active in crafting a cultural identity centered on Africa, for example, as a rich scholarly literature attests.[2] As I show further, these same leaders transformed Bahia's Afro-Brazilian Congress of 1937, where they took a dominant position in driving the course of Bahia's social sciences.

Yet much of Bahia's black community is not represented in the written record. Literacy rates in the state hovered at 20 percent in 1872 and increased only marginally to 27 percent in the 1950 census; given recent gaps between black and white literacy of almost 20 percent, we can only assume that such racial divides existed earlier as well.[3] Black Bahians have thus been even less able than other residents of the state to leave written accounts of their history. Widespread illiteracy helps explain why a black press never developed in Bahia as it did in other parts of Brazil and why we have limited sources to tell us how the wider black community thought about race. A larger history of black Bahia in the early twentieth century remains to be written and will require new types of sources.[4]

Even with such gaps in the historical record, it is clear that the cultural invention of Bahia has been powerfully shaped by the actions of the Afro-Bahian community. In addition, however, we must also posit a changing attitude toward race and Afro-Bahian culture on the side of policy makers and intellectuals who moved in political circles. This is particularly relevant given the overwhelming exclusion of blacks from formal political power.[5] This study therefore looks at Afro-Bahian cultural resistance, but it also examines how local and visiting intellectuals have shaped the understanding of race in various ways. Some of these intellectuals are Afro-Brazilian; many are not. By looking at race from this perspective in Bahia we can turn our attention to arenas that have much to tell us about racial ideology, such as medical discourse, or Bahia's representation of its past, but that have not received critical historical attention. A survey of these intellectual currents deepens our understanding of what race meant in Bahia. In the process, it demonstrates how Afro-Brazilian culture became a central battleground in a larger struggle for the renewal and revalorization of Bahia itself.

Bahia: From the Center to the Margins and Back Again

Bahia's status within Brazil has suffered dramatic shifts over time: its early colonial prestige collapsed in the eighteenth century and only began to recover in the last half of the twentieth. Bahia began by playing an instrumental role in the birth of Brazil; Pedro Alvarez Cabral's "discovery" took place on its southern coast in 1500, and its port city, Salvador da Bahia, became the colony's first capital. Salvador was not Brazil's oldest city, but it undeniably became the most important during the colony's first two centuries. As the Portuguese began to import African slaves to support the growing sugar industry, Salvador became the port of entry for a steady stream of forced labor. Sugar plantations grew to surround the city and financed the development of an immensely profitable export market as well as a wealthy slaving class.

The state's economic circumstances took a sharp turn for the worse, however, when sugar production increased in the Caribbean, and world sugar prices fell as a result. The decline of Bahia's fortunes also reduced its political importance, culminating in the relocation of the colonial capital to Rio de Janeiro in 1763. After Brazil's independence from Portugal, the imperial regime (1822–89) continued to dole out prestigious political appointments to Bahians, but economic fortunes declined rapidly. Bahia would turn increasingly to exports of tobacco, hides, and later cacao, but its economy failed to keep up with the growth of the South. By the late nineteenth century the former capital had become a backwater.[6]

Racial composition played a powerful role in the assessment of Bahia as backward, as did ideas of racial inferiority. Brazilian slavery resulted in the forced import of more than 4 million Africans. Bahia's economy incorporated many of these arrivals; in 1823 it had 20 percent of Brazil's total slave population, the largest share of any province in the country. This concentration helped make Bahia an epicenter of slave rebellion in the early 1800s, including Salvador's Muslim slave uprising of 1835. That proportion declined during the 1800s as slaves were resold to the expanding coffee industries of southern Brazil.[7] Yet even this exodus did little to change Bahia's racial makeup after almost four centuries of slavery. In 1872, according to that year's census, Bahia was 24 percent *branco* (white), 46 percent *preto* (black), 27 percent *pardo* (brown), and 4 percent *caboclo* (of both indigenous and white heritage). Only two other provinces—Amazonas and Piauí—had a lower percentage of whites, and Bahia early established its reputation, still held today, as the blackest province (and, since 1889, state) of Brazil.[8]

The final abolition of slavery in 1888 and the declaration of a new republic in 1889 promised to modernize Brazil's economy and political system.[9] Yet modernization combined with the legacy of Brazil's slaving past brought new worries at the turn of the century. Dire predictions from racial science sparked anxiety about Brazil's large population of blacks, and its extensive levels of *mestiçagem*, or racial mixing.[10] Southern Brazil led the way in sponsoring European immigrants during Brazil's First Republic (1889–1930), anxious to flood the labor market and push former slaves aside in a newly industrializing economy.[11] Bahia lost out in this drive for European whitening: its sputtering economy was not dynamic enough to attract significant numbers of immigrants, or to finance their arrival. Ultimately Bahia proved too poor, too black, and too traditional to compete for national power. Federal leaders gradually shunted Bahia's squabbling oligarchy aside for an informal governing pact between the cattle elite of Minas Gerais and the coffee planters of São Paulo.[12]

Bahia's fallen standing, which humiliated some members of the local elite, also energized efforts to deny the decline. In 1901 Bahia's literary journal *A Nova Cruzada* (The new crusade) acknowledged the state's diminished status but also declared its goal of ensuring that "the title of Athens, the illustrious city of Demosthenes, returns to [the city of] Bahia."[13] Such comparisons to classical rather than tropical civilizations were central to elite Bahians' vision of their state, and Greek and Roman first names were common calling cards of the upper class.[14] The largely white ruling class preferred not to acknowledge Bahia's black majority and instead imagined itself in a genteel white world of fantasy. By the turn of the century, however, despite their best efforts, Bahia had acquired a title far different from the one elite Bahians envisioned. The state became popularly known as "a mulata velha" ("Old Mammy"),[15] reflecting a national conception of Bahia as overwhelmingly nonwhite and, no less significant, as aging and tradition-bound.

During the Vargas era (1930–45), the federal government made valiant efforts to revitalize Bahia, but it ultimately failed to eliminate regional inequalities. Getúlio Vargas, installed by a coup in 1930 as Brazil's president, orchestrated national politics throughout this period with various degrees of authoritarian assistance, but Bahia remained on the national margins. Despite the state's position as economically and politically marginal, however, various actors began at this point to promote an image of Bahia as central to Brazilian culture. Surprisingly, in view of the modern ideal of progress and the racial determinism that shaped much of Brazil in the early twentieth century, promoters of Bahia came to exploit its claim to tradition and especially to an authentic Afro-Brazilian cultural tradition. Stagnation was rewritten as preservation: Bahia had preserved all that was valuable of Brazil's past. Such ideals gained particular resonance as the Vargas era sought to promote a rediscovery and celebration of a Brazilian national essence, or *brasilidade*. Dreams of European whitening began to fade, and Brazilians instead began to talk of their future in terms of a racial democracy. Brazil, in this vision, owed its strength to its diverse racial heritage, its *mestiçagem*, and its cultivation of exceptional levels of racial harmony, forces surely in evidence in Bahia.[16]

The restoration of democracy in 1945 brought a peak of interest in Bahia's traditions, interest that clashed in many ways with the renewed modernizing efforts of the next decades. Although Bahia began to develop a booming petroleum and manufacturing center in the last half of the twentieth century, however, the state's image as an untouched historic preserve only gained momentum. With racial democracy now a national mantra, Bahia came to be seen as a guardian of national traditions long corroded in the more industrial regions of the South. These trends consolidated in the 1950s and intensified under Brazil's military dictatorship (1964–85) and Bahia's subsequent development of its tourism industry.

What is fascinating in this story is Bahia's remarkable creative energy in reinventing itself: it began its life at the political center of Portugal's largest colony, languished on Brazil's margins for more than two hundred years, and then successfully fashioned itself as the cultural heartland of the nation. In essence, as ideas of race changed, so did ideas of Bahia, but this tautology fails to account for the extent to which individuals in Bahia played a proactive, energetic, and creative role in changing ideas of race, and in promulgating particular visions of Afro-Brazilian culture. Ironically, the core elements of the originally derisive nickname, "a mulata velha," persisted: Bahia was still focused on the past and it was still not white. But attitudes changed over the course of the twentieth century so that the past and Afro-Brazilian culture began to represent not an obstacle but a treasure. This book addresses this transformation as Athens lost its claim of privilege over Africa. The twentieth century witnessed a refashioning of Bahia's identity, one that depended on creative new formulations of race and culture. Examining these efforts, and the debates they incited, is the heart of this work.

Cultural Struggles and Racial Inequalities

Much of this story was impelled by energetic actors in Bahia's capital. The port city of São Salvador da Bahia de Todos os Santos, most often known simply as Salvador, or Bahia, has long attracted and concentrated the state's political and intellectual power. In contrast, the arid *sertão*, or backland, that stretches beyond the sugar regions of the coast remains overwhelmingly rural and intellectually marginal to the state. The *sertão* erupts in Bahia's consciousness periodically with devastating droughts that flood migrants into the state capital. The most spectacular eruption, however, was the religious rebellion that shook the northern community of Canudos in 1897. This event prompted a largely sympathetic account of the rebels in the national epic by Euclides da Cunha, and some embarrassment for the era's coastal elite, who viewed the episode as a retrograde movement by a mixed and degenerate population.[17] Whenever possible, Bahia defined itself in terms of its capital, where aristocratic sugar clans and merchants regrouped by the end of slavery and where they continued to rule into the late twentieth century. This book thus looks primarily at the intellectual projects of urban Salvador, as it was here that the energy of the state and its ruling elite was most focused.

Salvador also was at the center of a long tradition of Afro-Brazilian cultural dynamism and resistance. Indeed, Bahia's cultural refashioning owes its most important debt to Afro-Brazilians themselves. Uprooted originally from their homelands across Africa, forced into labor, and enduring considerable cultural and physical repression, African slaves in Brazil carved out cultural autonomy for themselves against tremendous odds. Practices of drumming, capoeira (martial arts), and African-based religions such as Candomblé—widely denigrated and frequently repressed—represented resistance to the dehumanizing force of enslavement, as well as to the European white ideal that the elite wished to promote. Elites anxious about the rise of African themes in Bahia's carnival at the turn of the century complained to the local press that such displays threatened to "Africanize" the festivities and erode Bahia's "civilized" Athenian image. State authorities agreed: Bahian police declared the use of African costumes and drumming illegal for Bahian carnival beginning in 1905.[18] As historian Kim Butler and others have emphasized, these struggles were not simply to keep an original, African culture alive but also to reinvent or create traditions to keep a hybrid culture vivid and meaningful.[19] Such struggles can only be seen as a success, as Bahia today highlights its role in maintaining African cultural traditions and in developing new types of cultural expression that draw on an African ideal. As Bahian scholar Antônio Risério observes, Bahia's carnival, to cite only one instance of Bahia's contemporary cultural dynamic, has been "reafricanized."[20]

Today a visitor to Bahia cannot help but marvel at the stupendous success of this renewal. Bahia currently attracts millions of international and Brazilian tourists to a land portrayed as a living part of Brazil's past. The state's tourist board touts Bahia's claim as the "birthplace of Brazil" and the cradle of Brazilian traditions. Furthermore, capoeira and Candomblé, practices once earnestly repressed by Bahia's elite, are now promoted as cultural experiences to draw in visitors. The tourist board itself distributes lists of *terreiros*, or temples of Candomblé, where travelers looking for an authentic vision of Afro-Brazilian culture may observe the continued force of the African heritage in Bahia.[21] This sense of cultural inclusion and pride is a significant achievement for Bahia and sets the state apart from much of Brazil.

Yet visitors may also notice an alternate vision of Bahia that raises troubling questions. Much of Bahia's Afro-Brazilian population lives in poverty. A visit to a *terreiro* is a visible reminder of Afro-Brazilian resistance, but it also poignantly attests to the lack of infrastructure in some of Bahia's poorest (and blackest) neighborhoods. And if visitors look a little deeper, they will observe that Afro-Bahians, as a group, have not fared well with respect to basic social indicators. In part such indicators are the inevitable result of an impoverished Bahian treasury. But even Bahia's relative poverty fails to explain its social failures. While Afro-Bahians have increasingly become a powerful focus of Bahian cultural identity, they have not fared as well in the state system of public welfare.

One striking example of this discrepancy is literacy. The literacy rate for Bahia in 1991 was just 60 percent. Already lower than the average for Brazil, that figure conceals significant racial inequalities: while the overall literacy rate for those labeled as *branco* (white) was 69 percent, that number fell to 58 percent for *pardos* (browns) and 52 percent for *pretos* (blacks).[22] This gap between black and white literacy becomes even more disturbing when one considers Brazil's exclusive voting requirements: Brazil's modern political regime, beginning in 1889, barred illiterates from the vote until 1988. Thus Bahia's modern trajectory reveals a central dilemma: How did Afro-Brazilian culture become so valued while Afro-Brazilians themselves remain excluded from participation in public schools, and indeed, from Brazilian democracy itself?

As Edward Telles has thoughtfully proposed, the "enigma" of Brazilian race relations is how exclusivity may persist in some spheres but be absent in others.[23] Telles shows that while social interactions in Brazil may be shaped around notions of inclusiveness, economic indicators and other levels of welfare reveal significant racial exclusion. While Bahia takes pride in its cultural inclusion, I will demonstrate how the particular development of this ideal has often worked to limit economic and social reform. Though the heart of this book addresses changing conceptualizations of race, it also reveals how particular notions of culture and race influenced—and often halted—impetus for social change.

My study begins at the turn of the century with the most important arena for racial thinking in the era: the field of medicine. Bahia boasted one of only two medical schools in Brazil; since Brazil would not establish universities until 1934, these institutions provided the primary intellectual forum for debates about the nature of race. Indeed, medical research in Bahia posed some of the most important challenges to racial determinism in nineteenth-century Brazil.[24] Beginning in the 1860s doctors and researchers in Bahia, known as the Tropicalistas, insisted that Bahia's problems had their roots neither in climate nor in African heritage and therefore could be solved by larger social reforms addressing poverty and tropical disease. As I argue in chapter 1, the medical community split into two factions around the start of abolition; both claimed Tropicalista allegiances and both continued to insist on the need for reform. On the one side were the public health optimists, with a neo-Lamarckian view of heredity that emphasized the benefits that a healthy, sanitary environment might bring for all Bahians. On the other side, practitioners of the new discipline of legal medicine argued for more targeted reform, based especially on race. Strict views of racial inequality held by Raimundo Nina Rodrigues and others in this group privileged the role of heredity and saw it as central to Brazil's promise. A nuanced reading of Nina Rodrigues reveals, however, that his racial determinism was moderated by a surprising and often contradictory belief in the power of the surrounding environment. This allowed him to join public health reformers in advocating for modernization of Salvador's cityscape. As I argue, these reforms offered real promise, left unfulfilled, for improving basic welfare. Medical reformers of the turn of the century proved critical advocates for the city's poor, and thus critical supporters for many improvements that would have benefited the black majority.

In the 1930s the study of race moved from a matter of medical concern to a new topic of interest for Brazil's budding social sciences. Chapter 2 examines the evolution of racial thought in the 1930s and studies how intellectuals in the social sciences began to frame studies of race in terms of culture. Gilberto Freyre played a critical role in this transition, and the 1934 Afro-Brazilian congress he organized in Recife, the capital of the northeastern state of Pernambuco, gave the movement one of its most important statements. The congress marked a shift in racial thought, but scholars moved only hesitantly away from biological determinism: the new cultural framework retained many of the same hierarchies as its biological predecessor. This chapter then turns to the Second Afro-Brazilian Congress of 1937, this time organized by Afro-Brazilian intellectuals in Bahia. As I show, these two congresses reveal an intense struggle for legitimacy and power in the field of race. Though Freyre attempted to claim Recife as the locus for the budding field of Afro-Brazilian studies, Bahian intellectuals, and especially the young Afro-Brazilian ethnologist Edison Carneiro, argued that Bahia represented the true center of Afro-Brazilian culture. In making this bid for Bahian primacy the organizers claimed Nina Rodrigues as the earliest scholar of Afro-Brazilian culture and thus the founder of an authentic Bahian "school." This movement for Bahian authenticity provided a powerful rhetoric that began to portray Bahian racial identity not as a biological problem but as a cultural treasure. Furthermore, this chapter reveals the formative role played in the congress by leaders of Bahia's Candomblé community. Their efforts reshaped ideas of African heritage and privileged especially ideas of authentic African tradition. Working alongside Bahian intellectuals, their efforts led not only to the consolidation of a cultural rather than biological framework for understanding race but also to a new shift in the image of Bahia's African roots.

Bahian intellectuals in the Vargas era (1930–45) moved these ideas of Bahia as an Afro-Brazilian cultural treasure beyond academia to the arts. Chapter 3 reveals that leaders in the arts were anxious both to establish Bahia as the most authentic center for Brazilian traditions and to distinguish a Bahian identity distinct from the rest of Brazil. I show how race influenced the formation of Bahian identity through a close examination of one of Bahia's most dynamic artistic institutions of the time, the newly reorganized Bahian State Museum. As I demonstrate, the director of the museum, José do Prado Valladares, played an important role in cultivating this nascent sense of regional identity and moved between the realms of art and history as he sought to rewrite the way Bahians thought about their past. The museum promoted indigenous and African culture as central to Bahia's history and developed a vision of racial harmony with deep roots in Bahian traditions. Through its exhibits, its publications, and its very organization, the museum ensured that the idea of racial democracy became intimately tied to an idea of an authentic Bahian tradition. During this time Bahia came to be seen as a living museum and ultimately an unchanged portrait of an idealized past. In the end, however, Valladares's efforts were stopped short by protests from Bahia's white elite. A reorganization of the museum in 1946 continued to emphasize Bahia's traditions, but it also unveiled a vision of tradition tied to a white planter past. Both views of Bahian tradition, however, saw reform and social change as eroding Bahia's unique identity.

Despite such hesitations by the local elite, beginning in the late 1930s Bahia's self-promotion as the locus of Afro-Brazilian culture attracted a wave of foreign researchers. These outside observers, largely social scientists from the United States, included then-unknown scholars such as the sociologist Donald Pierson and the anthropologist Ruth Landes, as well as those established in the field of race such as Melville J. Herskovits and E. Franklin Frazier. Chapter 4 shows that Bahia became contested ground once more, as scholars debated whether Afro-Bahian culture had deep ties to an African past or was a particularly Brazilian creation. This debate moved beyond the realm of mere academic rivalry, however, since the question had particularly high stakes in Bahia. Though U.S. scholars brought their own agendas, it is no coincidence that the idea of Bahia as a museum, as a site of living tradition, is a leitmotif in their writings. These researchers were deeply influenced by the Bahian intellectuals who guided them through the Bahian landscape, and when they deviated from the carefully constructed view of harmony they suffered censure and disapproval. Scholars like E. Franklin Frazier who advocated that little of an African tradition remained were edited out of the discussion and given little credence in Bahia. Even scholars such as Ruth Landes, who argued that the past needed to be understood alongside an equally dynamic process of contemporary change, were controversial. Afro-Bahian culture was a meaningful building block in Bahia's past, but it was an uncomfortable, unresolved issue for Bahia's present and future.

The next chapter examines this central issue—the clash between tradition and reform, between racial harmony and potential racial unrest—as it played out in the 1950s. It was during this period that the worlds of academia and the state came fatefully together: Secretary of Education Anísio Teixeira invited the U.S. anthropologist Charles Wagley to study the "primitive" people of Bahia so that state's efforts at reform could target their modernizing efforts more precisely. And it was in this same moment of modernization that the United Nations Educational, Scientific, and Cultural Organization (UNESCO) began to ponder its research agenda on race relations. Chapter 5 examines how these trends collided in the UNESCO studies of Bahia and revealed the power of the Bahian myth of tradition. Charles Wagley, already in Bahia, became one of the leaders of the researchers who, with Bahians as their guides, painted a portrait of racial harmony grounded in Bahia's traditions. It was here that the conflict between tradition and twentieth-century modernity came out most forcefully. Although Wagley and others included descriptions of racial discrimination in Bahia, they portrayed them as intrusions from the modern world. These were products of modernization, and in order to stop them Bahia needed to stop outside forces of industrialization, change, and modernizing reform. Bahia's intellectuals over the twentieth century molded a powerful ideology that successfully prevented radical social change. Though they championed racial harmony, this concept was built on ideas of tradition and the past that ignored present inequalities and discrimination. Efforts to define Bahia as an exceptional enclave for Brazilian values proved successful, but such efforts also created obstacles for larger programs of social reform.

The book concludes with an assessment of Bahia in the second half of the twentieth century. Ideas of tradition continued to be instrumental to the military government of the 1960s. Indeed, the military period opened up surprising space for Afro-Brazilian culture in Bahia. Yet inherent in this development was an acceptance of an old doctrine. If Bahian tradition was to be preserved, social reform should not be on the agenda. As the elite of Bahia built up a powerful image of their state, drawing strength from a racialized past and harmonious tradition, anything that imperiled such traditions threatened to disrupt the racial harmony of Bahia as well.

RACE IS BOTH a social and historical construct, but it is not necessarily a national one. We must ground the constructions of race in their local settings to understand how individuals created, used, and contested ideas of race in strikingly original, and local, ways.[25] Only from such focused, regional analysis can we begin to understand the full complexity of racial thought in Brazil. Though the vast majority of studies of race in Brazil have aimed to provide a national overview, they often base their conclusions on the economic and cultural centers of power—São Paulo and Rio de Janeiro. This extrapolation neglects the question of how race is understood outside of these intellectual poles, and, even more significant, how race is understood in areas where Afro-Brazilians have long made up the vast majority of the population. As the historian João Reis observed in 1988 at the hundred-year commemoration of abolition, while Bahia represents the heart of the question of race in Brazil, it has been curiously overlooked in modern historical studies of race and race relations.[26] Since then scholars have begun to answer this call and have turned increasing attention to this center of the African diaspora. This book aims to continue this legacy and to begin to unravel the tangled strains of race, reform, and *baianidade*—a distinctly Bahian identity.

In our churches kisses murmur
promiscuously in all corners, on
the images, on the altars. . . . And
from the religious kiss, innumerous
afflictions are transmitted. In the
saliva that drops from the lips that
kiss the feet of an icon there are
thousands of malicious seeds,
microscopic germs, that remain
in the shadow of the niches, waiting
for other lips to carry them away.
—OTHON CHATEAU,
"O beijo nas imagens,"
Gazeta Médica da Bahia, 1906

CHAPTER 1

Finding a Cure for Bahia

Bahia's public health reformers never convinced Catholic authorities to take action against the malicious germs lurking in their sanctuaries, but goals of disinfected and hygienic churches remained symbolic of their modernizing, reformist vision for society as a whole. With the final abolition of slavery in 1888 and the advent of a new federal republic the following year, Bahian society entered a particularly anxious era that fostered ambitious views of modernization and reform. Doctors had long been authority figures in Salvador, the site of one of only two medical schools in Brazil. With the turn of the century, however, they insisted increasingly on the need for radical social change and entered politics as energetic, reformist governors and advisers.[1] In 1889, the first year of the republic, medical doctors and public health reformers in Bahia swept into political power with hopes of curing Bahia of its backwardness.

Many would have agreed with the vision of Bahia as a retrograde state in need of change. Salvador's Afro-Brazilian majority might have pointed to continued police persecution of their religions, to a depressed economy that kept most of the city in overwhelming poverty, and to the exclusion of blacks from political power despite the formal end of slavery. The city's traditional white oligarchy, in contrast, might have bemoaned the failure of Bahia's police to enforce the standards of "civilization," the economic collapse that made them marginal in the national sphere, and the new fluidity of a society without any formal legal divisions to protect their status. More significant, Bahia's white elite saw Bahia's backwardness as intimately tied to its racial makeup.

Indeed, as the twentieth century began, blacks were commonly viewed across Brazil as racially inferior. It was this assumed connection of whiteness and progress that convinced São Paulo's elite to seek out "modern" European immigrants to replace "traditional" black workers in the 1880s.[2] Bahia, in contrast, lacked the economic dynamism to attract immigrants in any significant numbers, but the idea still held appeal. Although isolated Brazilian intellectuals periodically protested that the races were equal, they confronted an ever-growing body of Western research which asserted—with all of the authority that such "science" could muster—that whites ranked above blacks and that Brazilians of mixed heritage, *mestiços*, were a horribly unstable and degenerative category. Brazilians struggled to reshape such racial orthodoxies to their own realities, and, as the century progressed, acted creatively on a variety of fronts to form their own theories of race.[3] But at the turn of the century few of Bahia's elite doubted that the state's African heritage was a serious obstacle to their vision of progress. Deeply skeptical about the capacity of Afro-Brazilians to participate as full members of society, they instead placed their faith for the future in exclusive social policies.

In contrast, Bahia's medical reformers of this era demonstrated faith in Bahia's population and mistrust of its reigning social order. They refused, therefore, to view Bahia's backwardness as an inevitable result of its blackness. This position, while radical at the time, carried significant weight: the medical profession was the foremost authority on matters of race in Brazil until the rise of the social sciences in the 1930s. The most egalitarian views came from the field of public health, yet, remarkably, even Bahia's emerging field of forensic medicine—indelibly marked by racial determinism—also stressed the transformative role of social reform. Thus while the Bahian elite sought progress *despite* Bahia's racial makeup or through quixotic European immigration programs, medical reformers insisted that the existing population be taken seriously as a basis for Bahia's future. Bahia's problems were not racial, they believed, but social; they diagnosed a broad swath of problems that could be remedied with energetic reform. Passionately, they denounced the city's deficient schools, insufficient public sanitation, and neglected infrastructure. Aiming to transform Salvador into a progressive capital in a European mold, they touted a vision of social medicine that targeted social ills as much as disease.

These visions gained a unique opportunity to be put into practice. Medical authority seemed to have a particular affinity for politics in the restricted world of the Bahian elite in the late 1880s. The last provincial president of Bahia was a member of the medical school, and the sudden transition to a republic in 1889 changed little in this regard: of the first four civilians to hold office in Bahia at the start of the republic, three were medical doctors. These medical reformers, however, ultimately failed to effect the change they had hoped for. Threatened by the idea of a more inclusive social order, Bahia's traditional oligarchs chose to preserve their privilege rather than risk change. Reforms that would have improved the quality of life for Bahia's black majority, many of them newly liberated from slavery, remained stymied, frustrated dreams. Doctors were eventually politically eclipsed by lawyers, who occupied the governor's palace in Salvador continuously from 1896 to 1930.[4] But while its impact in the politics of Bahia was short-lived, medicine played an important, and thus far underestimated, role in shaping the early republican era.[5] The debates in Bahia's medical community give insight into the racial controversies that shaped Bahia in this pivotal moment after abolition, as Brazil's new republic ushered in a vibrant period of medical activism.

This chapter gives new attention to Bahia's dynamic medical reformers of the turn of the century and unravels the views of race that shaped their hope for change. It looks at a variety of contexts in which issues of race and medicine commingled and explores the reformers' view of themselves as central to an expansive, and eclectic, assortment of causes. Doctors in this era saw the need for intervention in matters that ranged from sewers to education to questions of religious tolerance. We will follow these doctors in their diverse arenas of interest and examine the reformist spirit that shaped their generation. Turning first to the nineteenth-century roots of medical reform in Bahia, this chapter looks particularly at the controversies over educational reform proposed by one of the most prominent leaders of Bahia's public health movement. I then examine the growing divisions between the fields of public health and forensic medicine. I argue that despite such divisions, there was often surprising common ground in Bahia. Even the most racially deterministic of Bahia's medical reformers, the forensic expert Raimundo Nina Rodrigues, agreed that social change was necessary and saw a formative role for the environment. Bahia's medical reformers differed in the weight they gave to race, according to their field of specialty. Remarkably, however, they often came together despite these differences to push for changes that might have improved the quality of life for Bahia's black majority. The chapter concludes with an assessment of this turbulent, yet particularly reformist, early era for Bahian medical and racial science and shows that Bahia's doctors played remarkable roles as advocates for social change.

Nineteenth-Century Legacies: The Tropicalistas

The energy of turn-of-the-century medical reformers built on the legacy left by a Bahian circle of doctors known as the Tropicalistas. The Tropicalista "school" of medicine departed from European science to argue for attention to local realities. In the process, these thinkers challenged deterministic ideas of the tropics and of race.[6] The school had simple origins: it began as an informal consortium of doctors, with only three founding members in 1865. By the next year, the group had expanded and produced the first edition of its journal, the *Gazeta Médica da Bahia*, which would become one of the most prominent medical publications in Brazil. From their first issue the editors stressed their commitment to not just local medical realities but social engagement: all scientists, they insisted, had a basic obligation to contribute to progress and the common good.[7]

It is notable that such innovations happened, despite, not within, Bahia's medical school. A later admirer, Nina Rodrigues, viewed the Tropicalistas as explicitly in conflict with Salvador's traditional medical training. As he wrote of Bahia's medical establishment in 1903: "the method was detestable. It was the repetition of science made for other races and for other climates. It was the repetition of what we received from across the ocean. . . . [One day a group of respected doctors] decided to break with routine and study medicine, not in European books, but in the sick themselves, and it was in this way that that the famed [Tropicalista] school was formed."[8] Bahia's medical school may have offered sterile foundations for academic innovation, but it was one of the few options for advanced study available across Brazil: higher education clustered primarily in two fields—medicine and law—until Brazil's first university finally formed in 1934.[9] Even these courses of study were fairly late developments due to regressive colonial policies: it was not until the transfer of the royal court to Brazil in 1807 that the Portuguese king, Dom João VI, allowed the creation of courses in medicine in both Rio de Janeiro and Salvador. These courses were consolidated into formal medical schools—modeled on those of Paris—in 1832.

The efforts by the Tropicalistas to address Brazilian disease were formed in part as a reaction against the exceptionally Francophile orientation of Brazil's medical training. The three founding members in particular—Otto E. H. Wucherer, John L. Paterson, and José Francisco da Silva Lima—brought new attention to local problems of hookworm and beriberi and produced dramatic research breakthroughs for tropical medicine as a whole. Their efforts to reorient the profession from European to particularly Brazilian concerns were, however, a peculiar type of intellectual nationalism: all three were European-born and only one, Silva Lima, who graduated from Bahia's medical school, completed his training in Brazil. The Tropicalistas by no means rejected European medicine altogether; many of their advances came from their adherence to the most recent advances in microscopy from abroad. They used these tools, however, for significantly different purposes than their European colleagues. Most important, they broke from European assumptions about the inherent insalubrity of the tropics.[10]

Yet while the doctors diagnosed the tropical setting as healthy enough, they campaigned actively for social reform and sanitation improvements. Unlike the latitude, Brazilian society and the streets and ports of Salvador could not be granted a clean bill of health. Moreover, Tropicalista doctors did not just diagnose reforms for the city. They used the *Gazeta Médica* as a forum to advocate decentralization of politics under the empire and to decry the continuation of slavery. And as the historian Julyan Peard argues, the Tropicalistas consistently resisted facile racial typologies. While deterministic racial categories dominated the science of much of the Atlantic world, such assumptions were generally deemed irrelevant by the Tropicalistas.[11] It is not that their research attempted to prove or advocate racial equality. Rather, they set race aside as a meaningful factor at all, demonstrating a bold independence in the heavily racialized contexts—Bahian, Brazilian, and beyond—in which these doctors lived and worked. Social reform, rather than climatological or racial theories, was the focus of their agenda up to the close of the nineteenth century.

The end of the century was also the end of the Tropicalista era of tropical medicine. In its place came a new activism driven by much of the same urgency for reform. The focus, however, was different. Instead of tropical disease and climate, Bahia's medical reformers of the 1890s shifted their attention increasingly to the field of public health and epidemic disease. Such discussion was not entirely new: outbreaks of yellow fever in Rio de Janeiro and São Paulo in the 1880s had already made such concerns a primary topic of discussion in the *Gazeta Médica*. They received even more attention as changes in bacteriology seemed to promise an imminent solution for many of these public health scourges.[12]

Notably, however, bacteriological research remained less important than sanitation reforms for Bahia's public health advocates. In part this was because Bahian doctors continued to view most ills as originating from miasmas, or mysterious gases that might emerge from rotting materials. In fact, as Peard shows, although other views of disease were increasingly accepted, miasmatic theory continued to work particularly well with the vision of tropical redemption and social reform originally advocated by the Tropicalistas. The Bahian medical reformers thus abandoned miasmas somewhat later than the international medical establishment.[13] They poured their energy into assessment, debate, and reform of Bahia's environment and dedicated little of their research to bacteriology. Furthermore, not only did they believe in the power of sanitation to halt disease, they also viewed public health regulations as central to any national progress: sanitation measures, they proposed, were the true measure of a "civilized country."[14] Bacteriological research never became a central concern for these doctors, who instead focused their efforts on civilizing Bahia through ambitious initiatives of public health regulation and policy. These agendas continued to be pursued in their medical journal after the Brazilian Republic was born in 1889. But they also received new attention in the highest ranks of Bahian political office.

The Republican Transition: Education as Social Medicine

The doctors would get their chance to enforce their own vision of civilization as they led Bahia through the first years of the republic, especially under the reformist administration of Governor Manuel Vitorino Pereira. Acceptance of the republic in Bahia, however, came reluctantly, and only through a military uprising.[15] The first appointed doctor-governor was Virgílio Damásio—head of Bahia's Republican Party and a founding editor of the *Gazeta Médica*. This choice was rapidly vetoed by federal authorities, who imposed the appointment of a different doctor, this one not even a republican. Manuel Vitorino, a member of the Liberal Party, was a frequent contributor to the *Gazeta Médica*, a brother of its editor, Antônio Pacífico Pereira, and grounded in the Tropicalista school. Vitorino accepted the position of governor reluctantly, but once in office he displayed little hesitation in using his power.

Manuel Vitorino almost immediately began a radical remolding of Bahian society, including a far-reaching educational overhaul that proved one of the more controversial elements of his regime. While it might seem that educational plans had only distant connections to reigning ideas of public health, for Vitorino and other medical reformers they were intimately linked. In fact the Vitorino educational reforms are particularly revealing of Bahian conceptions of race and medicine in the turbulent time around abolition; it is in these farthest social reaches that the core ideas of Bahia's public health movement become clearest.

Vitorino's vision of dramatic social reform was central to the broader public health movement but ultimately proved too threatening to Bahia's elite to allow his continuation in office. Indeed, Vitorino's governorship proved so controversial and so radical that he was forced out of office by a threatened coup almost immediately. Though his policies offered plenty for elites to disagree with, his ideas of race and reform in Bahia's schools undoubtedly proved a key element in elite disapproval.[16] Vitorino saw schools as a site for social uplift and sought to extend schools to a broad swath of the population, including former slaves. This policy was dismantled immediately after his ejection from office.

On 30 December 1889, only six weeks into his term, Vitorino established a major new tax initiative to fund Bahia's schools. The very next day he issued a decree that completely reorganized the education system. Vitorino's radical reforms took their greatest inspiration from Bahia's homegrown public health movement and, more specifically, one of its foundational figures, his older brother Pacífico Pereira. The sons of immigrant furniture makers from Portugal, the Pereira brothers themselves had witnessed the social mobility possible through education. Both brothers edited and frequently wrote articles for the *Gazeta Médica*, but Pacífico Pereira, as chief editor in 1878, dedicated a particularly impassioned series of articles to the question of educational reform and hygiene.[17] The reforms advocated by the Pereira brothers encapsulate much of the thinking for Bahia's public health movement in the late nineteenth century; let us turn first to the early model set by Pacífico Pereira.

Pacífico Pereira and the Need for Educational Hygiene, 1878

In 1878 Brazil was considering changes to its educational program, and Pacífico Pereira called for the *Gazeta Médica* to intervene to direct the course of this change.[18] His extended article, "School Hygiene," filled many pages with dramatic rhetoric and concrete plans for reform. Drawing frequent contrasts between the practices of "civilized nations" and those of Brazil, Pacífico Pereira deplored that Brazilian educators and administrators seemed to ignore the scientific consensus on the benefits of hygiene and physical education. "It is intolerable," he wrote, "for those of us outside of a civilized country" to watch schools open without any concern for such issues and to be forced to observe pedagogues develop a veritable "homicidal education."[19]

The wrath of Pacífico Pereira focused particularly on the unhealthy conditions of Brazil's ill-adapted school buildings as well as the dangerous neglect of physical education. Such conditions destroyed the mental, spiritual, and physical capacities of children, leaving them poor, wasted beings, or "shabby, decadent organisms."[20] Such degradation would only be inherited and passed down to future generations. A follower of Lamarckian views of evolution, Pacífico Pereira viewed the direct passing of genes to be only part of the genetic equation: equally important were environmental and social influences that could mark an individual and be inherited by the next generation.[21] Pacífico Pereira added moral vigor and spiritual dissolution to this assortment of inheritable traits. His view of evolution was ultimately hopeful, expressing a deep faith in the potential for change, but it also underscored dangers such as those found in Brazil's schools. These institutions, if not carefully controlled, might not only corrode today's youth but also start a much larger cycle of degeneration.

The priority he gave to environmental change also had important repercussions for thinking about racial difference. After all, if even a genetically perfect white child might become hopelessly apathetic and physically degenerate simply through the influence of the schools, then the contribution of genetics and race could be given less weight. In sum, this view saw the body, mind, and soul as dangerously mutable. Given this potential, Brazil's racial heritage held little danger for the nation, but an inappropriate social and physical environment might threaten Brazil's future. Controlling environmental factors here took priority over any initial genetic makeup and thus reflected a Tropicalista interest in redeeming the potential of the Brazilian, and especially the Bahian, setting. For Pacífico Pereira and others interested in public hygiene, improving Brazil's social institutions was the key to reforming and bettering the Brazilian "race" as a whole.

Though the public health reformers were optimistic about the potential for change if their dictates were followed, they were positively morbid about the consequences of inaction. The faith in environmental improvement was tempered by warnings about the peculiarities of the tropical climate, where the reformers believed air circulation and air quality to be worse than in colder or temperate climates. This tropical distinctiveness demanded greater government intervention than in other regions. Already the lack of hygiene made walking across the threshold of a Bahian school equal to "crossing over into the entrance of the cemetery." Students' satisfaction at graduation was marred by the fact that they would "often take with them the germ of death or inevitable suffering for their entire life."[22] And life itself might be short indeed. In the first installment of his series Pacífico Pereira compared students in the classroom to geese being fattened so that their livers might be used to make pastries.

These hyperbolic claims were intended of course to spur immediate reform. One such reform aimed to ensure adequate air circulation and ventilation in the classroom, but Pacífico Pereira also worried about the damage that a fixed, inappropriate desk height could cause for both vision and body alignment. His recommendations, elaborated in excruciating detail, intended to resolve these problems with new mandates for school buildings and school furniture. Schools should be located in airy plazas when possible, but certainly away from tall buildings that might block air flow and light. As ventilation would come through numerous windows, spaced according to the proportions devised by the Mackinnel system, exposure to humid winds or the miasmas of swamps or drains should be avoided. Room height was fixed at 4.5 to 5 meters, and each child in the room would have 1.3 to 1.5 square meters of space around them. School furniture in Brazil was so ill-equipped for its mission that it should be tossed into the fire and replaced with desks proportional to each age, with a ten centimeter difference in the height for each year.[23]

Pacífico Pereira went beyond these infrastructure concerns to advocate dramatic changes to Brazilian pedagogy. Most important in his view was to shorten the school day and make physical education an integral part of the curriculum. Physical education offered the only solution to the health problems perpetuated by the schools themselves: according to a Lisbon authority, poorly equipped schools "add[ed] new ills to hereditary sickness, which . . . should be combated victoriously by gymnastic processes."[24] Another cited expert insisted that there was "only one recourse to avoid the progressive degeneration of the human species: . . . rational gymnastics."[25] Pacífico Pereira closed his study by citing statistics for blindness, muteness, and insanity from Brazil's 1872 census. In his assessment these indicators and others highlighted the painfully "evident signs of the physical degradation" suffered by the nation. Pacífico Pereira concluded with a stern and dramatic warning: "It is necessary to repeat, in no other country is it [physical education] more necessary, and perhaps in no other people [*povo*] can such manifest signals of a precocious physical degeneracy be noted."[26] Schools, if reformed according to hygienic and medical standards, could answer Brazil's most pressing problem: the physical deterioration and degeneration of its citizens. The public health reformers would have to wait twelve years, however, for their ideas to be put into action.

A Dream Fulfilled? The Reforms of Manuel Vitorino Pereira, 1889–1890

After his appointment as governor in 1889, Manuel Vitorino followed much of his brother's outline for reform closely, but Brazilian society had witnessed important transformations since 1878. Chief among them was the final abolition of slavery, enacted in 1888. Since slaves had been banned from schools of any sort, abolition not only established freedom from slavery but for the first time opened legal access to education for all of Brazil's population. Opening schools to the masses meant that Vitorino's reforms would occur in a very different context. When his brother had ambitiously sought regenerate Brazilians through the schools, the schools still served only the very elite. Indeed, in 1886 just 1.1 percent of Bahians attended school, and many of those irregularly.[27] Even if Pacífico Pereira's program had been incorporated, it would have "regenerated" only a select few.

Manuel Vitorino abandoned this selectivity with his education law of December of 1889. Primary education, he declared, would be free, obligatory, and secular.[28] Each of these dictates individually were revolutionary. Together they threatened the traditional hierarchy of Bahian society. Vitorino's reform would have extended literacy to nonwhite masses only recently eligible for public education. Far from aiming to regenerate only the state elite, as the 1878 program had intended, Manuel Vitorino insisted on opening the reforming potential of the schools to all. The new education system would ostensibly be capable of regenerating all Bahians—elite or poor, black, white, or brown. Just as important, it could enfranchise Bahians who now, as illiterates, were barred from the vote.

The 1889 reform was marked by a surfeit of detail on some issues and a surprising silence on others. The requirements for the height of the school desks were exceptionally detailed—they should be provided in five different sizes, with two to three centimeters of height added to each size—and accompanied by an elaborate chart, but the subjects to be taught in the schools remained undetermined.[29] Similarly, the reform offered minutely detailed specifications for school buildings and their locations—with amounts of air space required for each student—but the goals of education were discussed only in general terms. The role of science and hygiene was most apparent in the elaborate health regulations outlined for the schools. These regulations created a complex hierarchy of health officials to police the schools and the students themselves, granting a much expanded role to medical officials and medical science. The establishment of an educational health service, pronounced in a separate decree, merited twice as many pages as the law that ostensibly reshaped all of the state's educational system.[30]

Clearly the law aimed to demolish the existing system of education in Bahia. It created a new school financing tax as well as a new school census, obligatory attendance, and the penalties to enforce it. Yet perhaps the most important element in the educational law was a clause explicitly acknowledging the policies that were left to be determined. Questions concerning the length of the school day, subjects to be taught, and anything else concerning the "normal evolution of child intelligence" would be decided according to "the general precepts of science and the particular study of race and climate."[31] The use of the singular "race" rather than the plural "races" suggests that the law intended to address Brazilians as a race, while emphasizing that Brazilians, and Bahians, would need to tailor their schools to their particular context. This notion of scientific action guided by local realities bore the clear mark of the Tropicalista agenda. Yet the inclusion of even amorphous ideas of race in shaping education signaled that changes were under way.

The ideas of science and race came together in one health regulation in particular. This article required that each school keep a complete record of hygiene. First and foremost in this record was a somatological exam. Somatology at this time indicated physical anthropology, a discipline whose research focused on bodily measurements.[32] Bahian records for each student would include not only basics such as nationality of parents and date of birth but also "height, weight, cephalic measures [the index between length and width of the head], circumference of the chest, diameter of the thorax and the transverse diameters of the body, force of traction, constitution, temperament, [and the] color of skin, eyes, and hair, carefully classified."[33] These measurements were core components of racial indexes of the time. The schools would thus make available massive, state-of-the-art data on Bahia's racial composition.[34] In fact, Bahia appears to be the only Brazilian state that created such exams, which were notably absent, for example, in the much heralded educational reforms in Rio de Janeiro the following year. Though such exams came into wider use in Brazil with the push for physical education in the 1920s, and intensified under the semifascist Estado Novo, the Bahian reform was early in its attempt to introduce racial classifications in the schools.[35]

The hygiene regulations as a whole represented the particularly medicalized concerns of Bahia's doctors, the chief campaigners for public education in Bahian society, and revealed that ideas of race were gaining credence as a factor in Bahian medical discourse. Nonetheless, the reform represented a powerfully inclusive idea of education. Though the schools might be used to study the racial dynamic of Bahia's population—perhaps a concession to Raimundo Nina Rodrigues (discussed later in this chapter), who expressed regret that the initiative eventually failed—the schools marked a new departure by viewing education as a public good that should reach all of Bahia's children, even those of its recently freed slave population.[36] Schools were to be shaped by the local racial and geographical realities, but the optimistic view of the public health reformers allowed Manuel Vitorino to advocate that all Bahians be shaped into citizens. In the context of the years immediately following abolition, this alone made him a radical force for change in Bahia.

Manuel Vitorino's efforts at inclusion provoked a dramatic response: he was removed from office and four days later his entire array of educational reforms was revoked. Vitorino's concept of social environment, however, would continue to haunt Bahia's debates about education. Another medical doctor, Sátiro Dias, would use the same idea to forestall the democratization of Bahia's schools. Dias, as state director of education, charged in 1890 that the reforms were impossible to enact "by virtue of their radical dispositions" and "the absolute transformation they would cause for education."[37] In his view Vitorino had crafted a set of reforms that were impractical and too ambitious: "Deficient in some points, backward in others, sophistic in many, badly executed everywhere, [the reform] need[ed] to be recast in accord with [Bahia's] social environment."[38]

This idea of social environment, used alternately to foment and to limit reform, revealed a profound divide over Bahia's possibilities, particularly its racial potential. Sátiro Dias not only insisted that Bahia could not support a wholesale expansion of its educational system, he worked to further restrict it. He radically reduced state responsibility and financing for education with a decentralizing reform that made primary education the exclusive care of municipal, rather than state, authorities. Federal authorities had already disclaimed any responsibility for primary education; now Dias rejected any further involvement for state government and subjected all school funding and oversight to local coordination.

Such a move fit well in the larger context of political decentralization in Brazil's new republic. Yet many Bahians must have predicted that such a transfer would doom primary education altogether: Bahia's municipalities had little income of their own, and local bossism, or *coronelismo*, created local authorities more interested in personal gain than in public welfare or racial justice. This reform, at this particular political moment, signaled a disturbing effort by the Bahian state government to shirk its most basic obligations. And it revealed a shocking willingness to neglect any meaningful agenda for racial equality in the critical years following abolition. Since voting was restricted to the literate, Dias's actions were not only socially undemocratic but directly contradicted political democracy. Access by blacks to schools and to the polls was an idea too radical for Dias and the wider Bahian elite at this time. In arguing that Bahia's "social environment" was not ready for "radical" ideas of universal education, Dias surely had the context of abolition and the state's racial makeup in mind.

The Dias reforms functioned predictably. By 1898 official figures revealed that school enrollment had decreased, and the percentage of the total population served by Bahia's primary schools dropped below 1 percent. Bahia's literacy rates from 1872 to 1920 remained at roughly 20 percent.[39] The passage of fifty years, the abolition of slavery, the start of a new republic, and the promise of free and obligatory education had done nothing to incorporate the majority into Bahia's schools. Bahia's environment was viewed as incapable of supporting a dramatic change in educational access, and the racial views of elites played an important role in slowing the expansion of full, obligatory education.

Conflicts that surfaced in education arose in the wider Bahian medical community as well. As the 1890s began, the *Gazeta Médica* found itself increasingly divided on the importance of race. A rift formed between those—such as the Pereira brothers—who insisted that race played a minimal role in shaping disease or behavior and those—most extremely Raimundo Nina Rodrigues—who argued that race was the most important factor in Brazilian life. This ideological split formed along a parallel disciplinary divide. Nina Rodrigues, who turned his focus to forensic medicine, believed that race mattered; the Pereira brothers, who studied epidemics and public hygiene, believed that it did not. These tensions between two developing fields—forensic medicine and public health—came to the fore in Bahia's survey of medical knowledge at its 1890 medical congress.

The Third Brazilian Conference on Medicine
and Surgery: Bahia's Racial Schism

In 1890 the Bahian medical community gathered itself for a great event: the Brazilian Conference on Medicine and Surgery, inaugurated in 1888, had scheduled its next meeting to be held in Salvador. The *Gazeta Médica* announced the congress as a forum to address the "special character" of Brazil and to analyze specifically national problems. Core members of the *Gazeta Médica* editorial board—Silva Lima, Pacífico Pereira, and Nina Rodrigues—formed the organizing committee for Bahia and thus held considerable power in setting the agenda for the congress and for formulating the most critical questions for Brazil's doctors to debate. The organizers were well aware of the intellectual latitude and the pressure: they worried openly about how to equal the success of the previous congresses, both held in Rio de Janeiro in 1888 and 1889.[40]

The event came at a moment in which the political influence of Bahia's medical authorities seemed under threat. By the time the announcement for the conference was published, Bahia's doctor-governor Manuel Vitorino had been driven from office. His resignation, forced by the threat of a military intervention, took effect on 26 April 1890, and his successor, Marshal Hermes da Fonseca, was not a doctor but a soldier. This context heightened the claims for medical authority as the Bahian doctors gathered in November of that same year. In essence, as Lamarckians, Bahian doctors viewed themselves as a critical part of the social environment and believed their intervention could affect the course of change. They stressed that though evolution moved slowly in both biology and society, human action might quicken the pace. If correctly and energetically guided, what ordinarily could take centuries might be coaxed to develop in little more than a decade.[41] The doctors clearly saw themselves as the ideal guides for accelerated Bahian progress.

The conference organizers developed a program that defined the nation's problems in terms that echoed many of the central concerns of the *Gazeta Médica*. Tropical disease, a mainstay of the journal, received a significant share of the program, for instance, with many panels on beriberi, hookworm, and malaria. School hygiene in Bahia figured as a special topic, not surprisingly given its current importance in the state reforms, and since it was Pacífico Pereira's own area of interest. Also significant was the attention given to forensic medicine, a status that certainly owed much to Nina Rodrigues. Though criminology would gain much attention across Latin America at the turn of the century, the field, then known as legal medicine, still remained in its early stages of development and addressed controversial claims.[42] Indeed, by the late nineteenth century, legal medicine had moved closer to racial determinism: its most notorious practitioner, the Italian Cesare Lombroso, theorized that physical development and heritage predetermined some for a life of crime and others for a life as productive citizens. Previous congresses had not included legal medicine as a topic of study, nor would the next national congress, held a decade later. Nonetheless, when the Bahian organizers divided medicine into six broad categories, one of the six was dedicated to legal medicine. Since legal medicine was still a relatively unformed field, its inclusion in the congress was a victory for its proponents.[43]

Brazil's next congress, for example, held in Rio de Janeiro in 1900, pushed aside the topics of legal medicine and race. The event, organized to coincide with the four hundredth anniversary of Brazil's discovery, defined the proceedings around three central questions: Brazilian pathologies, Brazilian treatments or drugs, and original studies of Brazilian hygiene.[44] Tailored even more closely than Bahia's conference to specifically Brazilian concerns, the Rio organizers—in a marked contrast to those of the Bahia congress—steered clear of questions of race and criminology. Bahia's conference and its emphasis on race shows how very central the issue was in the immediate aftermath of abolition, and how critical it proved for Bahian medical scholars.

Bahia's congress not only highlighted the question of race directly, it also aimed at a broad diffusion of the topic. Publishing the program in the *Gazeta Médica* enabled the editors-cum-organizers to keep their colleagues in Bahia—as well as their readership in the larger Brazilian medical community—abreast of the event. They reached further, however, in also appealing to the daily press to publicize the conference and publish the agenda. This effort gives us some indication of the journal's readership: although abysmal literacy rates in Bahia (20%) meant that any publication had a very limited diffusion, the *Gazeta* writers obviously believed they at least had an audience among Bahia's intellectuals and journalists.[45] And given the *Gazeta*'s political commentary and biting critiques of local sanitary and city conditions, it would have behooved politicians to maintain some familiarity with its pages.

Appealing to the local press meant a broader exposure to the ideas deemed important by Bahia's medical profession. While the general public may not have attended the congress, the titles of the papers for the conference were enough to give any casual newspaper reader an impression of the medical view of race. One panel, for example, proposed to study the "physiological effects of acclimatization by foreigners resident here and their descendants."[46] Another sought to determine "the influence that the slaves of African race imparted on the Brazilian *povo*; their ethnic, moral, pathological, and social effects."[47] These questions spoke to the interests of Nina Rodrigues especially, as did the panel that debated whether the Brazilian criminal code should be "modified in accord with the progresses of medicine and sociology."[48]

Such statements, though brief, give the reader some indication of the new medical view of racial difference in Bahia. For example, while medical authorities determined to study immigrant "acclimatization," the impact of African slaves was framed in less adaptive terms. The study of Africans, rather than centering on their own acclimation, instead turned to the question of their larger outside impact, "their ethnic, moral, pathological, and social effects."[49] In sum, the panels drew a contrast between adaptive immigrants—merging and changing to fit the environment—and African slaves, deemed polluting, and assumedly pathological. The topics of medical responsibility in legislation, particularly the criminal code, completed the evocative portrait. In fact, such discussions were relevant to Bahia's own political dilemmas: in the next few years the Bahian state government attempted to bring in European immigrant labor to replace African workers. The policy, while pursued at the national level, now had local intellectual endorsement and scientific authority. Though the effort ultimately proved unsuccessful in Bahia, it revealed an activist agenda for those interested in racial difference there. Let us turn now to the foremost scientific proponent of racial difference, Raimundo Nina Rodrigues, who ironically may have been of mixed racial background himself.[50]

Nina Rodrigues

Nina Rodrigues was one of the most important pioneers of legal medicine in Bahia, and indeed, in all of Brazil. Though many of his research interests diverged from those of his colleagues at the *Gazeta Médica*, he was undoubtedly rooted in the Tropicalista commitment to both science and social causes. Like his Bahian colleagues in public health who wanted to modernize and reform Bahian society, Nina Rodrigues believed in the benefits of strong government programs and established himself as an important advocate for public health reforms. Yet he departed from his Bahian colleagues by speaking frankly, openly, and aggressively about race and by insisting on the centrality of racial and genetic heritage.

In fact, Nina Rodrigues is often invoked as the most racially deterministic thinker in Brazil; scholars have often pointed to him as the most open Brazilian proponent of racial difference. Yet his legacy is complicated by the fact that he also produced some of the earliest, and still valued, ethnographic descriptions of Afro-Brazilian religion and African-based culture. This uneasy balance between racial pessimism and cultural engagement has long been noted, but there is further depth and complexity to Nina Rodrigues that deserves to be considered.[51] Notwithstanding his highly problematic racial theories, Nina Rodrigues also advocated important public health reforms that could have brought real benefit to the city's poor. He further saw deep problems to be resolved in Bahian society itself; for all of his racial determinism, he believed race to be mediated and altered by a host of environmental and social influences. The fact that he saw the presence of modern medical institutions, a balanced political system, and a developed public infrastructure as critical for Brazil show his thinking to be surprisingly multivalent: his anxieties often centered as much on these "environmental" factors as on matters of race. This focus on the environment, broadly conceived, surfaced early in his work and continued to dominate his thought until his death in 1906.

Born in 1862 in the state of Maranhão, Nina Rodrigues began his training at Bahia's medical school but transferred to Rio de Janeiro midway through his program and received his final degree there. He returned to Bahia's medical school to assume his first academic position, first as a professor of clinical medicine before switching to legal medicine in 1891. Though his research was ambitious and far-ranging, his confrontational nature may have isolated him in the medical school; the approval of his annual report in 1897, traditionally a formality, was rejected by his colleagues. With his typical fervor for exposé, Nina Rodrigues had used the report to denounce the institution's lack of original research and to assault the pedagogy as excessively theoretical rather than practical.[52]

Despite, or perhaps because of, his affinity for scathing critique, Nina Rodrigues was well connected in medical and political circles. He was chief editor of the *Gazeta Médica* from 1890 to 1893, and he married the daughter of José Luís de Almeida Couto, an influential Tropicalista politician who had served as Bahia's last provincial president under the empire. Nina Rodrigues took a vivid interest in Bahian public policy and, whether through his reputation or his connections, was named to several prominent positions. In 1892 he became part of a council to outline a new state plan for the administration of public health in Bahia, and he campaigned constantly in his writings for reform and change.[53] Though few of his initiatives had much success, Nina Rodrigues had the ear of prominent politicians and administrators, many of whom were his colleagues in the medical school and familiar with his work and research.

Nina Rodrigues nonetheless fit uncomfortably with those members of the Bahian elite who wished to promote an image of Bahia as a white state in a classical European tradition. He published a series of articles in 1896 that asserted precisely what these elite did not wish to hear: that Bahia was neither European nor Catholic but rather very much black and exceptionally connected to African-based religions.[54] The series, "O animismo fetichista dos negros bahianos" (The animistic fetishism of black Bahians) paid serious scholarly attention to Bahia's Candomblé tradition for the first time. Bahia's ruling class viewed Candomblé as barbaric and attempted to shut it down with violent police raids and frequent denunciations in the Bahian press. Nina Rodrigues stood apart from this elite by adopting a pragmatic stance: Candomblé, he insisted, was so deeply ingrained in African culture that police repression and elite complaints would never succeed in stamping it out and instead only pushed the practice underground. Furthermore, he argued, Brazil's constitution guaranteed religious freedom, and therefore Bahians who tried to repress Candomblé were illegally attacking personal liberties.[55]

Not only did his frank discussion of race and constitutional rights put the Bahian elite on the defensive, it also fit awkwardly with the environmental focus of Bahia's public health reformers. While Nina Rodrigues is often cited in studies of racial thought, he has most often been viewed as a national intellectual, rather than being considered in his Bahian context. Not only was his research conducted almost exclusively in Bahia, however, he was also a well-connected figure in Salvador.[56] Indeed, the uneasy relationship between Nina Rodrigues and the Bahian medical community may be seen in his obituary in the *Gazeta Médica* after his death in 1906. While the editors emphasized his dedication "to the study of our environment," his work with Afro-Bahians was an effort that the medical journal—for all of its focus on social involvement—did not altogether support. The eulogy diligently reported his research interests as "the arduous problems of general and criminal anthropology, morbid psychology, criminal responsibility, professional liberty, Brazilian *mestiçagem* [racial mixture], African fetishism and Catholic monotheism, psychological conditions of criminal mutilation, and many others."[57] This remarkable array of topics went without comment, however, falling far short of the intellectual Festschrift traditionally given to Tropicalistas in memoriam. The work of Nina Rodrigues needs to be considered in the Bahian setting, where he treated topics uncomfortable for the Bahian elite, as well as in the medical setting, where his racially deterministic ideas surely led him to butt heads frequently.

In fact the uncertain treatment of Nina Rodrigues by his colleagues is an important indicator that his legacy is far more complex and ambiguous than traditionally acknowledged.[58] As his warning about illegal attacks on Candomblé revealed, Nina Rodrigues often was a proponent for integration as much as segregation and for progressive health reforms as much as racially regressive policies. Such a contradictory figure cannot be fully treated in all of his complexities here, but I emphasize here his view of social reform, which in fact urged dramatic improvements in public health for Bahia's most needy. Nina Rodrigues, though he gave a much greater priority to race than his colleagues in public health, embraced a view of social medicine that also aimed to improve living conditions and bring about social change. With this in mind, let us examine here some of his earliest work.

A CALL FOR REFORM

In 1889 Nina Rodrigues published one of his first articles in the *Gazeta Médica*, an extended study of leprosy that suggests the roots of his later interests and his insistence on the need for political and social reform. It further reveals an activist side of Nina Rodrigues that is often forgotten. Nina Rodrigues used his article not only to document his medical findings but to expose the pitiful conditions of lepers, who suffered from shocking official neglect.[59] According to his report, the state governor of Maranhão continued to assert the existence of a hospital that had not been in operation for over a decade, while lepers languished in unsanitary quarters with exceptionally high rates of mortality.

In this report, as in many others, Nina Rodrigues denounced the health conditions suffered by those in state facilities and sought to remedy disturbing patterns of neglect and illness that officials often tried to cover up. In 1904, for example, a similar effort occupied him in saving patients in Salvador's insane asylum, who were dying in massive numbers. A recent outbreak of beriberi among the patients had attracted outcries from the daily press, but Nina Rodrigues argued that the authorities had become deaf to the pleas of journalists, and he aimed to use his medical authority to incite action. In a journal of Bahia's medical school, he claimed he wrote with "the declared intent of provoking the attention of the public powers."[60] Nina Rodrigues reveled in the exposure of uncomfortable truths, but the ultimate objective of his exposé was reform and ultimately improved survival chances for the sick. The humanitarian side of his advocacy has often been overlooked, but it is a key to understanding his complexities. Beyond his pleas for decreased mortality for patients in state institutions, Nina Rodrigues saw a much wider arena for change.

In dealing with leprosy in 1889, Nina Rodrigues expressed hope that Brazil's new republic and its decentralized regime meant that public hygiene would be taken seriously soon. As he saw it, leprosy should be treated by intensive state efforts, including a strong dose of hygienic instruction and the strict regulation of marriage. Yet though the state formed the answer for the future, it had largely failed its responsibilities in the past. Maranhão had fallen into decadence, he wrote provocatively, as a result of "complex political and economic factors" that could not be fully addressed by his own research.[61] He noted with sharp irony that the state had been able somehow to marshal funds for animal vaccination centers but had ignored human welfare, whether in terms of leprosy or in broader public nutrition and malnutrition. These social and political problems formed the basis of his critique, a format well accepted in the *Gazeta Médica*; like his Bahian colleagues, Nina Rodrigues viewed disease as a problem to be solved by state intervention. Rather than blaming the sick for their genetic problems or lack of self-control in marrying, Nina Rodrigues saw these as expected, even natural difficulties. What he saw as mutable was state action to prevent future outbreaks and contagion to the rest of the population, and to establish a better basis for human welfare as a whole.[62]

THE DILEMMA OF BRAZIL'S RACIAL MIXTURE

Nina Rodrigues also used his study of leprosy to insist that the nature of immunities raised important question of race, and especially *mestiçagem*, that demanded further medical research. In his view, it would offer "great advantages from the medical perspective to define the ethnological origin of the predispositions and immunities that were transmitted to us." Addressing this medical question, however, required some knowledge of the degree and type of racial mixture in Brazil, and Nina Rodrigues expressed skepticism about how much scientists thus far had been able to uncover. In his opinion, Brazilian racial mixing was so widespread, with such a long history, that weighing the influence of any one race proved a most uncertain task. Scholars faced "the difficulty and almost impossibility of rigorously delineating the diverse types of *mestiços* in our population."[63] Though Nina Rodrigues denounced the lack of scholarly attention to Brazil's racial makeup, he also dismissed the findings of preliminary studies of race, insisting that there were few remaining examples of Brazil's original races—defined as black, red, and white. The question still needed further study to determine "the products of crossings of diverse races that will contribute and are contributing to the peopling of the empire and from which natural selection will have to choose in definitively shaping the future national type."[64] Though Nina Rodrigues initially framed his interest in race as a question of differential immunities, the topic that truly captured his attention was the larger question of racial legacies in mixed race populations.

This contrarian position on the nature of *mestiçagem* not only challenged the findings of his colleagues who had ventured to study race, but also questioned the very idea of Brazilian whiteness itself. His assertion that there was little left of racial purity in Brazil was a controversial affront to those who prided themselves on their white, "superior" heritage. Instead of seeing *mestiçagem* as a problem afflicting a portion of Brazil's population, Nina Rodrigues defined it as central to all of Brazil's inhabitants. For this reason, he believed the question of *mestiçagem* to be of critical importance, not only for the present but also for the nation's future. Nina Rodrigues defined this question, however, in terms that moved between biology, culture, and the environment in often contradictory and interesting ways.

THE ROLE OF THE ENVIRONMENT IN DEFINING RACE

In establishing the framework for the "problem" of racial mixing, Nina Rodrigues initially focused on biological ideas of race. His broad definition of *mestiçagem* came in part from what he viewed as a long history of genetic intermingling and intermixing in Brazil's population. He believed that the crossing of races created a "truly *mestiço*, intermediate way of being" and that it would be impossible to separate out traits from any one race, as some might disappear and others might become dominant. If mixing continued, one intermediary *mestiço* type would emerge, a type that "no longer ha[d] well-defined ethnological characteristics."[65] Yet Nina Rodrigues also departed significantly from this biological framework of race. For in the next moment, he distanced his idea of the *mestiço* from simple racial categories of "red, black, and white" and adopted a much more complicated view of the Brazilian environment as formative.

This focus on the environment led to some surprising conceptions of how a *mestiço* might be defined. For example, turning to the wider population of the state of Maranhão, Nina Rodrigues opined that even families of European origin that had attempted to conserve their racial "purity" could no longer count themselves as pure original types because they had lived for at least a generation in Brazil. With his typical relish for unveiling unpopular truths, Nina Rodrigues insisted: even "if we can't say that the population of the province of Maranhão is entirely *mestiço*, we should at least consider it rigorously Brazilian."[66] In this framework, even Portuguese families that had carefully intermarried for generations were no longer pure whites but Brazilians. The blurring of the categories of *mestiço* and Brazilian revealed a powerful role for the Brazilian environment in creating a *mestiço* type, even from ostensibly "pure" races.

For Nina Rodrigues, racial heredity therefore depended as much on contact with an original culture or environment as the biological framework of "blood": fresh influxes of European culture and white blood brought only a short-term racial effect and ultimately surrendered to the power of the environment, becoming Brazilian or *mestiço*. Furthermore, Nina Rodrigues noted, in the whole of Brazil, there had been no arrival of "genuine" Africans since the ending of the slave trade, and Brazil's indigenous populations had virtually disappeared. The lack of any new racial influence from abroad meant that Brazil was forced to confront the realities of its current population, which was inevitably altered by the Brazilian setting.

This idea of a Brazil dominated and defined by its *mestiço* population had some parallel outside of medicine. Nina Rodrigues cited the literary critic Sílvio Romero, who also insisted in the "future of the ethnic Brazilian type" as *mestiço* and proposed in the 1880s that Brazil study and embrace its *mestiço* roots.[67] But while Nina Rodrigues agreed with the need for further study of *mestiçagem*, he held more pessimistic views on Brazil's future. Sílvio Romero pointed to the *mestiço* as a new stronger national type. Nina Rodrigues, himself a *mestiço*, continued to see danger in mixing; in contrast with those who believed in the inevitable "progress" of whitening in racial mixture, he believed that mixing could eventually lead people to return to either the white or black race.[68] Although he believed there might be "*mestiços* who had returned to being white," in his view the parallel and less desirable alternative was that of *mestiços* turning black.[69] He further emphasized this idea of racial deception in his article the next year in the *Gazeta Médica*, titled "Mestiços brasileiros." There he warned that even individuals who appeared to be white might actually be black.[70]

These fears of the unstable nature of racial mixture and the potential of "turning black" placed Nina Rodrigues in opposition to the reigning Brazilian racial ideology. By the turn of the century a belief in the potential "whitening" of Brazil's population was the new best hope for many elites hoping to jumpstart progress, provoking Brazilian intellectuals and state authorities to increase importations of European immigrants. In this view, Brazil's emergency transfusion of white blood would eventually heal the nation's enervating and dangerous dependence on black blood. On the one hand, increasing state sponsorship of immigration would mean white numeric dominance. On the other hand, inevitable racial mixture would eventually lead to the "triumph" of white blood because of its "superior" qualities. One of the primary advocates of this theory was the Brazilian scholar Manuel de Oliveira Lima, but as historian Thomas Skidmore has shown, such ideas gained wide acceptance across the Brazilian elite.[71] Whitening, while fundamentally racist, nonetheless was a creative response by Brazilian intellectuals who dared to confront the European dismissal of the *mestiço* with a positive reassessment of their own reality of racial mixing.

For those who believed in the theories of whitening, *mestiçagem* was to be encouraged as it promised a brighter, whiter future for Brazil: this biological idea of progress was a key element of the nation's prosperity. Yet the theory also endorsed a vision of social change that happened principally in the arena of race and demographics, not in the institutions or framework of society itself. For those who saw progress in terms of whitening, the social conditions of Brazil's blacks were of little concern, as they would be remedied biologically. Inequalities between blacks and whites would be solved not through social critique or social reform but through intermarriage and procreation. In this view blackness was a problem that would be solved by the laws of the natural world: genetics would do the heavy lifting of social improvement. Those who saw whiteness as the ultimate key to the nation's progress could sit back and let nature take its course.

Nina Rodrigues disagreed with the two basic fundamental elements of this vision. First, he believed that *mestiçagem* did not always result in whitening and that even the whitening it produced might be illusory and unstable. In his view, therefore, *mestiçagem* alone would not bring social progress. Second, Nina Rodrigues believed that the social setting mattered, as his views of whites "becoming" *mestiço* by living in Brazil expose. For all of his emphasis on the centrality of heredity, Nina Rodrigues believed social environment to be formative in counteracting the role of genetics, which he did not see as a necessarily benevolent force. In his view, Brazil's racial future needed social reform.

THE URGENCY OF SOCIAL REFORM:
TAKING NATIVE BRAZILIANS SERIOUSLY

This background, then, helps us understand the calls for reform that Nina Rodrigues made in his early study of leprosy. His agenda was in part humanitarian and in part aimed at extending the state's control over its citizens, but his ultimate message was to emphasize that Brazilians needed to take their existing human potential seriously. He made this point most emphatically in deploring the extreme disrepair of the state hospital, where resident lepers, forced outside of the uninhabitable central complex, were forced to improvise cabins along the periphery of the grounds. As he wrote with some despair: "So long as Brazil is not a civilized country, with a real sanitary organization in place, as long as the primitive cabins of American Indians or of black Africans are not replaced with modern scientific hospitals, as long as the promotion of demographic expansion is nothing more than the spectacular introduction of batches of immigrants with the aim of becoming noticed by Europe and the Argentine Republic, we will continue to be just one of those semibarbaric or barbarous countries."[72] Nina Rodrigues called for a modern public health code, modern scientific institutions, and, most significant, dedicated attention to Brazil's existing population, rather than a showy importation of white immigrants. Whitening—whether by racial mixing or by bringing in European immigrants—was not the answer. Brazil, he argued, needed to confront its own reality and improve conditions for its own citizens.

It is all the more remarkable, then, that Nina Rodrigues believed leprosy to be in part genetic, as his calls for the control of marriage for lepers reveal. Yet his analysis moved beyond a strict genetic or hereditary focus to what he viewed as the underlying social problems. Nina Rodrigues sought to improve Brazil's standards of civilization, and, as is not often acknowledged, to improve the quality of life for the sick. In this sense he saw Brazil's social makeup as problematic but improvable through controls and modernization. The answer for him was not to be found in substituting whites for blacks or engaging in massive attempts to engineer whitening. Brazil should take its existing population's health and well-being seriously, he argued, and improve demographic growth through native policies rather than foreign solutions.

Nina Rodrigues further demonstrated his faith in policy and reform in the curious conclusion he attached to his article on leprosy. Here his provocative statements highlight the transformative role of politics and the broader social setting. Referring to the spread of disease in the Middle Ages (presumably the Black Death), Nina Rodrigues traced the problem, cryptically, to a "demoralization of the spirit." Perhaps, he mused, the "extremes of centralization" under Brazil's empire had created a similar situation in his country. And if so, he suggested, Brazil's demoralized spirit (and the health of its people) might be remedied with its new decentralized republican regime. Here, in this almost mystical explanation of disease and its causes, Nina Rodrigues revealed a critical foundation for his beliefs: political climate was critical to the health of a civilization. If state actions could prevent and cure disease, an inappropriate political system could also provoke physical symptoms of despair, or even death, among the citizenry. Rather than seeing the chief causes of disease in medical indicators, Nina Rodrigues saw them in the political and social setting of Brazil. And thus ideas of environment and culture, in their broadest social and political sense, were critical components for his views.

LEGAL MEDICINE

The contradictions that Nina Rodrigues revealed in his early article on leprosy gained further expression in his later studies of legal medicine. He was most influenced by Italian approaches to the field, where practitioners attempted not only to determine physical evidence in cases of crime but also to predict crime itself by uncovering supposed links between race, genetics, and criminality. Nina Rodrigues complained in 1892, however, that though there was great enthusiasm for the Italian school of criminology in Brazil, the contribution of Brazilian scientists had "been almost nil or at best very insignificant."[73] For Nina Rodrigues such a gap was unfortunate, as the Brazilian setting, though very different from that of Italy, offered perhaps even richer fields for observation: "our population—in the midst of formation by the crossing of three distinct races, mixed in very variable proportions—[and] our social environment—in which gradations of civilizations so different from one another can be found in conflict—necessarily offers a completely distinct field for the study of the criminal, as much in the biological realm as in the sociological."[74]

Bahia took an early national lead in these new efforts to address criminology. Indeed, Nina Rodrigues gained international attention and earned praise from the father of the field, Cesare Lombroso, as the most insightful of its practitioners in all of the Americas.[75] Yet, as we have just seen, Nina Rodrigues viewed both biology and sociology as important to criminology. In contrast to Lombroso, who attempted to read the potential for crime in the shape and measurement of a skull, Nina Rodrigues allowed a much greater role for the social environment. In his analysis of the skulls of nonwhite criminals, Nina Rodrigues repeatedly acknowledged that society and poverty, rather than physical or biological markers, might predominate in determining criminal behavior.[76]

This focus on the social environment convinced him that structural changes to Brazilian society were paramount. Nina Rodrigues worked tirelessly to address Brazilian criminality through legal reforms. His work on legal matters, however, also revealed the most racist strains of his work. His first book, *As raças humanas e a responsibilidade penal no Brasil* (The human races and penal responsibility in Brazil), had weighed in on legal questions in 1894.[77] Clearly here Nina Rodrigues put limits on role of the social environment: in this formulation of law he professed that Brazilian civilization could not hope, in a few generations, to change the African cultures brought with the slave trade. Ranking civilizations with an evolutionist eye, he believed that primitive civilizations held primitive visions of right and wrong, and although these might develop over time, people from these civilizations remained generally mired in a primitive morality that prevented their ability to understand and adhere to more advanced legal and moral dictates. Nina Rodrigues here imagined ideas of civilization and race in overlapping ways. In his view, Africans and *mestiços* were not necessarily capable of following the same legal norms as whites, or even of understanding them, in part because of their race but especially because of their "inferior" levels of culture. Active in promoting these ideas, he addressed his plans for reform repeatedly to governmental commissions in Bahia in 1896 and in 1901 to national reformers of the civil code.[78]

Although Nina Rodrigues believed that Africans had primitive levels of civilization and culture, he also believed that this culture needed to be understood. While he continued to measure skulls and worry about racial indexes, he also turned to a new research strategy: ethnographic observation. His analysis of the "primitive" practice of Candomblé had been first published in a series of articles from 1896 ("The Fetishistic Animism of Black Bahians"). By 1900 he had extended his interest from religion to broader questions of African culture and begun to publish research based on his experience in Bahia's black community. This ethnography also relied extensively on Afro-Bahian informants, who came to serve as esteemed experts and respected figures in his works (I will discuss the most important of these informants, Martiniano do Bonfim, in chapter 2). His shaping of this latest research into a book was cut short by his death in 1906; his unfinished work, later collected and published as *Os africanos no Brasil* (Africans in Brazil), revealed all the contradictions of his thought.

In this work Nina Rodrigues made belief in black inferiority abundantly clear. Although he allowed that a few individuals might sometimes break from the norm, he saw "the cultural value of a race" as fixed.[79] "If we know black men or men of color of indubitable merit, endowed with esteem and respect," he wrote, "this fact should not obstruct us from the recognition of the truth: to this point blacks have been unable to establish civilized nations."[80] In the case of Brazil, Nina Rodrigues believed that the presence of Afro-Brazilians, despite what he saw as their valuable contributions to Brazilian civilization, would "always be one of the factors in our inferiority as a nation."[81]

For all of his focus on racial inferiorities, however, Nina Rodrigues devoted much of his analysis to culture. His focus on the cultural rather than the biological value of a race reveals some of this interest. Indeed, ultimately it was a cultural question that motivated Nina Rodrigues to conduct his research. His ethnological attention to the African origins of the slaves imported to Brazil and the extent of African survivals was intended to assess the influence these cultures might play in the Brazilian nation. In the conclusion of *Os africanos no Brasil* he made his views clear:

> In the meantime, as instructive as it would be to know the unequal evolutionary and civilizing capacities of blacks and whites, today this does not fully address the question of blacks in Brazil. Given [on the one hand] their absorption into the composite population of the country, and, on the other hand, the different capacities and grades of culture among the imported blacks, it is clear that their influence on the American people whom they helped to form will thus be that much more damaging the more inferior and degraded the African element introduced by the slave trade. Now, our studies demonstrate that, contrary to what is generally supposed, the black slaves introduced in Brazil do not belong exclusively to the most degraded, brutal, or savage African peoples.[82]

Here Nina Rodrigues revealed the multiple paradoxes of his beliefs. On the one hand, blacks and whites were assumed to have differential biological and cultural capacities. On the other hand, he asserted that this was besides the point for Brazil given its high degree of racial mixing, which had created a "composite population" with different characteristics. Furthermore, culture had a powerful role to play, and Nina Rodrigues proposed that though damned by the *quantity* of African slaves imported, Brazil was somewhat redeemed by the *quality* of its African slaves. Although he believed in racial determinism, Nina Rodrigues saw the need to distinguish between Africans of different ethnic and national origins, an effort that would be taken up by social scientists such as Gilberto Freyre, as we will see in the next chapter. Engaged in an elaborate search for Brazil's founding cultures, both Nina Rodrigues and Freyre worked to create a potentially redemptive view for Brazil's future.

It has not been emphasized enough that in his ethnographic research Nina Rodrigues sought to predict the capacity of Brazilian civilization based on a careful ranking of African cultures. This ranking showed the interaction of his most racially deterministic ideas with cultural differences he viewed as profound and thus revealed the primary significance of the social environment to his worldview. In this sense Nina Rodrigues believed social change was still a necessary and positive force in Brazil, but he rejected solutions that focused on the simple substitution of European immigrants for Brazilians. Brazilians had potential, but their potential needed to be shaped by reforms that revealed an understanding of the country's racial and cultural makeup.

In typical fashion, Nina Rodrigues urged that race was a factor which needed to be addressed rather than avoided, and he warned that Brazil had to confront "the sphinx of our future—the problem of the 'negro' in Brazil." The process would not be easy: "for some it will be a delicate topic and dangerous to treat, easy to wound respectable feelings. For others, driven by fantasy or imagination . . . [it will be] an ethnic problem inexistent in Brazil."[83] Though some might wish to avoid discussion of the topic, and others to deny Brazil's racial reality, Nina Rodrigues insisted that it was only through a direct, honest study of the "problem" that some "cure" for the future might be found.

This treatment of race as a serious object of study was not embraced by the Tropicalistas or by their followers in the public health movement, who instead saw the environment as entirely formative. Nina Rodrigues argued that blacks and black culture were not uncomfortable side notes in Brazilian society but important elements in Brazil's future that needed to be studied and understood. Though racial determinism was undeniably central to his work, Nina Rodrigues defies easy categorization, for he also saw the possibility of significant modification through the social environment and pushed for extensive social reforms, thus revealing his ultimate allegiance to the Tropicalistas and the public health movement.

Conclusion

Bahia faced a difficult moment at the turn of the century as the scientifically endorsed racial doctrine that blacks and Africans were a drag on a truly "civilized" state grew ever more emphatic. This belief was easy to find in much of the science across the Atlantic, and it was easy to find in the hopes of whitening so fervent in São Paulo. Race, as a category, became increasingly important for scientists at the turn of the century, and particularly for physicians, Brazil's foremost authorities on the question at this time. Thus it is worth highlighting that many Bahian doctors turned skeptical eyes to the question of racial determinism. Racial determinism was by no means overturned in Bahia, but it was not seen as meaningful by public health authorities. Furthermore, a careful reading of Nina Rodrigues reveals that even one of the most doctrinaire of racists gave the capacity for cultural and social change significant weight. Both sectors of the Bahian medical field, therefore, questioned determinism, creating room for the transformative role of the environment, for culture, and for political and social reforms that might shape Bahia into something progressive and modern.

In the midst of these modernizing projects, public health reformers showed an early concern for public welfare, focusing on urban improvements that could benefit all of the city's inhabitants. They acknowledged significant problems for Bahia: it had no real system of sewers; its population lived in poverty that made it susceptible to disease; and as a tropical port city it proved vulnerable to epidemics such as yellow fever, influenza, and cholera. They believed that such problems could be solved by comprehensive city sanitation efforts and by far-reaching social reforms that would lift the quality of life for all the city's residents. Though they diagnosed problems in Bahia, they focused blame not on the tropical environment, or on Bahia's nonwhite population, but the larger social setting. Disease in their view could be overcome, but only through significant new actions by government and health leaders to improve social welfare, particularly for the most vulnerable in the population, the very poor. Led by the brothers

Antônio Pacífico Pereira and Manuel Vitorino Pereira, the public health reformers advocated urgent change, stressing measures to bring education to all Bahians, to reduce poverty, and to improve sanitation. In the midst of a racialized scientific moment, the Bahian doctors who held power in Brazil's new republic took a remarkable stand by insisting that social institutions such as schools, not eugenic population policy or racial controls, would improve the population as a whole.

As the 1890s dawned these specialists in the field of public health found themselves increasingly at odds with a rival worldview that was gaining prominence in Bahia, one that departed in significant ways in questions of race and followed European racial science with interest and enthusiasm. It saw race and heredity as fundamental categories ordering the world. Indeed, Nina Rodrigues saw the races themselves in terms of hierarchies, with whites the pinnacle, blacks the nadir, and *mestiços* an unstable and undetermined enigma.[84] If Bahia's capital was to aim for a civilized, modern ideal, its racial population needed to be studied and accounted for in social and legal institutions. Yet, as I have argued, the legacy of Nina Rodrigues is multivalent and complex, viewing racial difference as fundamental but granting a significant role to environmental factors in genetics and in society more broadly. Ultimately this vision of environmental change as formative created significant cooperation and agreement with the public health reformers: Bahia's capital could be made modern by reforming not only its population but also the city itself.

While historians have recognized the importance of the Bahian medical scene, our understanding of these rival fields and their impact in Bahia has remained incomplete because we tend to see these fields as isolated from one another, or as removed from the Bahian context altogether. This chapter instead has emphasized how these two radically different visions of race and social change developed and interacted with one another, coming together in a particularly vibrant form of social medicine that aimed to harness medical knowledge for the advancement of the social good. The early twentieth century marked a unique moment for social activism in Bahian medical circles, as public health reformers like the Pereira brothers worked closely with more racially deterministic thinkers such as Nina Rodrigues. This cooperation, evident in the shared editorship of the *Gazeta Médica* and the joint organization of the 1890 Bahian medical congress, indicates some significant common ground. Most obviously, these scholars were brought together by a belief in the power of environmental forces, by a shared passion for reform, and by a conviction that Bahia needed social medicine more than racial doctoring.

The "social medicine" that Bahians adopted had its most famous proponent in the German doctor Rudolf Virchow (1821–1902), who in 1848 declared famously: "Medicine is a social science, and politics is nothing more than medicine on a grand scale."[85] Bahian doctors not only paid tribute to Virchow with elaborate celebrations of his life in Salvador (his eightieth birthday was rung in with speeches, poetry recitations, a Latin address, and a band that played the German and Brazilian national anthems), they devoted much of their energy to this ideal.[86] They believed, as Virchow had, that medical professionals could best guide society to a modern, civilized paradigm. Ironically it was the doctors of the turn of the century, with a still very Eurocentric ideal of progress and no explicit campaign for racial equality, who would offer the most powerful vision of social change that Bahia would witness for much of the twentieth century.

The 1920s introduced deeper divides in racial thought across Brazil. On the one hand, racial determinism enhanced its scientific standing in international circles and in Brazil itself. Eugenics, a field of science that purported to refine the human race through selective breeding, gained ground in Brazil, albeit with more of an allowance for environmental factors than would be found in the rest of Latin America or the United States.[87] On the other hand, Brazil's public health movement also gained increasing momentum as federally funded initiatives attracted more and more national attention. One of the most dramatic early moments came with epic expeditions by doctors through the backlands of Brazil beginning in 1912. Their conclusions, widely publicized, declared that Brazil's population suffered from a shocking array of chronic disease and undernourishment. Brazil, proclaimed one medical reformer, "is an immense hospital." Unlike the diagnosis of racial degeneracy, this verdict of disease came with a promise of redemption: Brazil's population had potential, but it badly needed medical attention.[88]

This was what Bahia's reformers had asserted, but by this point the movement was no longer based in Bahia. Although the expedition targeted Bahia's backlands, and though one of its medical leaders was himself Bahian, the entire project was organized and funded through Rio de Janeiro and the federal government. Indeed, although Bahia had some approximation of a public health initiative during this time, this occurred only because federal health authorities began to focus on the state in the 1920s and, with help from the Rockefeller Foundation, sent their own officials to Bahia to force health and sanitation reforms.[89]

The decline of medical authority in Bahian politics was in part due to the fact that turn-of-the-century ideas of curing Bahia through social change held limited appeal for the elite, who enjoyed their own position in the status quo. In fact, a focus on the environment was antagonistic to the elite, who much preferred a strict hereditary perspective. The view that status, or the lack thereof, came from family genes rather than social opportunities endorsed the hierarchy of elite white rule. Furthermore, the doctors' early determination to portray themselves as experts, and to create an extensive role for themselves as bureaucrats and public authorities, may have threatened, rather than inspired, the existing political elite: by proposing such extensive overhauls during the governorship of Manuel Vitorino Pereira, the medical reformers made clear their vision of a government shaped by medical authorities rather than a traditional oligarchy.

Indeed, the broader political context of Bahia played a significant role in blocking reform. As the historian Luiz Castro Santos points out, early medical campaigns for reform corresponded with profound disorganization among Bahia's ruling powers: meaningful or effective governmental action in Bahia was an elusive dream for most of the early twentieth century.[90] The political context of immigration further shaped Bahia's inability and reluctance to advance social change. States such as São Paulo and Rio de Janeiro pushed through urban reforms with the hope of attracting European immigrants; Bahia never had the threat or hope of immigration to encourage change. Beyond these ideological obstacles, the poverty of the state government further limited the nature of reform.

Ultimately the call for social and environmental reform proved unsuccessful on all fronts in Bahia. To take only the most prominent example, the public health movement failed to convince Bahia's public authorities to make sewers a priority. Reformers probably played some role in bringing the issue up for debate, and even in pushing the municipality to initiate Salvador's first sewer construction in 1906. Sadly, the municipality stopped payment before completion of the project and the reform stalled: construction resumed in 1916 and again in 1926, but it was never completed. This early lack of infrastructure continued to plague the state capital and proved difficult to make up for as the city expanded. Even as recently as 1995 only 26 percent of the population of Salvador had access to sewers, and many of these were open, uncovered drains, subject to flooding during rainy periods.[91]

Social reform too met obstacles. While Nina Rodrigues's most extreme versions of legal racial divisions made no headway in Bahia, neither did his ideas of humanitarian reforms for the treatment of lepers or the mentally ill. And the reforms of the Pereira brothers, who proposed education for the masses, were accused of being "too radical." It appears that the Bahian elite may have felt uncertain about biological difference, but certain that they wished to preserve the social and economic hierarchies that they had worked so hard to create. Embracing talk of the "social environment," they used the idea as an obstacle to change rather than a hopeful field for government intervention. This too has had lasting repercussions. The early failure to develop an educational infrastructure surely played a role in keeping Bahia's literacy rates among the lowest in Brazil over most of the twentieth century: even the resumption of state oversight of education in the 1920s, under the energetic efforts of Anísio Teixeira, did little to alter Bahia's languishing literacy rates.[92] These rates remained essentially static into the 1940s, ensuring the effective disenfranchisement of Bahia's masses and sealing the political exclusion of Bahia's Afro-Bahian majority.

Sometimes retrograde science can serve a useful medical and social purpose.[93] Such was the case of Bahia's public health reformers and scholars of legal medicine, both of whom engaged in scientifically questionable theories, whether of miasmas or racial difference, to drive a vision of social medicine that was in the end more socially radical than most of the elite-centered reforms of the rest of the twentieth century. Even Nina Rodrigues, who worried about the retrograde influence of blacks, argued that they needed to be taken seriously as part of Bahia's makeup. This concern for human welfare, for basic provisions such as clean water, access to hospitals, sewage treatment, and education came from some questionable scientific dictates. But these dictates produced a vision of social reform that offered improvement for all of Bahia.[94] Nina Rodrigues and the public health reformers pursued modernization plans that aimed to make life safer, healthier, and ultimately more in line with the "civilized" nations of Europe. Yet these Eurocentric views of progress held some faith that Bahia's population could prosper—with a greater or lesser role for genetics depending on the field. Clearly, some of these dictates, particularly those of Nina Rodrigues, might have introduced significant racial divides. The fact remains, however, that public health reformers and Nina Rodrigues found much to agree on, and their views must be seen in all of their complexity.

The medical field's ability to shape questions of race declined as the twentieth century moved forward. The new authorities on race in the intellectual world would come from the social sciences, which, though delayed in their arrival by the lack of a university system, would nonetheless emerge from Brazil's museums and from professional congresses. The congresses of the 1930s, the subject of the next chapter, show the shift in discussions of race from medicine to the new fields of ethnology, sociology, and anthropology. Ironically, Nina Rodrigues would be taken up as a mentor in these fields—despite his tendencies toward biological determinism—and social scientists would reinvent his legacy in order to shape an emerging Bahian legacy of their own. A different spirit of reform, however, guided these social scientists, who instead organized their activism around questions of cultural integration rather than changes in Salvador's cityscape. Stepping away from a European ideal to a nascent sense of Brazilian pride, these reformers aimed for cultural inclusion in *brasilidade*, or Brazilian identity, and worried less about matters of basic welfare.

CHAPTER 2

Contests of Culture

Brazil's revolution of 1930 ushered Getúlio Vargas into the presidency and shifted power away from the nation's traditional oligarchies. Bahia's elite faced the future uncertainly as federally appointed governors, or interventors, replaced them in office. They referred scornfully to Interventor Juracy Magalhães (a native of Ceará) as a *forasteiro*, or foreigner, and used him as a foil to what they deemed an "authentic" Bahian identity. Such rhetoric about the outside disruption of true Bahian ideals concealed real fears about the future: the revolution's vague agenda of centralization and national regeneration offered unclear benefit for Bahia. Furthermore, the populist appeals made by Vargas surely unsettled an elite that had most often aimed to conceal, rather than to mobilize, the black Bahian majority.

Ultimately populism had its limits in Brazil, however, and especially in Bahia; while traditional oligarchs may have suffered from their political marginalization, the transformations of the era only minimally broadened state electoral politics. Women won suffrage in 1932, but the barring of illiterates from the vote still meant that many Bahians were excluded from the elections of the Vargas era (1930–45). And as Vargas grew increasingly sympathetic to fascism, he suspended elections altogether: his inauguration of the Estado Novo, or New State, in 1937 created an effective dictatorship until the return of democracy in 1945.[1]

While the realm of politics remained restricted, the cultural policies of the Vargas era did offer new opportunities for mass participation, at least symbolically. Vargas and his cultural ministers aimed to fuse a heightened sense of *brasilidade*, or Brazilianness, inspired by folk, popular, and even Afro-Brazilian cultural traditions. Europhile elite cultural practices began to lose status, while the Afro-Brazilian melodies of samba rose to national prominence; the African-inspired martial art of capoeira became elevated to "national gymnastics"; and folk tunes became fodder for new nationalist compositions. Although the Vargas cultural program inevitably suffered from cooptation and control, it nonetheless granted new value to native, rather than foreign, cultural movements. Such nationalistic leanings had their intellectual roots in the 1920s, with events such as São Paulo's Modern Art Week and Gilberto Freyre's Regionalist Movement, but the Vargas era brought new state interest in Brazilian identity and culture.[2]

Bahian promoters used this national moment to argue for a new role for their state as the birthplace of Brazil and the cradle of authentic Brazilian traditions. By the time Vargas made his first visit in 1933, he was able to draw on nativist pride by evoking Bahia as "the birthplace of our nationality" in his speeches and appeals.[3] Such imagery of Bahia as central to Brazil had in fact been encouraged not only by elite intellectuals but also by popular samba and its utopic Bahian refrains. Indeed, samba itself was rumored to have been created by Bahian migrants relocated in Rio de Janeiro's slums.[4] But if Rio de Janeiro was samba's birthplace and the center of the nation's budding recording industry, Bahia was its muse and a central motif for sambistas. Those lyricists unlucky enough to have been born outside Bahia made up for such deficiencies by praising Bahia all the more. The composer Ary Barroso, for example, wrote lyrical rhapsodies about Bahia with only the most marginal knowledge of the state; he visited only after his themes were already well developed.[5] Most relevant to Bahia's importance in this popular music scene was Dorival Caymmi, an Afro-Bahian musician who skyrocketed to national prominence during the 1930s. Caymmi composed sambas that portrayed Bahia in idyllic terms and made praising the region his principal lyrical theme. As Bryan McCann argues, his efforts imparted an "apparent folkloric authenticity" to samba as the Northeast—and especially Bahia—came to be seen as a pristine repository for Brazil's truest traditions.[6]

For the majority of blacks living this in this land of tradition, such valorization was undoubtedly influential, but it had its limits. Indeed, there was still much left to be gained. Blacks in Bahia were a distinct underclass in the 1930s, economically, socially, and politically. And Afro-Bahians battled enduring racial prejudice made all the more malignant by the often subtle form it took. Bahians themselves rarely commented on the inequalities that divided the population largely along lines of color. But select foreign observers evocatively portrayed the racial dynamic of the time. Such depictions demand careful treatment, of course, for U.S. scholars in particular could not help but be influenced by comparisons with the severity of segregation and racial oppression in the United States.[7] But while U.S. observers of Bahia in the 1930s noted a surprising absence of racial tension, they often described social divisions that failed to match the writers' rosy conclusions.

In fact, despite general assertions of racial harmony, academic chroniclers such as Donald Pierson and Ruth Landes (both treated further in chapter 4) could not help but be struck by the harsh inequalities of Bahian life, and their own evidence often revealed significant racial exclusion. Although both ultimately concluded that race was not important in blocking access to goods and status, their ethnographic detail revealed that life for most Afro-Bahians took place in painful poverty and under significant racial stigma and exclusion. Exceptions existed, of course, which allowed these authors and others to argue that much depended on factors beyond race such as education, class, and lighter skin color. Yet the portrait of Bahia by these researchers, when examined closely, revealed the rise of a few exceptional Afro-Brazilians, especially among those of mixed heritage, whose accomplishments seemed virtually unattainable for an enormous black underclass with little possibility of upward mobility. Blacks, according to Pierson's estimates, made up 0.4 percent of Salvador's "intelligentsia" but 75 percent of the lower class. Whites were in the opposite position: they made up 84 percent of the intelligentsia but only 1.5 percent of the lower class. And people of mixed heritage fell in the middle, with 16 percent found in the intelligentsia, 23 percent in the lower classes, and the majority located in the middle sectors.[8]

Pierson noted in a paper presented to Salvador's Afro-Brazilian Congress of 1937 (treated later in this chapter) that "blacks in Bahia, according to occupational indices, still make up the greatest portion of the lower class and find themselves progressively less represented according to the proportion that we move up on the occupational scale. . . . whites still occupy the majority of preferred occupations."[9] In his book *Negroes in Brazil* he elaborated: blacks dominated in professions such as porters, laundresses, masons, dockworkers, domestics, candy peddlers, cobblers, newsboys, and shoe shiners. "Mulattoes" tended to be concentrated in positions such as barbers, musicians, street sweepers, and to a lesser degree clerks and police and army officers. Whites, at the top of the social ladder, dominated positions as bank employees, priests, businessmen, lawyers, politicians, and doctors.[10] This dominance by white elites was all the more remarkable given their small numbers in the city. Whites made up roughly a quarter of the population of Salvador in 1932, while *pretos* made up another quarter, and *pardos* the remaining 50 percent.[11] Blacks were completely unrepresented among the very rich of the city, according to one tax collector interviewed by Pierson, and Pierson's own counts showed them to be absent from the city's most prestigious social club, elite political galas, and even from passing cars.[12] White students responded overwhelmingly that intermarriage with blacks was not appropriate (93%), and the majority (66%) refused to consider even the possibility of dancing with blacks.[13] Such ideals constituted an extreme vision of social and economic segregation that aimed to cloister the small white minority away from the city's majority population.

This setting of exclusion and racial division made the events of the 1930s dynamic and complex. On the one hand, like much of Latin America, Brazil was beginning to embrace a multiracial identity. On the other hand, here, like elsewhere, society itself remained marked by strict hierarchies that belied much of this developing cultural acceptance.[14] Nonetheless, the cultural reimaginings of Brazil are important, particularly in terms of thinking of race. Certainly they sparked a significant shift in Bahia. Building on the new cultural movements of the era, Bahia began to claim links to African and folk traditions with new pride.[15] The turn-of-the-century observer Raimundo Nina Rodrigues had noted Bahia's exceptional role in maintaining Brazil's cultural connection to Africa at a time when such pronouncements profoundly disturbed and embarrassed Bahia's elite. By the 1930s, social scientists and Afro-Bahians themselves worked to dispel this stigma and found themselves in a more fertile historical moment.

This is most clearly evident in a pair of congresses that called academics together to discuss the African contribution to Brazil. The first Afro-Brazilian Congress, held in 1934, and the second, held in 1937, both attracted top scholars. Press coverage and the publication of their proceedings disseminated the debates that occurred there more broadly. The congresses aimed from the beginning to move discussions of race from biological terms to the language of culture and sociology. Despite their common aims, however, their outcomes were very different, and the results critically influenced Bahia's trajectory. The first congress, held in Recife and organized by the U.S.-trained sociologist Gilberto Freyre, attempted to move beyond biological and racial determinism but revealed the scholars to be in the midst of an uneasy transition. Some scholars moved only partially beyond the framework of racial determinism, and many others turned instead to various forms of cultural determinism. The second congress, organized in Salvador by the young Afro-Bahian ethnologist Edison Carneiro, showed a more definitive break with determinism, moved sharply away from biological language, and sought to involve Afro-Brazilians themselves in the event. In the contests over the meaning of culture, Bahia's African heritage moved from being viewed as a problem to becoming a treasured part of the state's traditions.

The Birth of the Social Sciences: New Languages of Race

The Afro-Brazilian congresses of 1934 and 1937 took place at a critical moment in the development of ideas of race and the birth of the social sciences. While biology was the original foundation for studies of race, culture had become a new priority for scholars. As the 1920s unfolded, Brazilian discussions of race began to broaden from the realm of medicine to the social sciences. To be sure, the division between medical science and the early social sciences remained somewhat fluid, and fields such as physical anthropology bridged the two. Both congresses played a critical role in ensuring that culture, not biology, would become the new framework for talking about the Afro-Brazilian contribution to Brazil.[16]

Nonetheless, the First Afro-Brazilian Congress in 1934 revealed a still unsettled consensus on race in the social sciences. Though the organizer of the Recife congress, Gilberto Freyre, insisted that ideas of racial supremacy had been disproved, the question continued to drive many of the congress participants. And though Freyre made an important intervention in discussions of Brazilian identity by highlighting the contributions of African and indigenous culture to the nation, he was still far from accepting such cultures as equal. The French scholar Roger Bastide later wrote that the first congress served to "lay the foundations for a distinctive Africanology" as Brazilian scholars began to "break the umbilical cord to Europe [and] suddenly became aware of the value of cultural traits which had come from Africa."[17] In fact, these foundations remained shaky. While scholars have viewed Freyre and the movement toward culture in the 1930s as a sharp break with older, racially deterministic approaches, the Recife congress shows that determinism was slow to be cast aside. Instead the congress revealed that hierarchies of biology had been largely replaced by hierarchies of culture. Though key scholars such as Freyre and Edison Carneiro valorized Afro-Brazilian culture in the 1934 congress and celebrated it as central to Brazil, they both were uncomfortable with its relation to African culture, a contribution which they viewed as primitive and no longer central to the Brazilian context.

Despite the reliance on cultural hierarchies at the first congress, the shift to cultural terms marked a significant change. Most important, it opened the door for Afro-Brazilians to begin to participate in central academic debates. While medical discussions could not easily be entered by those outside the field, the realm of culture offered potential for broader participation. In fact, the late development of the social sciences in Brazil offered a unique opportunity for such participation. Brazil's first university opened only in 1934, and Bahia's first humanities program started only in 1942. Until then social scientists were often self-trained and depended on the occasional congress to attempt to consolidate their fields and their methodology. While anthropology established roots in a few of the country's limited museums, and physical anthropologists gained some training in medical schools, practitioners in fields such as sociology and ethnology were left to eke out an existence independently. With no formal academic training, no advanced degree, and no medical terminology to distinguish expert from layman, this new disciplinary focus on culture briefly offered a more democratic arena for discussions of the black contribution to Brazil. As we will see, by the second congress blacks themselves were contributing decisively to the conversation. The extrainstitutional development of the social sciences in the 1930s opened up surprising space for Afro-Brazilian contribution to the field.

Such possibilities remained latent in the first Afro-Brazilian Congress; they would materialize with the second in 1937. There, in a remarkable turn, Afro-Brazilians, particularly practitioners of Candomblé, became the new experts, contributing to both the Salvador congress and the development of the social sciences as a whole. Admittedly, such opportunities still depended on the goodwill and interest of more elite partners: Edison Carneiro, as organizer, played an important role in brokering this participation. Yet remarkably, thanks to Carneiro as well as the Candomblé community at large, the

Afro-Brazilian Congress of 1937 showed off Candomblé leaders as intellectuals and authorities in the realm of religious tradition. And these intellectuals, as well as the scholars who studied them, helped define a new role for Bahia, that of the nation's most important center of Afro-Brazilian culture. Emphasizing links to "authentic" African practices, both intellectuals and the Candomblé community agreed that Bahia needed special protection to preserve its valued, if threatened, traditions.

Leaving behind the Recife event's reluctance to abandon biracial typologies and its discomfort with African culture, the Salvador congress moved to a new cultural hierarchy that turned the standard established by the first congress on its head. African culture and African connections were now privileged; African culture represented the pinnacle of achievement. This valuation reversed the privilege given to Brazilian culture in the first congress by scholars such as Freyre and Carneiro. This chapter traces the uncomfortable attitude toward Africa in the first congress, then turns to the academic battlefield in which Recife and Salvador fought to be considered the center of the new field of Afro-Brazilian studies. Finally, it turns to the Salvador congress, where the black community rallied to endorse its own vision of African-based "authenticity." As this chapter reveals, the Salvador congress and the enthusiasm it generated ensured that Bahia emerged as the definitive locus of Afro-Brazilian tradition and the center of future efforts in Afro-Brazilian studies. Let us turn first to its predecessor.

The Recife Afro-Brazilian Congress of 1934:
Cultural Rankings and the Dilemma of African Culture

In 1934 the U.S. anthropologist Melville J. Herskovits received an invitation for an ambitious series of events to be held at the First Afro-Brazilian Congress later that year. The invitation aimed to bring together scholars from across Brazil and even Europe and North America to "study problems of race relations in Brazil and to trace African influence in the cultural development of the Brazilian people."[18] The clear emphasis on sociological, rather than biological, questions resulted in large part from the framing and organization of the congress by the young scholar and Recife native Gilberto Freyre.

In 1934 Freyre had just published his first book, *Casa-grande e senzala* (*The Masters and the Slaves*), where he drew on a variety of intellectual currents, particularly the groundbreaking anthropology of Franz Boas, to argue that Brazil's racial mixture and tropical climate did not doom its future. Despite its often impressionistic nature, the work was an important attempt to valorize the indigenous and African contributions to Brazil.[19] While Freyre's analysis in *Casa-grande* incorporated elements of the reigning scientific views on race and race mixture, his focus on a Brazilian hybrid culture signaled a shift away from the biological effects of racial mixing, or *mestiçagem*, and a new emphasis on the sociological and cultural results of this mixture. Freyre insisted that, regardless of the tone of Brazilian skin, the Brazilian soul retained black imprints: "every Brazilian, even the light-skinned fair-haired one, carries about with him on his soul . . . the shadow, or at least the birthmark, of the black."[20] Whatever the biological result of *mestiçagem*, elements of indigenous, Portuguese, and African culture remained etched in Brazilian identity, and these contributions, including black contributions, would not gradually disappear through repeated mixing.[21]

In the preface to his work Freyre claimed Franz Boas as a central influence on his views of the primacy of culture. A leader in anthropology in the United States, Boas concluded from his studies of immigrant children that culture and environment proved formative, while categories of "race" were less stable and significant than scientists had assumed.[22] Freyre had studied with Boas for his master's degree at Columbia University in 1922, but he was far from alone in admiring Boas and his emphasis on culture.[23] Indeed, the 1930s witnessed a dramatic shift as many Brazilian scholars began to reconsider ideas of race and to give added weight to the role of culture.[24] The congress encouraged a decidedly cultural approach.[25] According to the invitation, the event intended to examine "problems of ethnography, folklore, art, sociology, and social psychology" and would also include exhibitions by artists.[26] Clearly, part of the primary objective was to foster the social sciences, and the congress was a particularly important forum for these still embryonic disciplines.

The First Afro-Brazilian Congress revealed deep divisions, however, about the state of Afro-Brazilian studies and its methodology as scholars moved to bridge the divide between biological approaches to race and newer attempts to unravel the influences of culture. Many scholars remained mired in the biological concerns of an earlier era and still attempted to assess the results of *mestiçagem* in the strict scientific terms of the era, using extensive anthropometric measurements. Geraldo de Andrade, for example, a recent graduate from the Recife Medical School, used cranial indices and color indices to conclude that the mulatto population of Pernambuco was whitening.[27] His research represented one branch of scholarship that sought to quantify the results of racial *mestiçagem* and report back optimistic findings that minimized black or "regressive" influences.

Other contributors to the congress departed from this concern over physical indicators, however, and questioned the ultimate relevance of race. Juliano Moreira, trained in Bahia and a follower of the Tropicalista school, used intelligence tests and other evidence to argue that environment, not race, was the most important factor in mental development.[28] Moreira, the former director of the National Mental Asylum in Rio de Janeiro, had died in 1933, but his research was seen as so relevant to the conference that his widow presented a paper with selections from his work over the previous thirty years. The summary of his research concluded with a ringing endorsement of nurture over nature. In his opinion, barring physical defects, "it is certain in every case that an individual removed from a socially inferior setting and moved to a better environment at an early point will develop in a surprising manner."[29] Biological studies of race continued to be important, but their results were increasingly challenged by scholars who stressed the formative role that the Brazilian environment—and culture—might play.

Africa Debated

Though many scholars grappled with cultural questions, three are most central to the field of Afro-Brazilian studies and, ultimately, to the story of Bahia traced here: Gilberto Freyre, Edison Carneiro, and Arthur Ramos. Ramos and Freyre were perhaps the most distinguished Brazilian scholars to attend the conference. Carneiro, though still unknown at this point, would become one of Bahia's most important intellectuals. Though the three addressed different themes in the papers they presented to the congress, they were united by an uneasiness in treating the impact of African culture in Brazil. Freyre presented only one formal paper, "Bodily Deformations in Black Fugitives," which studied runaway slave advertisements from nineteenth-century Brazilian newspapers.[30] Freyre argued that the physical descriptions of the slaves' bodies shed light on the conditions of Brazilian slavery; slave owners, anxious to ensure the return of their human property, carefully documented injuries, deformities, and distinguishing marks to help authorities identify individual slaves. In an exhaustive and sometimes overwhelming catalog of physical ailments and problems, Freyre attempted to diagnose the ills faced by slaves in Brazil. While some assessments showed real medical insight, others were purely speculative, an effect heightened by his neglect in citing sources.[31]

The paper highlights Freyre's efforts to refute racial science as well as his struggle with the retention and role of African culture in modern Brazil.

Freyre worked to dispel notions that the African contribution to Brazil had been negative: "although of course we cannot forget that in some cases [blacks] are carriers of African defects and illnesses, these are found in far less significant numbers than the carriers of illnesses and vices acquired here—in contrast with the image of the socially pathological black, the figures who appear throughout the announcements are, in great number, admirably eugenic: black men and women who are strong, tall, attractive, well-formed, their teeth white and perfect."[32] This "admirably eugenic" praise makes clear that Freyre did not dismiss the role of race and biology altogether but rather found blacks to be a noble, rather than an inferior race. His priorities are also clear in his discussion of pathologies: African disease, in his view, was unimportant in the face of broader and more immediate Brazilian ills.

Freyre had by 1933 developed a neo-Lamarckian view that saw traits originating in the surrounding environment and society as influential and inherited. Lamarckians believed that the environment could bring about changes in an individual that could then be passed on as a genetic heritage to the next generation.[33] Freyre's understanding of Lamarckian ideas had important implications for his analysis presented at the congress. Most significant, it allowed him to insist that Africans had arrived in good form but that their physical and social advantages had been altered by the effects of slavery and the Brazilian setting. Freyre's views of heredity assumed that abuses under slavery not only had been destructive originally but continued to degrade the black population of Brazil. Thus, for Freyre, neither race nor African culture could be blamed for degradations often viewed in racial terms; instead, the corrosive influence of slavery and the Brazilian social setting was the source of contemporary problems.

Freyre finished his paper by warning that while Brazil's African ancestors should not be romanticized as faultless "demigods," it was time to absolve them from blame for the "ills and diseases they developed, since they would have probably developed in another race imported and subjected to the same regime of slavery in a nation of monoculture."[34] In the end, for the purposes of his article, Freyre saw little use in tracing African characteristics or discussing problems of race. Brazilian culture and the abuses of slavery were the most important factors in shaping the Afro-Brazilian population and negated any distinctiveness about African culture: the problems faced by slaves were not African in origin but more recent. This in some ways contradicted the arguments advanced in *Casa-grande*, where he devoted more attention to African roots: indeed, he attempted to differentiate among African cultures in order to argue that Brazil had absorbed only the most "advanced" African civilizations.[35] Yet in both arenas, Freyre ranked cultures: Brazilian culture was, for him, by far the most formative and important. The message for African culture was paradoxically both redemptive and dismissive as Freyre attempted to dismantle racial arguments for the condition of blacks in Brazil.

The Afro-Bahian ethnologist Edison Carneiro presented two papers at the Recife congress that differed considerably in tone and emphasis. Only twenty-two years old, Carneiro lacked the formal academic and scientific affiliations held by many of the other congress participants. He had earned his degree in law but made his living as a journalist and also had considerable contacts with practitioners of Candomblé in Salvador.[36] Carneiro's interest may have stemmed from his own mixed racial background, but it had probably been furthered by his immersion in the culture of Salvador, as well as the interests and guidance of his father, Souza Carneiro, a local expert in Afro-Brazilian folklore who collected folktales in Salvador and its environs.[37]

Carneiro contributed an article on Candomblé to the congress and also offered a more general paper on the status of Afro-Brazilians. The two articles shared the same general conclusion: Africa had little bearing on the lives of Afro-Brazilians. In his article "Xangô," Carneiro analyzed the practice of Candomblé. The bulk of the article was dedicated to a description of the deity Xangô and built on the work of an earlier Afro-Bahian self-trained in ethnology, Manuel Querino. Querino (1851–1923) was a founding member of the conservative and traditional Instituto Geográfico e Histórico da Bahia (Geographic and Historic Institute of Bahia, or IGHB) who wrote about the African past in essays such as "The Black Colonist as a Factor in Brazilian Civilization," first published in 1918. He paved an early path for intellectuals who would take Afro-Bahian culture as a serious topic for study, especially black scholars such as Carneiro.[38]

Carneiro wasted little time discussing Africa and instead emphasized that whatever the origins of Afro-Brazilian religion, it had changed considerably in its new environment. Its mythology, he emphasized, had been "created under different conditions than those of the primitive habitat."[39] Afro-Brazilian beliefs preserved basic associations of the African Xangô, but, he argued, the deity had gathered new associations in its new context, many of them with Catholic saints. Carneiro's work seems at first to lack methodology, and his approach appears more descriptive than analytical. In fact the article was a powerful rejoinder to a paper presented to the congress by Arthur Ramos, in which Ramos argued that Candomblé represented the survival of a primitive mentality from Africa.

Arthur Ramos was born in the state of Alagoas in 1903 and moved to Salvador in 1921 to attend medical school.[40] Though Raimundo Nina Rodrigues had been dead for more than a decade, his legacy still held sway in Bahia, and Ramos followed closely in his footsteps, specializing in clinical psychiatry and forensic medicine. His thesis examined insanity and criminality, and after graduation he continued his research in Salvador, with a five-year association at the Nina Rodrigues Institute. In 1933 he relocated to Rio de Janeiro, at the invitation of the educator Anísio Teixeira, to oversee "mental hygiene" in Rio's public schools. His research and writing during this time spanned a variety of topics from social psychology and education to the role of African culture in Brazil. He would become more famous for his work in the latter sphere, and the first book of his four-volume series *O problema do negro no Brasil* (The problem of the black in Brazil) appeared in 1934.[41]

As a psychiatrist, Ramos had posited the existence of primitive subconscious survivals whose roots were to be found primarily in Africa.[42] In contrast, Carneiro looked at the practice of Afro-Brazilian religion not as a psychiatrist but as an ethnologist. His article demonstrated that he saw mentality as largely irrelevant and social environment as paramount. Though he himself assessed African culture as primitive, Carneiro neatly argued that it had little influence in what was essentially a Brazilian creation. Ramos's focus on mentality and the subconscious had allowed him to trace long connections back to Africa. Carneiro's sociological focus placed all responsibility and causality on the Brazilian environment.

Carneiro emphasized the Brazilian setting throughout his article and worked to ground the beliefs of Candomblé in a specifically Bahian geography. He cast aside questions of the Afro-Bahian's mental landscape and instead focused on Bahia's physical and geographical landscape, drawing connections between beliefs and everyday life and practice. Carneiro was also careful to specify the location of devotion, noting, for example, that the goddess Iemanjá, the second-most popular *orixá* in Bahia (after Xangô), resided in a lake in the Salvador. The world of Candomblé was not a primitive mental state that flowed uninterrupted from Africa; it was an active and living social practice with extensive ties to the community and the real-world Brazilian context. Furthermore, by mentioning white practitioners and believers in his article, Carneiro may have intended to highlight the fragility of

African roots. After all, if even whites participated in the practice, it could not be linked with an exclusively African mentality or a distant African past. Carneiro's approach differed from the psychoanalytical and mental survivals of Arthur Ramos. His focus was not African continuities but the everyday realities and beliefs of practitioners in Brazil, and more specifically, in Bahia.

Concern with contemporary realities is even more evident in the other paper Carneiro presented, "The Situation of the Black in Brazil." In an assertive opening he charged that the abolition of slavery had "resolved the problems of whites, but not of blacks." According to Carneiro, legal equality granted empty privilege and meant only that "blacks, as well as proletarian whites and *índios*, had the right to die of hunger."[43] Capitalism, he proposed, had provided simply another form of slavery, and while Carneiro did not romanticize Brazil's slave past, he argued nonetheless that it had at least offered basic sustenance, something the market rarely provided. According to Carneiro, blacks, exploited through market capitalism, had fallen into alcoholism, vagrancy, fetishism, and criminality. Carneiro's communist leanings shaped his belief in the power of market forces, but much of the degradation he lamented was social and cultural.

Carneiro viewed Freyre's ideas of cultural hybridity with a cynical eye. He argued that if Brazil had incorporated Afro-Brazilian elements into its culture and its society, this had happened almost always against the will of the "white master." In direct opposition to Freyre's ideas of a cultural and social *mestiçagem*, Carneiro stated: "The black has been, and continues to be, a being apart, almost an animal [*bicho*] that the mayors permit only to pass through the streets and work for the white. And nothing more."[44] Freyre's ideas of cultural fusion were blasted with a stark vision of separate races and a powerful statement of existing racial prejudice.

This separation, according to Carneiro, was the root of contemporary problems that stemmed from not racial difference but socioeconomic injustice. "The deplorable situation that blacks find themselves in within Brazil," he wrote, "absolutely does not testify against the *raça negra*. We know today that race does not have the importance in social development that one [often] wants to give it. . . . What exists is not fixed racial inferiority or superiority . . . but inequality of economic development. . . . the lack of conditions to help [blacks] effectively, humanely, meant that the blacks' absorption process of the superior culture of the white suffered a slowdown that set blacks even further back."[45]

This attempt to dismiss race as a determinative category fit with the trend of the rest of the congress, but Carneiro set himself apart by arguing that the solution to economic inequalities and resulting social problems lay in blacks' accepting and integrating themselves into mainstream (white) culture. Carneiro's critique of postabolition inequalities highlighted not only an exploitative economy but also cultural and social degeneracy: his proposals for integration were marked as much by disdain for black culture as by righteousness for equality.[46] For him, fusion represented a solution, but it was far from being a reality. His argument represented a line of analysis parallel to that of the African American sociologist E. Franklin Frazier in the United States: the race problem was cultural and the result of an incomplete acceptance of white culture.[47] Carneiro perhaps went one step further in his Marxist emphasis on poverty as a barrier to this mainstream culture, but his focus on problems of culture, rather than race or biology, was central to his view of race relations.

Carneiro's evaluation of Afro-Brazilian culture was by no means positive, as he believed the position of blacks had fallen to a humiliating level. In the Candomblé article, he concluded that the magnitude of Xangô's feats was further heightened by Afro-Brazilian tendencies toward exaggeration and overdramatization. The radical and frank tone of Carneiro's statement differed considerably from the other papers. Its treatment of a political present as well as its denunciation of inequalities set it apart from the rest of the studies, which focused, if not on the past, at least on trying to minimize difference and current inequalities, albeit often in biological terms.[48]

In the end, though the shift to culture turned away from racial determinism, it was still not a relativist position. Brazilian or "white" culture came to the fore as most prominent and most advanced, while African culture sank to the primitive level envisioned by Ramos or Carneiro or had to be swept away by assertions of the primacy of Brazilian culture. Brazilians, and indeed most scholars, were not yet ready to embrace a culturally relativist position that gave equal status to all cultures. Racial equality was an admirable and noble idea; cultural equality was an idea that had not yet gained currency. Indeed, Freyre, Ramos, and Carneiro all argued at various points that African culture was primitive and sometimes savage. Highlighting Brazilian identity as the most formative gave these thinkers increased relevance in a highly nationalistic moment. For Freyre and Ramos, whether intentionally or not, it allowed a continued hierarchy of Brazilian culture that in some ways challenged but by no means overturned the status quo. For Carneiro, asserting the force of the Brazilian context and culture was the surest way to unite all Brazilians under one redeemed, de-Africanized culture. The first congress pushed the social sciences away from biological categories, but it also exposed the struggles of scholars still uncertain of how to weigh the role of culture.

Although scholars at the first congress turned to culture as a category to replace that of race, these categories and their importance continued to overlap and bleed together. New priorities ushered in attention to African culture rather than racial studies of the "negroid," but also brought new dilemmas. Arthur Ramos, for instance, in trying to redeem the turn-of-the-century scholar Nina Rodrigues, would later claim that though the work of Nina Rodrigues was grounded in the scientific racism of his time, it retained all of its relevance if modern readers simply substituted the concept of race with that of culture.[49] This substitution of terminology, however, did nothing to eliminate the prevalent idea that some groups were superior to others, whether due to racial background or culture itself.

Reinventing African Traditions: Bahia's Candomblé Community

If some academics had expressed discomfort with the role of African culture in the Recife congress, the 1937 congress in Salvador moved to new acceptance of African traditions, driven, in large part, by a much greater participation in the congress by African descendants themselves. A sense of pride in African roots was not altogether new to Bahia, but it gained momentum in the 1930s. The U.S. sociologist Donald Pierson conducted extensive field work in Bahia from 1935 to 1937 and provides ample documentation of a sense of African pride felt by Bahia's black community. Such pride was perhaps most developed in the realm of Candomblé, where claims of African authenticity were the ultimate praise for a *terreiro*, or house of worship. Thus Procópio, a Candomblé leader, or *pai-de-santo*, "proudly boasts" in Pierson's study that all of his paternal line came from Africa. Although his mother, a *mãe-de-santo* (Candomblé priestess), had been born in Brazil, Procópio took great care to specify that her sister was from Africa.[50] This type of genealogical precision in asserting African ties, far from unusual among Candomblé leaders, was especially developed by the two most powerful figures in Candomblé in Bahia's 1930s, Eugênia Ana Santos (known more commonly as Aninha) and Martiniano Eliseu do Bonfim (known as Martiniano). The two reinforced each other's legitimacy, and Martiniano played a significant role in establishing Aninha and her temple.[51] Together they increased the status of African connections and of religious practice centered on ideas of African authenticity.

Martiniano was born in Brazil in 1859, but in the Candomblé community he was greatly admired for his intimate ties to Africa. Pierson introduces him as "known and thoroughly respected throughout the fetish world for his piety and sincerity and his knowledge of African customs and traditions." So respected was his expertise that he was often called to the neighboring state of Pernambuco, where there was no one of his status or authority to perform select religious rites.[52] As a key informant for most of the early scholars of Candomblé, he played an immense role in shaping academic knowledge, appearing as a central figure in the narratives of scholars such as Raimundo Nina Rodrigues, Donald Pierson, Edison Carneiro, E. Franklin Frazier, Lorenzo Turner, and especially Ruth Landes.[53]

Martiniano's knowledge owed much to his time spent as a young man in Lagos. His parents, both freed Africans, determined to educate their son in their native land. Taken by his father to present-day Nigeria in 1875, he stayed there for eleven years, attending a Presbyterian school taught by African missionaries. Though his school educated him in English, and he later taught the language to students in Bahia, he also became fluent in Yoruba. According to the biography collected by another U.S. scholar, the African-American linguist Lorenzo Turner, his training in Yoruba made a deep impact: in the early 1940s, more than a half-century later, Turner reported that Martiniano spoke Yoruba as fluently as Portuguese.[54] Carneiro himself trained in Yoruba under Martiniano, one of the few options available for the study of any African language in Brazil during this time.[55]

Yet the Yoruba language was only part of a larger cultural legacy that Martiniano drank in: he also trained as a *babalawo*, or diviner of Ifa. It was this religious training and a wide exposure to the Yoruba "traditions" being cultivated by a cultural renaissance in colonial West Africa that Martiniano would call on in Bahia. The U.S. anthropologist Ruth Landes, who provided one of the most thorough contemporary portraits of Martiniano, wrote: "Passionately he condemned ignorance of African morals and traditions. He found it terrible that the new generation did not care much about cult practices, and that present-day standards for those practices were being lowered and cheapened. He felt that he was losing his footing and he was frightened. Not frightened for himself, he would say, but for his people, for whom he felt responsible, and upon whom he feared would fall the whimsical vengeance of the neglected African gods."[56] Martiniano's anxiety drove him to make energetic efforts in Bahia's Candomblé community, although his vision of protecting African traditions was more precisely targeted than Landes ac-

knowledged: Martiniano worked especially to ensure the prestige and continuation of his own Yoruba heritage.

In fact scholars have pointed to a variety of reasons why African roots, and
particularly Yoruba roots, became a central marker of legitimacy in Bahian
Candomblé by the 1930s. While scholars agree that the process originated
in the late nineteenth century, they disagree about the precise timing and
the causes. Indeed, despite the African heritage of Candomblé, it is critical to remember that it was not so much faithfully preserved as reinvented.
For anthropologist J. Lorand Matory, the African focus of Candomblé came
largely from transatlantic travelers impressed by a Yoruba cultural renaissance in West Africa in the 1890s. Matory points out that Martiniano was
not the only member of Bahia's black community to visit West Africa. These
observers arrived at a critical moment, one in which missionaries, Africans,
and colonial authorities collaborated in constructing an idea of authenticity and purity that privileged the Yoruba over other ethnic groups. Indeed,
part of this effort involved fashioning a sense of Yoruba identity from many
disparate ethnic allegiances.[57] For Matory, the idea of African tradition that
Martiniano inculcated was relatively recent and originated in initiatives that
he, his family, and a larger community had undertaken in modern Western
Africa. This was not, as many scholars once assumed, a preservation of an
African past transmitted faithfully from before the time of slavery.[58] Ideas
of African purity and tradition used by Martiniano and others like him were
not so much a remembered history as a history being crafted in the late
nineteenth century.

The anthropologists Luís Nicolau Parés and Stefania Capone agree that
Bahia's Afro-Brazilian religions were crafted, not preserved; they emphasize
that claims of African authenticity in Candomblé have been shaped according to practical and historical concerns. Yet while all may agree on agency
by the Candomblé community, Parés sees an Africanization that began
earlier than the 1890s, and he has argued that the impact of transatlantic
travelers must have been limited. For Parés racial tensions around the early
stages of abolition in the 1870s created a competitive environment among
Candomblé *terreiros* where leaders sought to distinguish themselves and
attract clients: claims of authenticity became a powerful way to advance a
particular Candomblé.[59]

The end result of this Africanization of Candomblé, which only further
developed in the twentieth century, was to ensure a vibrant place for Africa
in Bahia. Indeed, the esteem for Africa was such that many transatlantic

merchants specialized in providing imports to Bahian buyers anxious for authentic African products.[60] Martiniano brought African cloth back from his travels, while Aninha sold African goods to other members of the religious community in Salvador's center.[61] Pierson reports that her success owed much to her prestige and knowledge of African products: "since the members of the fetish world know that these articles must be, if she sells them, legitimate, the store does a thriving business."[62]

Aninha was not herself African, but her ties to Africa proved essential not only to her commercial success but also to her authority. As one elite patron of Candomblé (known by the title of *ogan*) proudly noted, "She knows African things better than anyone I know in Bahia." And she herself stressed this same idea. As she explained to Pierson: "'My *seita* is pure Nagô. . . . But I have revived much of the African tradition, which even Engenho Velho [a competing sect, or *seita*] has forgotten. Do they have a ceremony for the twelve ministers of Xangô? No! But I do.'"[63] In fact such a ceremony had been largely invented for this purpose by Martiniano, but Aninha's claims to rigorous adherence to tradition made her a legend in Bahia.[64] As Martiniano described her, shortly after her death, "I consider her to be one of the last great *Mães*. She really tried to study our ancient religion and reestablish it in its African purity. I taught her a lot, and she even visited Nigeria. . . . None of them [the remaining Candomblé leaders] do things correctly, as she did."[65] This orthodoxy became accepted among scholars as well. Carneiro, writing her obituary for the Bahian press, would emphasize that with the death of Aninha "African-origin religions lost one of their most learned and greatest interpreters. . . . She did much for the preservation of African traditions in Candomblé in Bahia."[66]

Aninha, however, was the leader not of a traditional Candomblé *terreiro* but a new one that she had founded herself. As an exceptionally young head priestess, or *mãe-de-santo*, she had not always been so respected, and her prestige by the 1930s owed much to her own assertions of African purity as well as to the interventions and endorsements of Martiniano. In fact Matory argues that the discourse of purity in Bahian Candomblé cannot be found in its African religious forebears, and he insists that it was largely constructed by Martiniano and Aninha working together in Bahia to reinforce their own status.[67] These efforts further served, most likely intentionally, to consolidate the dominance of Bahia itself in the larger Brazilian religious sphere. Aninha, for example, frequently asserted during this time that Bahia was the Black Rome.[68] Such a statement of authority served not only to further the prestige of her own efforts but also to prioritize Bahia as the leader, and the spiritual authority, for the entire African diaspora.

Aninha and others forged this pride in African roots at some cost. Their efforts are all the more remarkable when we remember that Bahia as a whole, and especially its elite, felt mostly embarrassment or disgust in relation to Africa. As Pierson reports, "if a Bahian wishes to be particularly insulting, he will aggravate the sting of 'Negro' by adding to it *de Africa* ('from Africa'). In this way he doubly accentuates his reference to the foreign origin of a black."[69] In the Candomblé community, in contrast, assertions of African authenticity conferred prestige, and were an important way to competitively demarcate one *terreiro* from another.[70] Nonetheless, if we examine some of the statements about African heritage and Candomblé during this era in Bahia, we begin to understand that asserting African roots took great courage and a strong sense of identity and self-worth in the context of broader Bahian society. Indeed, the movement, though conducted in the realm of culture, was highly political and highly confrontational. Certainly practitioners of Candomblé confronted the police directly, although they were sometimes able to gain allegiances and protection from select officers.[71] And they took on a public that urged repression of African culture more often than comprehension or coexistence. Editorials written in the Bahia press in 1936 deplored the existence of Candomblé: in one writer's view, when harmful "customs are linked with the persistent beliefs of African fetishism and constitute outrageous attacks on the moral and physical well-being of those that practice them, it becomes necessary to insist on immediate and complete suppression. This can be done in no way except by police action, energetic and persistent."[72]

Such characterizations began to be attacked the same year by the journalist Edison Carneiro in one of Bahia's leading newspapers, *O Estado da Bahia*. In January 1936 Carneiro began organizing a series of articles to educate the Bahian public about the logic and dignity of the Candomblé world.[73] But even more significant gains in public opinion came from his planning of Salvador's Afro-Brazilian Congress and from the direct participation of Candomblé leaders in the event. In contrast to the first congress, here Afro-Brazilians themselves took a leading role in fomenting increased acceptance for their culture and for their African heritage. And Carneiro, with his role in the press already established, took an important step in diffusing their efforts through his extensive reporting on the event. These joint efforts continued after the congress: the formation of the União das Seitas Afro-

Brasileiras da Bahia (Union of Afro-Brazilian Sects of Bahia) in late 1937 aimed to establish a self-governing body to oversee Bahia's black religious world. Together, Carneiro and the leaders of Candomblé's most prestigious houses capitalized on the favorable climate to win new political and cultural gains for Afro-Bahians.

The Second Afro-Brazilian Congress: Controversy Erupts

Carneiro began planning the Second Afro-Brazilian Congress in 1936 when he was just twenty-four years old. A central figure in Bahian radical intellectual circles, he was associated with the Communist Party and close friends with Bahian novelist Jorge Amado. Though Carneiro moved to Rio de Janeiro in 1939, partly to escape Bahia's persecution of suspected communists under the Estado Novo, he retained close ties to Bahia, and much of his later research and writing would focus on Bahian topics. He established deep relationships with the Candomblé community early. These relationships made his research possible but also ultimately proved vital for his own safety; when hunted by the Bahia's police in 1937 he took refuge in Aninha's *terreiro*, Opô Afonjá.[74] His most famous work, a study of Bahian Candomblé, would be published later by the State Museum of Bahia, as I discuss further in chapter 3.

The proposal to host the second congress in Salvador was audacious; Bahia at the time lacked a scholar with national standing to bring credibility and attention to the conference, and Carneiro himself was not yet well known. Although it is unclear who first had the idea, Carneiro took much of the initiative in organizing the congress, along with one of his closest friends, Aydano do Couto Ferraz, a young intellectual described by Ruth Landes as the "son of an old white family of Bahia."[75] Carneiro further corresponded frequently about the event with Arthur Ramos, who certainly had the prestige to host a conference but was at that time based in Rio de Janeiro. The two began to discuss tentative dates in early 1936, and though Carneiro proposed September of that year, the event suffered delays and was eventually scheduled for January 1937.[76]

Before it began, however, the Salvador congress suffered a setback orchestrated by Gilberto Freyre. Scholars have noted that Freyre's attempts at sabotage were in part motivated by regional concerns: as a Recife scholar he feared the development of Afro-Brazilian studies outside of his geographical realm of control. Indeed, he pushed for some time to develop an academic institution in Recife that he could orient around his own regional interests.[77]

Such aims provoked him to discredit the Salvador congress in a most polemical way. What has attracted less attention from scholars is the response to Freyre's offensive by Carneiro, and especially Ramos, that used the figure of Nina Rodrigues as a central weapon. Let us turn first to the Pernambucan attack and then to the Bahian response.

It is unknown what role Freyre was asked to play in the Second Afro-Brazilian Congress, and precisely when he found out about it, but beginning in late 1936 he took an openly hostile attitude to the event. Freyre was remarkably possessive about the Afro-Brazilian Congress and believed *his* idea had been appropriated and misused. He wrote bitterly in December 1936 to Melville Herskovits, expressing his disappointment and his doubts: "As to the Second Afro Brazilian Congress I am afraid it will be too political. For that reason I am not taking an active part in it, though the idea and the initiative for such congresses are[78] mine. But it seems that political propagandists are giving a direction to the congress, entirely different from the one of the first congress—scientific, social, and political only in a broad sense, in its implications."[79] Though Freyre rarely expressed his sense of ownership about the congress so explicitly in public, he by no means kept his opinions to himself. He already had voiced these doubts and others in an interview with the newspaper *Diário de Pernambuco*.[80] In the interview, reprinted in *O Estado da Bahia* on 13 November 1936, Freyre spoke condescendingly of Carneiro and the potential of the Salvador congress: "The organizers of the present congress are only interested in the most picturesque and most artistic side of the topic: the "rodas" [circles] of capoeira and samba, the drum beats of "Candomblé," etc. This side is very interesting, and in Bahia it will have a unique color. But the program followed in the first congress was a more extensive program, including the element of scientific research and work—dry elements, but equally important to social studies."[81] These were harsh words indeed, and strange charges from a sociologist who had devoted so much of his own research to untraditional topics and, some might argue, impressionistic rather than scientific methods. He displayed clear condescension in depicting Candomblé and capoeira as merely picturesque "local color" (given the context of a congress on race, a strange choice of words). The organizers, in his view, had involved themselves only in quaint and superficial topics and would not truly engage with the "serious" scientific debates of the field. Though personally insulting to Carneiro and his associates, Freyre's comments drew a line as well about what was legitimate material for Afro-Brazilian studies and who might participate.

Freyre also believed, as he had noted to Herskovits, that the congress would be too political, a somewhat ironic critique given his own past involvement in the political scene of Recife.[82] In the newspaper interview, he declared that he "radically disagreed" with the relationship of the congress to the interventor of Bahia, Juracy Magalhães. The state had agreed to grant some financial support to the effort, and Freyre argued that this would corrupt the congress. He held up his own Recife congress as an ideal that had been "entirely independent of the government or any type of political organization." This point, which he had stressed repeatedly in his essay accompanying the papers of the Recife congress,[83] was misleading, since Freyre himself had former ties to the government, and since his cousin, Ulysses Pernambucano, a prominent participant in the Recife congress, held a head position in the state's mental hospital during this time. Yet the state in Pernambuco maintained a hostility to Freyre and his congress that would be absent from the event in Bahia.[84] This political endorsement that Freyre so resented was one of Carneiro's greatest accomplishments and a key to the success of the Salvador congress.

The matter of financing was only part of Freyre's critique, however; in the interview he also charged that Salvador's congress was driven more by racial politics than by the study of race:

> I believe that the problems of the black and mulatto in Brazil should be discussed and presented with the greatest frankness, with honesty and with firmness, indicating the social and even political effects of the oppression that people of color still observe among us. I think the fact that the Afro-Brazilian Congress of Recife faced the black and the black *mestiço* not as a problem of biological pathology, as was done by Nina Rodrigues himself—who was convinced of the absolute inferiority of the black and mulatto—but as a problem principally of social disadjustment, represents a notable victory for Brazilian social sciences and one with profound political repercussions. But it does not appear to me that the Afro-Brazilian congresses should slip toward the political or demagogic discourse of people of color.[85]

Whether this statement was intended as a direct attack on Edison Carneiro, who was Afro-Brazilian, is likely, but left ambiguous. It may also have been a warning against the participation of blacks in the congress and the perceived danger that such inclusion posed. It is clear, however, that Freyre intended to discredit the Salvador congress and the Bahian legacy of Nina Rodrigues in an inflammatory way as he charged that the black demagogues of the second congress would compromise the field's scientific focus.

It was a highly questionable premise that financing from the Bahian state government would affect the focus of the Salvador congress, but Freyre was correct in calling the second congress more political. Indeed, the Salvador congress provided the intellectual authority for the petition of religious freedom for Candomblé. Such actions were certainly political, particularly when we consider that the principal resolution of the first congress was to include a portrait of Nina Rodrigues with the published papers. Freyre, after all, though he proclaimed it necessary to study Afro-Brazilian culture, rarely sought to address questions of Afro-Brazilian political rights and their repression.[86] In fact his critiques of the second congress, when stripped of their reactive and defamatory context, were perceptive. His claim to possess the field *was* indeed being challenged by the Bahians; there was a cultural emphasis to the second congress that differed from the first; and Carneiro did indeed use the second congress for political objectives. Let us turn first to the claims to primacy, a tension central to understanding the two congresses.

Freyre's Claims to Primacy: Innovation in Recife

Just two weeks after the First Afro-Brazilian Congress, Freyre wrote glowingly of its success to Melville Herskovits, stressing that it had been a monumental event largely of his own making. As Freyre described it, the congress had been "organized by a group of students of race and culture problems in Brazil, and the suggestion was mine."[87] In fact, Herskovits had himself submitted a paper to the Recife congress, which suggests that he was already aware of Freyre's role in the event, but the letter reveals Freyre's desire to reinforce his role as the intellectual author of the congress.

The issue of control, and the question of whether the Recife congress represented a "new" initiative, can be seen particularly clearly in two sections of the published proceedings of the Recife congress: the preface, written by Arthur Ramos in December 1936 at the request of Gilberto Freyre, and an essay in the same volume that appears to date from slightly earlier, an assessment of the congress by Freyre himself. The result must have been infuriating to Freyre, for Ramos used the forum to draw out Nina Rodrigues as a founding figure for the field and to argue for the continued relevance, and dominance, of a Bahian "school" of analysis.[88] The two essays together provide insight into the regional and intellectual turf war sparked by the congress, as Freyre moved to claim Recife as the center of the field and Ramos countered with an assertion that Bahia had been, and always would be, the locus of Afro-Brazilian studies.

Freyre's essay, "What the First Afro-Brazilian Congress of Recife Represented," underscored that the congress had forged new academic ground. The very format had broken with previous models of conferences—its lack of pomp and pretension marked it as a new type of academic undertaking. Involving academics and *doutores* as well as local personalities, illiterates, and even Afro-Brazilian cooks, it had "attracted, simultaneously, the goodwill of the most simple people and the interest of the most learned."[89] Freyre emphasized that the conference had aroused the interest of some of the greatest names in the field, from Franz Boas to the most prominent Brazilian intellectuals.

For Freyre, however, the congress's most important contribution was not that it established a new, less pretentious tone for conferences but that it had blazed a new path for future studies. According to Freyre, at the end of the congress "it was felt that a movement of the greatest importance was defined for the life and culture of Brazil."[90] Elaborating, he spelled out the nature of this new movement: "The Recife congress, with all of its simplicity, gave new character and new flavor to Afro-Brazilian studies, freeing it from the academic exclusivity or scientificism of rigid 'schools,' on the one hand, and, on the other, from the surface interest of those who promote the topic for a simple attraction to the picturesque . . . without any intellectual or scientific discipline, without a more profound social sense of the facts."[91] Freyre contrasted the two extremes represented in the field—a formalistic academic approach and an amateur interest in the exotic—and advocated that his own approach carved a middle ground between the two. His dual technique of both celebrating the novelty of the congress and explicitly attacking other approaches established that his role in the making of Afro-Brazilian studies was central.

Freyre concluded his essay by referring to the inclusion of Nina Rodrigues's portrait in the volume, a resolution that had been voted on by the congress. As he described it, the resolution represented an "homage to Bahia's Medical School Professor, who gave such great impulse to Afro-Brazilian studies, demanding the respect of Africanists from all parts."[92] Freyre's use of "impulse" suggested that Rodrigues offered an *initial* propulsion to the field but no lasting contribution. This emphasis on Rodrigues as an early figure rather than a continuing intellectual presence was reinforced in the caption for his portrait, which identified him as "The Bahian Teacher, *precursor* of the studies about the black problem in Brazil."[93] These phrasings were by no means accidental. Freyre wished to diminish the role given to the Bahian

School and make it clear that Rodrigues and his approach, while historically significant, were no longer essential.

That Freyre intended to signal a break from Bahian approaches to Afro-Brazilian studies was therefore clear. But his silence spoke as eloquently about his position as did his barbs and insinuations. As Freyre was writing his epilogue, the Second Afro-Brazilian Congress was being planned for Salvador, but Freyre, strangely, made no mention of it. Here his competitive nature is particularly clear; the timing indicates that Freyre knew about the congress before the volume was published and chose neither to mention it nor to recognize it as a successor to his own congress.[94] Freyre's efforts at intellectual sabotage were undercut, however, when Arthur Ramos prominently mentioned the new congress in his preface. Ramos offered a decidedly different interpretation of the state of the field and the future of Afro-Brazilian studies—a vision that emphasized a central role for the Bahian school, and thus was flagrantly at odds with Freyre's.

Asserting Bahian Lineage: The Resurrection of Nina Rodrigues

The preface by Ramos attempted, audaciously, to trace the lineage of the Recife's First Afro-Brazilian Congress to Bahia and to the work of Nina Rodrigues. Written in December 1936, it was shaped by Ramos's involvement with the upcoming Second Afro-Brazilian Congress in Salvador, and also by his familiarity with Freyre's synopsis of the Recife congress. The first congress, Ramos carefully noted, was a "debt owed exclusively to Gilberto Freyre" and had brought "new angles of vision, new research methods, and new directions for future studies" to the topic of "the black in Brazil."[95] The distinction, subtly made, stressed that while the congress brought new approaches, the topic itself had a prior history. Building on this theme, Ramos declared that he wished to make a "small observation." "Since 1926," he wrote, "the name of Nina Rodrigues, the learned founder of Black-Brazilian studies, has been taken up again in Bahia with the firm proposition of a reinterpretation of the Black-Brazilian problem, [an interpretation developed] in the shadow of his great school. I have claimed his priority on other occasions and it is now tacitly recognized by the Recife group, both by the homage offered to Nina Rodrigues by Gilberto Freyre's article in this volume, and by the fact that the eminent sociologist of *Casa-grande e senzala* solicited from me these words of preface."[96] In this statement Ramos forcefully claimed the study of Afro-Brazilian culture as a Bahian invention. Attributing its origins to Nina

Rodrigues, he carefully noted when and where the topic had been reintroduced to scholarly attention. According to Ramos the discipline was reborn in Bahia in 1926—in other words, long before the publication of Freyre's works and long before the congress. Gilberto Freyre was portrayed as an upstart leader of the Recife group whose work was valuable but indebted to much larger Bahian forces. The geography of the two were frequently juxtaposed in Ramos's writing, but while he referred to the Bahian "school," he classified the Pernambucans as only a "group," without the history—or perhaps the authority—necessary to become a rival on equal terms.

As for the future, Ramos noted, somewhat aggressively, that while the first congress was a "magnificent initiative," it would not be the only one.

> Other Afro-Brazilian Congresses will follow. The second, to be held in Bahia, with Edison Carneiro at its head, should definitively consecrate the memory of the Bahian Master, [Nina Rodrigues, who was] already paid homage in the first. And then we will have the opportunity to correct the methodological faults that we have already pointed to in Nina Rodrigues's work on the black problem, and to which the studies of Gilberto Freyre have brought the confluence of modern and learned methods of cultural anthropology. Editing this volume . . . [requires this editor] to thank Gilberto Freyre for one more opportunity to render to the Brazilian black, under the protection of Nina Rodrigues, the scientific and human recognition that can no longer be postponed.[97]

While Ramos acknowledged Freyre's role in inspiring a new methodology for Afro-Brazilian studies, he argued that the methodology should be used to revise foundational work by Nina Rodrigues: the Recife group should dedicate itself to the problems indicated by the Bahian school. As a preface, the comments by Ramos stand out for their contradiction of the stance taken by the volume organizer (Freyre) and for their insistence on a role for Nina Rodrigues, who would otherwise have received only passing mention and a photo tribute. Resurrecting a medical scholar, dead almost thirty years, as the intellectual most critical to the field was a deliberate and strategic move by the Bahians. Nina Rodrigues was deemed a central precursor in part because of his contribution to the intellectual content of the field. Equally, if not more important, however, was his role in establishing Bahian primacy in the rise of Afro-Brazilian studies and the social sciences.

Ramos continued to stress the importance of paying tribute to Nina Rodrigues as the Bahian congress developed. Carneiro wrote to Ramos in December 1936 that he and other organizers of the second congress "adhere[d] to [Ramos's] idea of homage," and he proposed that Ramos read his essay on the Bahian school at the congress. The essay, read in Ramos absence, insisted that "the Bahian Congress should recognize that there is a Nina Rodrigues School reinitiated in the Bahian capital, under whose high inspirations the studies of the Black in Brazil are conducted, studies that had great resonance in almost all the states of Brazil and crossed our own borders, awakening the attention of North American, Central American, and European scholars."[98] The origins and continued dominance of the Bahian school, with its influence radiating out from Salvador to the rest of the world, was a recurring theme in the work of Ramos, who insisted that the Bahian school be central to all future Afro-Brazilian initiatives.

The Second Afro-Brazilian Congress: New Partnerships in Bahia

The opening essay in the published papers of the Bahian congress of 1937 set a defiant tone. Carneiro and fellow organizer Aydano do Couto Ferraz began by asserting that the Bahian school was still alive and had been reinvigorated by the involvement of younger scholars. Many in Bahia had at first doubted the potential of the congress, believing "that a congress of Africanology, to be realized with real benefits for the field, needed to have Gilberto Freyre at its head. They did not believe that a group of young men [rapazes] . . . would be able to unite a scientific enclave equal or at least comparable to that of Recife in 1934."[99] The results of the congress, according to the authors, had proven the naysayers wrong on both accounts: the young organizers were certainly capable, and Bahia did not need Freyre to host its own conference.

In fact Carneiro and his associates organized the congress strategically and ingeniously, appropriating elite spaces for Afro-Brazilian culture. All of the congress sessions, for example, took place in the Instituto Geográfico e Histórico da Bahia, the state's premier academic organization. Its president, thanked effusively by the organizers, may have been sympathetic to the cause: Theodoro Sampaio, an engineer and a scholar of indigenous cultures, was the son of a slave mother and a Catholic priest.[100] The institute's journal published primarily studies of elite genealogies and dry political histories: studies of popular culture and Afro-Brazilian culture only flitted across the pages of their journal in passing. Despite this tradition, however, Carneiro and Ferraz were able to secure not only a house for the congress but also extraordinary cooperation, demonstrated by the institute's further willingness to unearth a display of Candomblé items from its collection and open the exhibit to the public.[101]

This spatial appropriation moved beyond the congress headquarters as the organizers brought in diverse cooperation from across the city. One of Salvador's private regatta clubs opened its tennis courts to capoeira exhibitions.[102] Scholars from the Nina Rodrigues Institute welcomed congress-goers even after the event had officially ended, and both the School of Medicine and the Nina Rodrigues Institute sponsored the proceedings.[103] Bahia's radio station granted Carneiro airtime to announce the event. And Bahia's airwaves, most likely accustomed to samba, instead hosted the melodies and drumming of Candomblé, led by the Candomblé leader of Goméa, João da Pedra Preta.[104] Finally, since Carneiro was a journalist for the newspaper *O Estado da Bahia*, the press was predisposed to be sympathetic to the congress and gave it substantial coverage.

In fact an important difference between the two congresses was how much institutional and public support the second congress was able to garner. Freyre had made the first congress a largely personal effort dependent on contributions from individual members of the Recife community.[105] In contrast, Carneiro drew on a wide spectrum of involvement from all sectors in Bahia and proved himself a remarkably savvy organizer. His small grant from the government resulted from not a personal connection to the governor but an appeal to the state assembly, a move that may have encouraged some politicians to attend the conference and surely made them aware of it.[106] And the governor himself, Juracy Magalhães, inaugurated the events.[107] In sum, by the end of the congress, a critical number of institutions and people, both elite and popular, had been involved in the event or had heard about it. A sizeable percentage of Salvador residents now knew that Afro-Brazilian studies was a legitimate field of study, and that Bahia was the locus for those interested in the topic. Carneiro had conducted an effective and wide-ranging campaign for Afro-Brazilian studies and for Bahia.

In their introduction to the published proceedings, Carneiro and Ferraz stressed two elements they believed most critical to the success of the Bahian congress: the approval and participation of prominent scholars, especially those beyond Brazil, and the popular character of the congress itself.[108] In some ways this claim was very similar to the one made by Freyre for his Recife congress, but the Bahian organizers took the idea of popular participation to a new level. In their words, the popular aspect was "inimitable," with more than three thousand guests attending special events at Brazil's oldest Candomblé temple, Casa Branca, or Engenho Velho. And the festivities at other participating Candomblés "dazzled" all who visited.[109]

In their assessment, however, what marked the congress as truly "original" was the "direct contribution of the *pais-de-santo* and the other devotees as researchers of their own sects." Prominent Candomblé leaders, Aninha among them, took their place "alongside our greatest scholars, on equal standing."[110] Carneiro and Ferraz listed a host of experts who had generously shared performances in capoeira, samba, and *batuque* (drumming) with a prominent musicologist from São Paulo, as well as with the public at large. The inaugural address for the congress stressed these ideas of equality, noting that the theses of Melville Herskovits, Arthur Ramos, and Gilberto Freyre would be discussed alongside those of Aninha and the *mãe-de-santo* Escholastica Nazareth, Mãe Menininha. The emphasis here was on the collaboration of scholars and Afro-Bahians in all endeavors. Rather than separating scientific experts from scientific objects, the congress had brought Afro-Bahians into the process of defining themselves and explaining their culture. In the congress, Afro-Bahians were esteemed interlocutors and guides for their scholarly visitors rather than simply anonymous folkloric fodder for study. Indeed, the organizers called on Afro-Bahians to help them reject this outdated mode of study. The congress, they declared in their public inaugural address, boasted "a democratic orientation, all those present being able to enter into the debates surrounding the topics, and *even need[ing] to enter into these debates*, so as to better clarify the topics studied."[111]

Carneiro further emphasized the cultural authenticity of the Salvador congress three years later. While Freyre's congress had brought Candomblé and its music to the site of the congress, Bahia "did not fall into this error." Carneiro believed that transporting the religion's practice away from its sacred temples compromised "the purity of the African rites." Instead, when participants in the Salvador congress "made contact with *coisas do negro* [the realm of blacks] it was in [the latter's] original environment."[112] Carneiro clearly wished to show that the Salvador congress happened on the terms, and in the space, of the black community. Given that capoeira and samba were performed on the tennis courts of the regatta club, this was not entirely true, but he sought to highlight the importance given to traditions in Bahia. Years later he would refer to the period as representing an "era of black spectacle," and it may well have been the exported ceremonies of Recife that Carneiro had in mind.[113]

In concluding their introduction to the congress proceedings, Carneiro and Ferraz expressed extensive gratitude to all of those who had helped with the event, singling out especially Donald Pierson, Martiniano, the secretary of Bahia's Historic Institute, and all the practitioners of Candomblé, samba, capoeira, and *batuque*. Martiniano especially won a prominent place in the congress. He, like Pierson, contributed an article that was published in the proceedings. But his broader participation and presence earned him repeated accolades. The two organizers described him effusively in the preface: "the former collaborator of Nina Rodrigues, head of the *Afro-Negras* religions of Bahia, our friend, and (why not say it?) our teacher."[114] Furthermore, Martiniano had been named honorary head of the congress, and he was introduced in superlative terms in the event's inaugural address.[115] These eulogies reached a fever pitch in the dramatic tribute to Martiniano by the novelist Jorge Amado in the later congress proceedings.

Amado was part of a literary vanguard in Bahia, and he inaugurated numerous short-lived literary journals with Edison Carneiro and Aydano do Couto Ferraz in the late 1920s and the 1930s. His reputation reached beyond Bahia, however, when he began to write his novels in 1931. His work probed the world of the black underclass in Bahia, and in *Jubiabá*, his 1935 novel, the world of Candomblé.[116] Amado gave a euphoric tribute to Martiniano do Bonfim at the congress. Echoing much of the language of the inaugural address, praising Martiniano as the most esteemed black figure in Brazil, Amado also emphasized how critical his participation had been to the congress. A "powerful intelligence" and the "backbone of the purity of the religions of Bahia," Martiniano had vouched for the event for the black "masses," giving the congress a "guarantee of honesty." His collaboration had granted it "an absolute prestige among the black masses, making it so that the festivities celebrated in the most notable Candomblé *terreiros* of Bahia in honor of the congress have not only shone with purity of ceremony, enthusiasm, and beauty, but also represented and clearly showed the solidarity that the black race [*raça negra*] of Bahia gave to the Second Afro-Brazilian Congress in an absolute comprehension of its intentions and its ends."[117]

Martiniano's participation thus was a critical endorsement that not only allowed Candomblé rituals to be performed in their purest form but also ensured that the "black masses" supported the congress as a whole. A respected leader in the black community, and most especially in the Candomblé community, Martiniano had ensured the participation of a broader public. Indeed, Ruth Landes, another observer from the United States who arrived shortly after the congress ended, noted that the event continued to be talked about in the Candomblé community for some time.[118]

Aninha also occupied a privileged place at the congress, ensuring its success in the religious realm as well as the popular. She was cited in the introduction, much as any scholar would be, for coining the notion of Bahia as the "Black Rome."[119] The inaugural address emphasized her contribution to the event and highlighted her scholarly role as an authority in the debates on Candomblé.[120] When Aninha died early the following year, Carneiro authored her obituary for the Bahian press and praised both her adherence to tradition in Candomblé as well as the critical support she offered to the congress. He recalled approaching her the week before the congress, where "her reception of us exceeded expectations, for instead of a simple *mãe-de-santo* who looked favorably on the congress, we encountered an intelligent woman who accompanied and understood our proposals, who read our studies and loved our work."[121] With only a few days' notice, this most traditional of leaders organized a special celebration, outside the ritual religious calendar, and opened it to the public. Later in 1937, Aninha formed with Carneiro the Union of Afro-Brazilian Sects. Here, too, Carneiro believed her support to be essential, far beyond mere acquiescence.[122]

Carneiro asked Aninha to compile recipes of African foods used to nourish the gods of Candomblé for the congress proceedings. As the anthropologist Vivaldo da Costa Lima points out, such recipes would have exposed sacred offerings long kept secret, and Aninha would have revealed much of her own spiritual power in sharing them.[123] For all practical purposes, then, Carneiro's request was impossible. Nonetheless, Aninha submitted a list of dishes, published as "A Note about African Foods," without any accompanying ingredients or instructions—a somewhat awkward solution but one that Carneiro published.[124] Though she could not fulfill the letter of the request, she clearly saw importance in the effort and tried to participate as fully as possible within the limits of her faith.

The Bahian Agenda: African Roots and Religious Freedom

The scholarly contributions of the congress as a whole were varied and deserve further attention, but at least a third of the published papers focused on religious life. This focus on Candomblé leaders and the freedom of religion may not have had the support of the entire black community. Donald Pierson, who attended the congress and presented a paper on race relations, noted the critique of a black Bahian who suggested the congress should highlight the "deplorable" status of the blacks in Brazil and "ought to say to the black man that he is dying of tuberculosis, of the heavy labor of carrying weighty burdens, of passing up necessities, and of sorrow." The congress, in this man's view, "ought to break the chains of oppression. . . . It ought to ask the black man how long he wants to remain a slave."[125]

From Carneiro's statements at the first congress, it would seem that such a focus on daily realities and inequalities would characterize any forum that he organized. Yet the congress as a whole was more single-minded, focused less on economic status than on religious oppression. And Carneiro's work also reflected this shift. He submitted three papers, a tribute to Nina Rodrigues and two on Candomblé. One of his essays, "The Doctor of the Poor," revealed that poverty and suspicion led many Afro-Bahians to entrust their health to the Candomblé deity Omólú. Economic attention to the underclass thus continued to be a part of Carneiro's analysis, as it had been in the first congress, but the tone had become decidedly less confrontational and radical. Rather than calling for social reforms or increased government intervention, he pointed to the positive role that Candomblé could play in the broader life of the poor. While deploring the poverty faced by Afro-Bahians, he also pointed to the solutions they crafted. Notably, this was a move away from his sometimes negative portrayals of black religious life in the 1934 congress.

In a further departure, his articles on Candomblé turned not on religious innovation and Bahian grounding, as he had emphasized in his paper for the first congress, but on fidelity to African traditions. His "A Revision in Afro-Brazilian Religious Ethnography" argued that more continuity existed with African belief than had previously been acknowledged, particularly in the case of the deity Olôrún. Though Olôrún was the original god of creation in African belief systems, he was long thought to be absent from Brazilian practice. Carneiro argued, however, that attention to the Bantu religions of Bahia, long neglected, showed a distinct role and memory of the god, although perhaps one now eclipsed by the deity Oxalá. For Oxalá, the connection to Africa was still vivid. Again Carneiro turned to the geography of belief, but this time he emphasized similarities rather than difference. In Bahia Oxalá "lived precisely at the top of a mountain, as in Africa." In his words, belief in Oxalá "therefore existed in its pure state in Bahia . . . [and] came to have the same representation that he had for the blacks of the African Coast."[126]

In addition, Carneiro now emphasized African roots much more prominently, discriminating among the different ethnic contributions in the Bahian Candomblé community. He noted that the Bantu contribution to Bahia had long been ignored by scholars focused on the Yoruba of Africa's west coast. This lack of attention had meant that the "vestiges of Bantu blacks" in the social life of Bahia had been underestimated; Carneiro's conclusion urged more attention to these diverse African origins. His emphasis on the primacy of the Brazilian environment, so evident in his paper for the first congress, was altogether absent. African lineage and ideas of purity now assumed central importance in his work. Most likely, this emphasis came largely from the black community itself, and Carneiro's later essay reflected not simply a maturation of his focus but increased exposure to his informants' worldview.

Indeed, this emphasis on African lineage is prominent in the contributions by Candomblé leaders to the congress. Martiniano's essay told of the origins of Xangô's deification, relating his life as a heroic warrior among the Yoruba in Africa. In this narrative, after Xangô's disappearance from earth, his ministers of state formed a body of twelve representatives to maintain his veneration. They aimed to ensure that the "memory of the generations" never extinguished its "remembrance of the hero." This, Martiniano concluded, was what made Aninha's creation of a ministry of twelve representatives for Xangô so important. Her Candomblé was "the only one in Bahia—and perhaps in Brazil—to organize this celebration, which brings such good remembrances to the spiritual children of the African continent."[127] Martiniano grounded his analysis of Candomblé in Africa itself and reserved praise for those who took up African traditions most faithfully. In doing so, he built up not only the prestige of Aninha, whom he had advised about the process earlier that year, but also the prestige of Bahia. It was Bahia, in his view, that paid most faithful tribute to the African motherland. In fact Martiniano seems to have played a role not only in leading Carneiro to assess African tradition more positively but also in convincing him of the importance of Nina Rodrigues.

For scholars in the 1930s this posthumous celebration of the medical scholar was not without serious dilemmas. After all, Nina Rodrigues had been a prominent spokesman for racial difference. The essays in his honor at the congress dealt with this dilemma in various ways. For Ramos, this was an accident of the era; Nina Rodrigues's true legacy lay in his role as an "advocate" for blacks and the "first *ogan*," or official sponsor, of Candomblé. As Ramos described it, while the abolitionist movement lost itself in lyrical turns of phrase, Nina Rodrigues addressed the "very real problems of the Black" directly. His tireless search to uncover the truths and history of the black experience, the "seriousness, honesty, enthusiasm, and immense sympathy" of his studies compensated for his outdated scientific framework.[128]

For Carneiro this legacy was somewhat more complicated. His essay paying tribute to Nina Rodrigues, less didactic and more reflective, admitted his own struggle to assess the many sides of Nina Rodrigues's legacy. As Carneiro described it, Nina Rodrigues had first inspired him to explore the lives of blacks in Bahia; it was in response to his work that Carneiro set out on his own journey into the world of Candomblé. Beginning with one of the oldest and "best" *terreiros*, Engenho Velho, Carneiro and Guilherme Dias Gomes encountered Martiniano do Bonfim. It was this "most efficient collaborator of Nina Rodrigues who taught us to like [*querer*], even more than we wished to, the old master of Legal Medicine. And it was then that I was able to see that Nina Rodrigues, if he were alive, would be with us in the trenches, as a comrade, as one of us, without false attitudes in the defense of the black race [*raça negra*]." Carneiro here frankly expresses his initial resistance and misunderstanding, saying that he was "conquered" by Nina Rodrigues.[129] This was only possible because of Martiniano do Bonfim, an authoritative member of Bahia's black community.

Carneiro also praised Nina Rodrigues's intellectual honesty and dedication. He echoed Ramos in saying that the racial beliefs of Nina Rodrigues were "an error of his time," but he argued that in the end Nina Rodrigues's "personal tendencies counterbalanced his theoretical defects." In his friendship and collaboration with the Candomblé community, and his condemnation of the violent oppression of independent black life, Nina Rodrigues had contributed to the "democratic task of the *rediscovery* of Brazil." Carneiro highlighted that Nina Rodrigues, like Ramos and Freyre, was an intellectual allied with the "popular masses." And in a remarkable reinterpretation of his work, Carneiro said he believed Nina Rodrigues wished nothing more than "to serve the cause of the *blacks*." He continued, Carneiro insisted, to serve this cause thirty years after his death. Ending on a populist note, Carneiro proclaimed that Nina Rodrigues belonged "to the *povo* [people]. And the *povo* cannot die."[130]

Indeed, the *povo*, Candomblé leaders, and scholars came together in the congress and resolved to fight for religious freedom. One of the most important outcomes for Bahia's Afro-Brazilian Congress was the resolution to create a self-governing body for Candomblé.[131] Carneiro had imagined the possibility of such a union in the weeks leading up to the congress[132] and he took a leading role in its formation after the congress. He wrote to Arthur Ramos in July 1937: "I am organizing an African Council of Bahia that will be charged with overseeing black religion, removing the police from such tasks." Established with representatives from the Candomblés, and with

Martiniano as its president, the group planned to send a petition for religious freedom to the government. The request would be backed by the executive commission of the congress and a newly formed Afro-Brazilian Institute of Bahia.[133] Although the institute was never created, the council, renamed the Union of Afro-Brazilian Sects, did emerge.

According to Carneiro and Ferraz, this effort had been a principal motive for organizing the congress. As they wrote in the published proceedings, the congress had sought to further "increased comprehension of the need for liberty for the Afro-Negro-Amerindian religions, as well as the need for social rehabilitation for the Brazilian black."[134] The goals of the congress were thus expressly activist, aiming as much for social advances as scholarly gains. While it remains unclear how Carneiro and Ferraz imagined "social rehabilitation," their goal of gaining support for religious freedom was realized. Here the importance of Nina Rodrigues in the congress became clearer, for he established an example of not only early Bahian primacy but also early support for religious freedom. This was one reason that Carneiro rewrote him as an activist and began to use him to convince Bahian authorities that the idea of religious tolerance had legitimacy.

The formal petition for religious liberty was delivered to Bahia's governor in July 1937. The first statute established a general framework for understanding Candomblé in the diversity of religious practice. It argued: "Every *povo* has its religion, its special way of adoring God—and Candomblé is the religious organization of the blacks and people of color of Bahia, the descendents of black slaves who left them various African sects as an intellectual inheritance." The second statute justified this inheritance with scholarly authority. Nina Rodrigues, Arthur Ramos, and all the intellectuals who collaborated in the Afro-Brazilian congresses had protested against the repression of these religions, repression that was not only fundamentally wrong but violated Brazil's constitution. These scholars viewed the "religious freedom of blacks as one of the essential conditions for the establishment of justice among men." The third statute noted that only black religions had been subjected to police control, creating an inequality that further violated the constitution. The petition closed with a final appeal for recognition and the right for Candomblé practitioners to oversee themselves.[135]

The second congress as a whole combined activism and scholarly work. For example, a paper presented by Dario de Bittencourt, who had traveled from the south of Brazil to attend the congress, analyzed the legal history of religious freedom in Brazil. Although Candomblé had often been repressed by the police, Bittencourt followed Nina Rodrigues and pointed out that this violated the religious protection granted by Brazil's constitution.[136] If someone chose to register a complaint about a particular Candomblé, Bittencourt said, it should be deliberated by the courts, not the police. And his essay provided an ideal template for such a legal defense, carefully documenting the text of the law. Indeed, listeners in the audience could have taken away valuable ammunition to protect their own legal rights. Carneiro never referred to Bittencourt's work directly, however, and it seems that much of the inspiration for religious freedom came from local roots.

In fact, Bahian leaders of Candomblé had long been active in this struggle. An interview with the *pai-de-santo* Joãozinho da Goméa several months before the congress made the point emphatically. Bahia's policy at the time forced *terreiros* to apply to the police for permits to celebrate each religious festival. The police charged a fee for this permission, which could apparently vary in scale. As Joãozinho told the local press, "My final opinion is that there shouldn't be any payment at all. Candomblé should have the freedom to function when it wants. . . . I think the Congress should really study a means to resolve this question. What difference is there between the religion of the whites and the religion of the blacks?"[137] Clearly the support of the Candomblé community was critical to the formation of the Union of Afro-Brazilian Sects, but such public comments show that members also played a critical role in pushing for religious freedom before, during, and after the congress.

Carneiro sought to further buttress this popular activism with the endorsement of government figures and academic authorities. He appealed to Ramos in a letter dated 19 July 1937 to solicit the governor of Bahia personally, "reinforcing the petitions of the blacks."[138] According to scholar Vivaldo da Costa Lima, Governor Juracy Magalhães was rumored to have close associations with Candomblé, whether as a formal protector, or *ogan*, or merely as a friend to certain Candomblé leaders.[139] As Carneiro noted, Magalhães had already proven himself by endorsing the congress, and he seemed likely to approve the measure. Carneiro resolved not to take any chances. He decided to "attack from all sides," summoning the most prestigious scholarly supporters on whom he could draw. Believing that "the governor has a great [*bruta*] admiration for you [Ramos] and for Nina," Carneiro made certain to mention both scholars prominently in his petition.[140] He further suggested that Ramos send a telegraph of congratulations on the day of the inauguration of the Union of Afro-Brazilian Sects and arranged for Ramos to be named an honorary member.[141] Strategically appealing to the governor and mustering all the academic credentials at his disposal, Carneiro worked hard to solicit official legitimacy for the union.

The union attracted an even wider base of support. The announcement of its inauguration in the local press (accompanied by a photo of the event) noted that the session was presided over by a federal judge and that the governor had sent his own representative to the meeting. But even more impressive were the other organizations who had pledged their support: the Democratic Student Union, several university associations, the League to Combat Racism and Anti-Semitism, the Union of Bahian Intellectuals, and labor unions for "businessmen, hotel employees, etc."[142] With Martiniano do Bonfim as president, and a large number of Candomblé leaders as fellow members, the union won a truly remarkable level of public endorsement.[143]

The union was not without its tensions, of course. To make its case for the legitimacy of Candomblé, the organization distinguished between what it viewed as organized forms of black religion and what it deemed witchcraft and sorcery. Such a hierarchy had been present in the paper of Dario de Bittencourt, and ideas of authenticity were also key to Candomblé leaders. Scholars and many religious leaders thus still endorsed religious "policing" rather than true religious freedom. Such hierarchies between those religious practices portrayed as "authentic" and those derided as "magic" necessarily caused conflicts in a scramble to assert legitimacy. Vivaldo da Costa Lima points out that Carneiro's efforts were not supported wholeheartedly by all leaders of the Candomblé community; the union granted some leaders enhanced prestige while diminishing the official status of those deemed less traditional.[144] Aninha and Martiniano were among those who consolidated their status; it is worth considering whether the union's emphasis on authenticity may have come as much from Aninha and Martiniano as from Carneiro and other scholars.

Conclusion

Carneiro observed some years later, in 1940, that the coming together of academics and the black community was the "greatest glory" of the Salvador congress. Bitingly, he noted that this indeed "gave the discussion 'a unique color,' as Gilberto Freyre predicted."[145] Carneiro continued, "This 'unique color' had, at the least, an advantage: it ended the image of terror that the Candomblés represented for the so-called superior classes of Bahia. . . . they ended up learning that blacks didn't eat people, nor did they practice indecencies during their religious ceremonies. The publicity of the congress, in the newspapers and radio, contributed to create a setting of greater tolerance for these slandered religions of people of color."[146]

Carneiro's assessment is important, but the congress undeniably had its limits. Though ideas and acceptance of Afro-Bahians changed, their living conditions did not. Salvador's poor, Afro-Brazilian majority continued to live in areas of the city without paved roads or running water. As Pierson reported, much of the African-descended population could be found in the "less comfortable, less healthful, less convenient" valleys of the city, inhabiting "simple mud huts" with earthen floors. Mostly illiterate, they had little contact with newspapers, books, or telephones. The center of the city offered paved roads but "something approaching slum conditions" for hundreds of poor residents.[147]

This unequal and often prejudiced setting makes it all the more remarkable that Salvador's Afro-Brazilian Congress took place and garnered such extensive support. And given the hostility toward Africa shown at the first congress, it is also remarkable that the Salvador congress envisioned adherence to African traditions as worthy of respect. In fact, presenting their findings to a black audience well informed in the traditions of Candomblé may have led some scholars to reframe their findings. It is worth wondering whether presenting their findings to the populations they ostensibly "studied" pressured some scholars to discard racialist or biological approaches and disparaging dismissals of African culture. If Arthur Ramos had attended, would he have been so quick to label Candomblé as a psychological remnant of a primitive past? Certainly Carneiro had modified his own views of Africa by this time and now privileged African orthodoxies. This, too, might have been a result of more extended contact with the black community, and a certain reluctance to posit his views of black hyperbole and social disintegration in front of blacks themselves. The Salvador congress may well have made many scholars uncomfortable with their own dismissals of African culture as barbaric or irrelevant.

Indeed, members of the Candomblé community were familiar enough with these scholars to be able to launch their own attacks and corrections should they choose to do so. While the atmosphere of a conference may well have been intimidating, these same Candomblé leaders had long viewed themselves as the authorities on their traditions, and they had been treated as such by the scholars in the field. As Pierson remembered, Aninha was not shy in defending her religion and defending Africa. When charged by a Catholic priest that she lacked "spiritual authority" because she had not been ordained by the pope, "she quickly inquired if Moses, 'that great prophet and leader of his people, was ordained by the pope.'" Aninha insisted that Jesus himself must have had African heritage or very dark skin, because, as she argued, "If Jesus was not dark, how could they have hidden him among the people of Africa?"[148] Such intellectual sparring ability was not rare among Candomblé leaders and certainly would have served to check, or even intimidate, scholars who wished to discuss an African past in disparaging ways.

The complexities of the Vargas era played some role in making both congresses possible. The period granted nationalistic thinking and musings over origins a new priority and legitimacy. Its emphasis on popular culture and the incorporation of the masses fostered new cultural initiatives and marked a critical transition to increased official acceptance of popular religious festivals, many of them with explicit connections to Afro-Bahian culture and to Candomblé.[149] Carneiro thus picked up not only on broad national shifts, and the reflective intellectual currents initiated with Freyre, but a more sympathetic moment in Bahia in particular. The positive role granted to Africa that emerged in Salvador, however, owed itself to a unique moment of cooperation between intellectuals, state official support, and black religious leaders. The black community had fashioned an alternate cultural world in an often hostile environment. With the congress, and the support of scholars, they made the new respect granted to ideas of African authenticity a lasting legacy. As the next chapter reveals, this new mood in the aftermath of the congress proved influential in reshaping Bahia's Museu do Estado in the early 1940s. The debates that erupted over the museum's early popular and multiethnic focus show, however, that this legacy was far from fully consolidated.

And in museums and libraries, public and private, and in individual collections, Salvador probably preserves more of its colonial and imperial heritage from what it calls the "savagery of civilization" than any other city in Brazil with the exception of Ouro Preto.
—VERA KELSEY, *Seven Keys to Brazil*, 1940

Our biggest problem is to protect these treasures from modernization. We guard buildings, paintings and statues from the people who think only of progress and forget the glittering past. . . . Everything pertaining to the history and artistic life of Bahia is studied and catalogued, and in conjunction with Dr. Valladares here, we try to get everything movable under the roof of the State Museum. . . . We have much to work with too—Bahia is the richest state in artistic and historic relics.
—GODOFREDO FILHO, quoted in Jack Harding, *I Like Brazil*, 1941

CHAPTER 3

Preserving the Past

Bahia's Afro-Brazilian Congress had begun to alter the atmosphere of Salvador, but Edison Carneiro was not there long enough to savor its results. In 1939 he relocated to Rio de Janeiro to research the "regional ethnography of black and indigenous" cultures in several Northeastern states for the National Museum, returning to Bahia only for short research expeditions. The director of Brazil's National Museum, Heloisa Torres, gave him an official letter of introduction for his efforts, asking state and local authorities to cooperate with him.[1] Such introductions were increasingly necessary. The semiauthoritarian dictatorship of the Estado Novo (1937–45) monitored and repressed political dissent, especially by suspected communists.[2]

Carneiro was a confirmed communist, a dangerous allegiance at a dangerous moment, and this forced him to leave his home state of Bahia. Ruth Landes, an anthropologist from the United States who arrived in Bahia in 1938 and worked frequently with Carneiro in her research, stressed the climate of repression in Bahia: "Eyes were everywhere, tongues were everywhere, fear—yes, fear was everywhere. For occasionally word would come that a university acquaintance had been hauled into the jail near the city plaza, or that a Candomblé had been raided under suspicion of concealing a political enemy, and finally mysterious telephone calls came even for me." Carneiro took shelter in the Candomblé *terreiro* of Aninha, but this earned him only brief respite. As Landes reported, by the time she arrived Carneiro "had already been in hiding and in jail for his opposition to Vargas, and was to be jailed again during my stay."[3] Carneiro confirmed his political orientation in a letter to Landes but only after the fall of the Vargas regime, when he felt it safe to do so. "I suppose you guessed in Bahia that we are all communists," he wrote. "Well, we were, we are."[4]

Remarkably, Carneiro agreed to return to Bahia soon after his self-imposed political exile, and on a most unusual mission. He was charged by Heloisa Torres with meeting Bahia's chief of police to ensure the safe passage of promised donations to the National Museum. Torres had written to Bahia's police in late 1939, noting that she had heard of the department's policy of confiscating items from unlicensed Candomblé houses in the "elevated goal of moralizing customs." Appealing to the police chief's "patriotism and interest in the progress of science," she argued that the donation of these items to the National Museum of Rio de Janeiro would mean that the museum archive would be "greatly enriched, and at an exceptionally opportune moment, given the ethnological studies that are beginning to be dedicated to black religions in Africa and in Brazil."[5] This appeal proved at least partly successful, for less than two weeks later she replied to the same police chief, thanking him for anything he might be able to do for her collection. The correspondence also served as a letter of introduction for Carneiro, who carried the letter back to Bahia and who was given the responsibility of coming to an understanding with the police chief on Torres's behalf.[6]

It is likely that Carneiro himself first suggested this appeal to the Bahian police, but there was some irony in sending this former political prisoner back to his jailers for delicate negotiations. As Landes noted, Bahia's Candomblé temples had gained a reputation for harboring communists and police fugitives, and thus Carneiro's connections to both communism and Candomblé doubly damned him. Despite his official backing, Carneiro was just as likely to be dismissed, or even imprisoned, by the police chief as to gain a thoughtful hearing. It was no doubt with pleasure, however, that Carneiro returned with the official endorsement of one of Brazil's most powerful cultural institutions. Though we do not know what happened in that meeting, Carneiro was at least partly successful, for he returned with an especially precious cargo, a series of Bahian dolls in Candomblé dress. With some items reportedly damaged during the voyage, Torres decided that the effort merited her own intervention; two months later, in late January 1940, she departed for a two and a half week trip to Bahia.[7]

These Bahian acquisitions would ignite one of the many controversies of Heloisa Torres's career. She included the dolls in a collection sent to Lisbon later that year for an exposition of the Lusophone world but was harshly censored for her efforts. Brazilian critics worried that the Candomblé figures, among other items demonstrating African heritage, would give viewers an unfavorable impression of Brazil. Though Torres refuted such critiques,[8] they may have taken their toll: the new anthropology exhibit under her care unveiled in 1947 at the National Museum apparently incorporated nothing of Afro-Brazilian culture whatsoever, and the dolls were not mentioned in the detailed holdings of the new exhibitions.[9] Despite Torres's claims to the police about the rising interest in "black religions," the role of Afro-Brazilian culture in Brazilian identity continued to be controversial.

In Rio de Janeiro, despite occasional efforts by intellectuals such as Heloisa Torres, museums in the 1930s and 1940s continued to offer conservative visions of Brazil's past, seemingly insulated from the larger intellectual debates around them. Such was the case for the Museu Histórico Nacional (National Historical Museum or MHN) through the 1930s. As the historian Daryle Williams reveals, the institution organized its historical exhibits around elite-driven portraits of Brazil's past, and shied away from incorporating items that might provoke consideration of slavery or race: "What visitors to the MHN saw, instead, was a noble view of the Brazilian past where production and labor were largely absent and the faces were overwhelmingly white." Although the director, Gustavo Barroso, was himself interested in folklore and popular culture, he felt that such topics were inappropriate for a national history museum, and he suggested, in 1942, that a separate museum be developed to treat these questions.[10] Like Torres, he shirked from integrating black representations of Brazil into a national repository of memory.

We know less about how these debates over identity unfolded outside of Rio de Janeiro. Yet the role of Bahia in particular deserves more attention. For in Bahia during the late 1930s and 1940s a new museum culture was growing, nurtured by the exceptional curator José do Prado Valladares. Together with Bahian Secretary of Education and Health Isaías Alves, Valladares sought to bring popular culture and Afro-Brazilian culture into Bahia's Museu do Estado (State Museum) and into Bahia's official identity. This chapter shows that Bahia's state policy under the Estado Novo encouraged new inclusion of Afro-Brazilian culture, an inclusion all the more remarkable for the central role it came to play in the Bahian State Museum, the state's official preserve of memory and identity. Offering a view of Brazilian culture diametrically opposed to that put forth in Rio's National Museum, it highlighted popular culture rather than great military and political figures. Also in contrast to the National Museum, it included Afro-Brazilian culture—not just indigenous culture—as part of Bahia's history.

This period did not consolidate Afro-Bahians as a critical part of state identity, however. Indeed, the radical turnaround in the museum's focus only a few years later shows that Bahia was very much divided about how to portray its past. The cultural refashioning that flourished in the early years of the Estado Novo ended after Interventor Landulfo Alves was forced from office in 1942. The museum dramatically and rapidly changed course, abandoning the incipient popular focus and becoming a frozen repository of Bahia's sugar elite. As this chapter reveals, many elites of the era proved unhappy and uncomfortable with a popular and more inclusive *brasilidade*. And *baianidade*, which came to emphasize popular and Afro-Brazilian culture as its core, at this point confronted an elite that prioritized instead its vision of a sumptuous colonial sugar culture from which Indians and slaves were absent.

Preserving Bahian Traditions: A New Role for the State

Bahia's State Museum gained new relevance and attention under the Estado Novo and Bahia's new Interventor Landulfo Alves (1938–42). With official state sponsorship of culture a heightened priority, Alves wasted little time in forming the Office of Culture and Promotion for Bahia and charged his brother, Isaías Alves, with directing it. Isaías Alves, who also served as state secretary of education and health, was a firm believer in the ideals of the Estado Novo. He initiated a full-scale cultural campaign for Bahia, sponsoring school programs, conferences and lectures, art exhibitions, and journalism courses.[11] Furthermore, the Office of Culture and Promotion gave itself the ambitious mission to "oversee historic and social documentation and preserve the cultural heritage of the state."[12] This meant, most obviously, a program of *tombamento*, or the registering of historic sites and objects, a process that replicated the federal program under way in the nation as a whole during this time.[13] The protection of Bahia's heritage developed along more local lines, however. Leaders envisioned a survey of the state's social and economic conditions and new official attention to "the preservation of the shape and health of Bahian traditions."[14]

These traditions were to be promoted alongside modernization, an uneasy tension to be sure. In 1939 the Office of Culture created a new illustrated journal, *Bahia tradicional e moderna* (Traditional and modern Bahia). The journal's cover featured a drawing by the artist Luís Jardim, with a Baiana in traditional garb juxtaposed against the modern skyline of Salvador's port. It was precisely this contrast that the publication intended to highlight. As the introduction explained, the artist had captured the essence of the initiative. The journal's goal, which the writer admitted would be "difficult to faithfully execute," was to provide "documentation, particularly photographic documentation, of Bahia in all of its aspects, as much from the traditional and historic Bahia of yesterday as from the modern, progressive Bahia of today."[15] Despite this conflicted rhetoric, the cultural program for the state set the modern ideal largely aside. Tradition gained increasing prominence in Bahia's cultural agenda.

State officials organized efforts aimed especially at preserving popular traditions. The Office of Culture planned an exhibition of popular art in 1939 and defined it in broad terms. Isaías Alves remarked that though the exhibit was only a modest initiative, it boasted "a certain sociological, even economic, interest" and would motivate the "spirit of invention and abilities of our people [*nossa gente*]."[16] In his vision the event would display and draw on "the most varied aspects of the life of the people [*o povo*]. In the open air markets, on the farms [*fazendas*], in the Candomblés, in artisan workshops, in schools, as well as in private collections and preexisting official collections, [all of these locations] offer objects that should figure in this original ethnographic exposition. . . . All of this collected material and photographic documentation of it should later figure in the Museu do Estado."[17]

It is unknown whether this exposition ever took place, but the motives in organizing it are remarkable. The state, which a few years earlier had repressed Candomblé,[18] was now proposing to celebrate it in an exhibition and to give it a space in the State Museum. Bahia, which had long been focused on the elite culture of its medical school, its poets, and its politicians, was now turning to popular culture, and Afro-Brazilian culture in particular, as a valuable element in the state's identity. Furthermore, the state sponsorship of culture (despite the far-reaching claims of *Bahia tradicional e moderna*) came to prioritize tradition in place of modernization.

The policy represented a sea change from Bahian efforts of the turn of the

BAHIA

TRADICIONAL E MODERNA

1

Cover of the first issue of *Bahia tradicional e moderna*, 1939

century and into the 1920s, when elites struggled to extinguish celebrations of popular culture and to de-Africanize their public display. As the historian Wlamyra Albuquerque shows, the elite debate of the 1920s divided those who believed strong measures were needed to extinguish popular manifestations in local celebrations from those who believed such displays would die out naturally in a larger march toward progress. The debate, with often racialized undertones, highlighted the dilemma of popular culture for a ruling class (and especially for the members of Bahia's Historic and Geographic Institute) that wished to privilege elite customs and European rather than African roots.[19] The debates of the 1920s revealed an early, though limited, effort at valuing tradition rather than modernization, but the Bahian elite proved unable to conceive of tradition in any way other than as a reflection of its own idealized culture.

Bahia's moves in the 1930s to state-sponsored popular and African culture reflected national trends toward cultural fusion, but they also represented a significant local effort in Bahia itself. The official attitude toward Afro-Brazilian culture had shifted dramatically, influenced by Bahia's recent Afro-Brazilian Congress of 1937 and the sympathy it had created. At this time Bahia first began to use popularized and Africanized visions of itself in its promotion to the rest of Brazil and to the rest of the world. *Bahia tradicional e moderna*, for instance, was distributed to all areas of the country and sent abroad as part of a campaign by the Touring Clube do Brasil. The club also collaborated with the state in other initiatives, promoting Bahia to potential visitors and preparing pamphlets for tourist propaganda.[20] In this context of crafting a new identity, the State Museum of Bahia gained new life.

José Valladares and the Bahian State Museum: Defining Traditions

The museum took form under the direction of José Antônio do Prado Valladares, born to a prominent Bahia family in 1917. His father, Antônio do Prado Valladares, was a physician associated with the Tropicalista school of medicine and a member of the editorial board of the *Gazeta Médica da Bahia*. José went north for his education; after graduating from the Ginásio Pernambucano in Recife in 1932 he earned a degree at the Recife School of Law in 1937. While there he dabbled in journalism, reporting for the local paper, the *Diário de Pernambuco*.[21] Most likely it was in this context that he first met Gilberto Freyre, who had been a regular contributor to the same paper since the early 1920s. When Freyre organized the First Afro-Brazilian Congress in Recife in 1934, Valladares, then only seventeen, served as congress secretary and maintained correspondence with intellectuals across the Americas to invite them to the event. Given Freyre's vision of the congress as an interdisciplinary showcase of Afro-Brazilian culture, Valladares's position would have brought him into formative contact with the world of art as well; the congress mounted a small "exhibition of pictures and drawings of Brazilian black life" curated by his younger brother, Clarival (then only sixteen), and the artist Cicero Dias.[22] A few years later, in 1939, Valladares returned to Bahia to direct the Museu do Estado da Bahia, the task to which he would dedicate the rest of his life.

Valladares was not the first choice for director: the post was offered first to a professor from the Normal Institute who proved unable to take the position.[23] Yet while he may have lacked formal qualifications, and even an early vote of confidence, he did have one critical advantage for the job: roots in Bahia's intellectual elite. Educated at the most prestigious private schools in Salvador and Recife and then at the venerable Recife School of Law, Valladares boasted an impeccable pedigree that was apparently enough to overcome his limited experience.[24] In fact, given the limited opportunities for higher education in Brazil at this point, it is not clear what qualifications the state might have sought for a museum director: there was no formal museological training program in place at this time, and degrees in the humanities and social sciences began to be offered only in the 1930s in the South and not until the 1940s in Bahia. Whatever the limits of his experience, it is clear that Valladares's brief participation in the Afro-Brazilian congress proved formative for his effort to give new life to Bahia's museum.

Bahia's Museu do Estado had been legally established by decree in 1918, but in its early years it was underfunded with an unclear mission.[25] Although it gained a more detailed charter in 1922, administrative reorganizations shifted the museum from one division of the state to another. Not until 1931 did the institution obtain a formal gallery of its own and open to the public.[26] The museum's charter divided the museum into three sections—numismatics, history, and ethnography—and emphasized local identity alongside national concerns; the institution would "scientifically classify, conserve, and exhibit to the public—with the necessary indications—all of the objects that are of interest to the history of Bahia and of Brazil."[27] The numismatics section, predictably, would display paper and metal currency. The history section was given an equally formal, elite ideal; focused on the great men of the past, it would showcase medals, patents, diplomas, and letters as well as the "clothes of civilized people" and portraits or sculptures of important figures.[28] The ethnography section, however, opened up a potentially radically inclusive vision of Bahian history. It would contain "labeled and clas-sified indigenous artifacts, objects used by *sertanistas*, by Africans, and any others falling within this classification." Bahian society, as represented in the museum, would include contributions from all of its members, a fairly innovative idea for 1922 and for an elite that more often tried to stress its European heritage. At the same time, this inclusiveness had defined limits: the contrast here between history—with the accompanying mementos of "civilized people"—and ethnography—defined as particularly ethnic—was clear.[29]

In 1938, a year after the start of the Estado Novo, Isaías Alves, the secre-tary of education and health, assumed direct oversight of the museum's op-erations.[30] The administrative transition signaled a transformation of the museum's mission as it gained prominence in the state government's cul-tural agenda. Alves emphasized that the museum offered a tool to educate a broader public. Opportunities for adult education in Bahia were sorely lack-ing, and Alves complained that the "rudimentary" night courses for adult literacy did little to build civil and moral character. Since the state had no way to educate its citizens once children left secondary school, adults were left completely bereft of "intelligent and practical use of their leisure time" and without any development of artistic appreciation and spirituality.[31]

Alves could have proposed a variety of measures to remedy the situation for adult education; São Paulo, for example, was instituting an adult industrial training program that sought to transmit morality and patriotism alongside shop techniques.[32] Alves, however, chose to focus Bahia's efforts on only one program for this adult civilizing mission: the state museum, revamped with an educational focus on culture and Bahian identity. According to an early statement about the museum by José Valladares, Alves had pushed to "ori-ent the museum in its true sense; a living organ of popular education, center of historical and ethnographic studies, where one has abundant material about the social formation of Bahia at hand."[33]

The Museu do Estado was the only official state-sponsored museum and the only one that claimed an educational mission for the public. It had few parallels in Bahia or its capital: Salvador in the 1930s played host to only a few scattered private museums with somewhat eclectic collections. Those hoping to see a signed letter from Arthur Conan Doyle or a Buddhist shrine might venture to the private Nelson de Oliveira collection, first opened in 1919. Others might visit the Feminine Institute of Bahia, which boasted two museums: the Popular Art Museum, founded in 1929, displaying items re-lating to folklore in Bahia, and the Antique Art Museum, dating from 1933, with a series of exhibitions on jewelry, clothes, silver, and the contributions of Bahian women.[34] While the rest of Salvador's museums were controlled by private institutions, and operated principally as offshoots of larger organizations, the State Museum would be a public initiative unto itself. Its new director embraced the project with enthusiasm.

When Valladares assumed his position the museum had already enjoyed some public success. In 1932, after being open to the public only one year, the museum ushered in 11,500 visitors. By the next year this had doubled to 23,593 and visitation reached its all-time high in 1934 with 36,635 visits. The pace peaked in July, with students free from school on winter break and with commemorative events offered in celebration of Bahian Independence Day (2 July). Yet the visits throughout the year remained impressive. Although many of the visits may have been forced (such as by school groups), they nonetheless ensured a fairly wide exposure for the museum and its exhibits.[35]

Despite this proven popularity, Valladares reported some difficulties in getting the museum in order and believed that there was much left to be done. In 1939 he reported that the whole of his first year had been spent simply getting his bearings and bringing the museum up to a workable standard; his tasks included repairing the building, arranging and framing paintings, publicizing the museum, and classifying the collections. The collections themselves were almost certainly eclectic. During 1938 the state had marshaled funds for a curious assortment of acquisitions: an album of old photographs of Bahia, a pendulum donated by the secretary of education (previously belonging to the Jesuits), two oil paintings by Bahian artists, documents pertaining to a council of health held in 1838, and personal papers of an imperial counselor.[36] The new director of the museum must have been overwhelmed by the assortment of materials gathered over the years and faced a significant challenge shaping these objects into comprehensible exhibits.

An inventory of the museum holdings in August 1939 gives us some idea of the struggle Valladares faced.[37] The museum at this point represented a diverse array of objects in surprising juxtapositions. Its thirteen rooms were numbered, and the first two had a general religious theme: the first began with a collection of religious objects including an engraving of a saint, an oratory, some pieces of porcelain, a carved table, and an image of a crucifix. The second continued this religious theme with missals and photographs of churches but also included an iron fork made by a blind man in 1736. The third room had one of the most consistent groupings of items, with roughly forty objects relating to Candomblé. These included various items of dress for a *pai-de-santo* and necklaces for a *filha-de-santo*.[38] There were also a few presumably indigenous objects, such as arrows, and other items that related to the *sertão* and its Canudos rebellion of the 1890s. Surely the most dramatic item in the room was the skull from one of the *sertão*'s most famous outlaw bands, a companion of the bandit Lampião, who terrorized the Northeast with raids and rampages throughout the late 1920s and early 1930s.[39] Although the museum appeared to be fulfilling its mission of ethnography, it crowded most of the ethnic elements together in one small section.

Another room of displays held various historical souvenirs, including a signed bill of sale for a slave in 1886 and the telegram proclaiming the creation of the Brazilian Republic in 1889. Room six contained old photos of Bahia and pieces of porcelain; room ten grouped various indigenous items as well as the door of the house of the colonial Jesuit Antônio Vieira. Rooms eleven and twelve showcased collections of fossils, animal bones, stuffed birds and animals, agricultural samples of rubber and wood, a dissected hand, and the mummified head of a native from New Zealand. Interspersed among these objects was a marble statue of Venus.[40] Valuable relics mingled with long-forgotten keepsakes of dubious value and preserved human remains that bordered on the macabre.

Within months Valladares had ambitiously divided the museum into five new sections: history, ethnography, archaeology, natural history, and the fine arts. In doing so, he retained the focus on history and ethnography but cut out numismatics and added a focus on the natural world and a focus on art itself. While Valladares may have been in part attempting to give some semblance of order to the curious assortment of objects before him, he was also clearly aiming to create a broader, more coherent intellectual framework for the displays. In a newspaper column in 1939 Valladares insisted that there had been too much criticism of how poor the museum was. He believed that the collections had the potential to become one of the best sites to understand Bahia's "social formation." To realize this potential, however, the museum needed to focus on what "we have to offer as a culture that differentiates us from the others, [since our culture] results from a miscegenation practiced on a large scale, leaving its mark anywhere there is a palpable manifestation of life—in religion and in art, in literature and in cooking, in the history of clothing, in the methods of production."[41] Valladares noted that the museum included historical, numismatic, ethnographic, and art sections, but he offered telling advice to future visitors: "Don't forget to seek out the element that is as representative as the others, though not in glamorous dress. And then pause at the reproductions of our old architecture, our azulejos and engravings, in the clothing and banners of regional festivals, in the objects from the Afro-Brazilian domestic and cult world."[42]

It may have been Freyre and Recife's Afro-Brazilian Congress that first awakened Valladares's interest in the ethnic relations of Brazil. But clearly Valladares had gone beyond this interest to insist that miscegenation had left its mark on Bahia's culture especially. As director of a museum aimed at educating Bahia's adult population, Valladares held considerable power in shaping public conceptions of local culture. He used it by mounting inclusive exhibits, stressing the importance and significance of the Afro-Brazilian contribution and popular culture.

The appeal was clear to foreign visitors as well as local ones. Jack Harding, a traveler from the United States who wrote about his visit to the museum in 1940, responded especially to the ethnic exhibits and displays. His travel narrative—enthusiastically titled *I Like Brazil*—reported his adventures across the country, highlighted by a guided tour of Recife by Gilberto Freyre. Harding requested recommendations for an English-speaking contact in Bahia and had been given a letter of introduction to Valladares by Freyre himself. Fearing a "fusty old curator of forgotten relics" and a "pedantic" tour of a "depressing museum," Harding found himself pleasantly surprised by a young and charming guide who proceeded to show him around the city of Salvador over the course of a few days.[43] The highlights of his museum tour, in his view, included looking at the "Indian weapons and domestic articles; at *Baiana* costumes, Brazil's most colorful—it was a *Baiana* costume that Carmen Miranda wore in her United States tour; at *balanganas* [sic], those African bangle bracelets, very heavy, some made of precious metals" along with paintings done by Bahians, a wooden judge's chair, and a bronze bell used during the Dutch occupation of Bahia in the seventeenth century.[44] Valladares expressed some embarrassment at the limited number of exhibits, explaining that the museum had only recently opened, and that he was still collecting materials from across the state.[45] Whether or not all five of the planned divisions were already represented is unclear, but Valladares had certainly acted creatively in bringing the exhibits together and in choosing among the disperse holdings of the collection.

It is worth considering a few of these items in detail. The Baiana dress, for example, raises a series of questions. It seems unlikely that the item was a donation; the Baiana "costume" was daily wear for many Afro-Bahian women, and surely few of them thought of their clothes as items worth donating to a museum, particularly given the elite orientation of most museums of the time. The display of the dress in a museum was thus unexpected for two reasons: first, as an item of daily use, it was considered almost routine by its users and the inhabitants of Salvador; second, it was a representation of Afro-Bahian culture. Placing the dress in the museum served of course to exoticize it—as an object of curiosity behind glass—but also to underscore its value as an element of Bahian culture, worthy of sitting side-by-side with objects from the Bahian elite. Together in the museum, the elements presented a daring juxtaposition of popular and elite representations of Bahia, as well as a careful construction of a culture with African as well as Portuguese influences.

It is also possible that the exhibit had been shaped by national and popular conceptions of Bahia. The presence of the *balangandan*, for example, recalls a then-popular samba performed by Carmen Miranda that mentioned the items prominently. The song, composed and written by the Bahian native Dorival Caymmi, was titled "O que é que a baiana tem?" (What is it that the Baiana's got?).[46] The lyrics detailed the many attributes of the Baiana, from her swaying hips to her turban, full skirt, and necklaces. Included in the litany of items was the *balangandan*, a large silver belt of dangling charms that Caymmi apparently added for lyric effect, since it was no longer worn by Baianas, and he learned of them only through a relative who owned an antique jewelry shop.[47] In 1939 Miranda performed the song on-screen for the Brazilian film *Bananas de terra* (Bananas), customizing her dress to complement the song. With the performance, Carmen Miranda the icon was born; she would use her version of the "costume" throughout her career. The song, perhaps already familiar to Bahian listeners, became a national hit and, with Carmen Miranda herself, was later exported as a symbol of Brazil.

The U.S. sociologist Donald Pierson, who visited Bahia from 1935 to 1937, provides further description of the Baiana dress worn during the era. He too emphasized that the *balangandan*, "formerly an important instrument, has disappeared," and that many families had traded the item for cash during rough financial times.[48] It is possible that Valladares displayed the item as an antique of obvious beauty, but its presence alongside the Baiana dress raises another possible explanation: that Valladares had crafted a small exhibit based on Caymmi's samba. Such a move would appeal both to tourists from outside Bahia—who arrived in the state museum wanting to know more of the "Baiana" or of Miranda's inspiration—as well as to samba devotees in Salvador, attracted by an homage to Bahia's homegrown lyricist. Whichever the scenario, Valladares creatively worked to incorporate popular and Afro-Brazilian elements into the space of the museum and to make Afro-Brazilian culture a topics of education. Although it would be telling to know which of the divisions (if any) the display fell under, the intent of the exhibit was to emphasize the multiple contributions to Bahian history and identity. Furthermore, a visitor to Bahia's museum would be not only struck by the rich and varied portrait of Bahian culture but also encouraged to see, as in the case of samba, that Bahian culture was Brazilian culture.[49] This new elaboration of Bahian cultural identity was used to remove Bahia from the margins and insert it back into national identity.

This bold approach of bringing popular culture to the museum did not meet with universal approval. An article in a Bahian newspaper in 1941 expressed frank disappointment with the museum and its goals. Elysio de Carvalho Lisboa, a member of Bahia's Geographic and Historic Institute and the Numismatic Society, complained that the museum was far too eclectic, and failed to meet its potential. As a local example of what might be done, he mentioned the Feminine Institute, whose permanent exhibits boasted collections of clothes, art, and antiques. In contrast, he wrote, "an eclectic museum, like the gallery [of the State Museum], which brings together paintings, old documents, furniture, and old weapons, tools from Indians, instruments and fetish items from Africans, and zoological and mineralogical collections, does not appear to us to constitute an agreeable consortium."[50] Lisboa continued: "the ideal museum for Bahia would . . . translate faithfully the refined tastes of its elites from colonial times to the present" and document the skill of Bahia's artists. Lisboa emphasized that the city's "representative circles" had long wished to give Salvador a museum to "reflect the grandeur of yesterday's Bahia and the good taste of our ancestors." The present museum was nevertheless still "not perfectly defined" in its character or the types of objects that should be displayed.[51] To remedy the situation, Lisboa paradoxically recommended still more types of objects and suggested incorporating exhibits on coins, the military, and religion.

Lisboa's critique shows that the efforts by Valladares and Isaías Alves were not without controversy. Not everyone was comfortable with a state museum that prioritized popular culture over the "grandeur" of an elite past—as Lisboa put it, the legacy of "*our* ancestors." The museum's current focus, "imperfectly" defined, Lisboa deemed unacceptable, but his suggested remedy reveals that it was the diversity of the definition and not its eclecticism that offended. Lisboa's satisfaction with a museum of military honors, coins, and religious icons made clear that he would not object to an eclectic collection of *elite* objects. A collection expressing the range of elite lifestyles was highly appropriate, even desirable, but Lisboa rejected incorporation of popular, indigenous, or African elements. This approach was being promoted not only in the museum itself, but also in a series of museum publications edited and organized by José Valladares.

Shaping the Intellectual Scene: Bahia's State Museum Journal

Valladares's vision for the museum was further elaborated in a new museum journal inaugurated in 1941. If the museum was a material representation of Valladares's ideal, the existing collections and lack of financial resources made it difficult to shape. Valladares envisioned the journal as complementary to the mission of the museum and insisted that it not be limited by the scope of the museum's content. The journal's purpose was to promote publications of "local history," but while some of these studies might correspond to the collections themselves, the topics would not be restricted to the museum's physical holdings.[52] The journal represented an open field for Valladares, an arena that depended less on finances and acquisitions than on creative and intellectual energy. He pursued a highly select group of authors and texts, and in his journal, even more clearly than in his museum, he was able to craft an image of a multiethnic Bahia with rich popular culture and traditions.

According to Harding, the intrepid U.S. tourist, Valladares had described the museum as a collection of pieces of Bahia's history. Valladares further refined this proposition in the first issue of the museum journal: "traditional Bahia is the object *par excellence* of the State Museum. . . . if not the body of its patrimony then at least part of its soul."[53] His goal was to preserve and divulge everything "precious and unique of the old Bahia."[54] The first publication of the series in 1941, "Procissões tradicionais da Bahia" (Traditional processions of Bahia), written by the Afro-Bahian folklorist João da Silva Campos, fit well with these goals. In fact, Valladares wrote that the first publication of the museum series should have rightfully been a catalog of the museum's holdings, but the exceptional nature of Silva Campos's work—his dedication to "traditional Bahia" and to "everything precious and unique in old Bahia"—caused Valladares to change his plan.[55] Although the piece on processions was already scheduled to appear in another state journal, Valladares believed it so fitting a start for the museum series that he requested permission to publish it as well. In his view the museum and the cause of Silva Campos were closely linked; the author would have been proud, Valladares believed, to "initiate a new branch of activities for an institution allied with the study of that which was most dear to him."[56]

Silva Campos had already established his reputation with a publication on folklore in 1928, and his name was well recognized in the state.[57] "Procissões tradicionais" sought to document the many popular religious festivals of Bahia, as well as to provide historical research into their origins and trajectories. Silva Campos himself reminded the reader that the processions were hardly elite events: "A good part of the church festivals that used to be celebrated in this capital, maybe almost the majority of them, were promoted by the humble classes, blacks and mulattos, freedmen and slaves, artisans, day laborers, and others."[58] The focus here was not on orthodox religious performance: several of the processions detailed had been discouraged or outlawed by Catholic officials. Instead, the popular classes were the heroes of this story; the street, rather than the church itself, was the setting.

The early focus of the museum journal had an activist bent: while the collections focused on the past, the authors and Valladares urged their readers to protect traditions in danger of slipping away. The first issue, by Silva Campos, opened with a preface acknowledging that if processions shared one characteristic it was the apparent disorder and lack of reverence by the marchers themselves, a quality that had led to efforts at repression. Bahian observers in the nineteenth century had marked their disapproval, and Silva Campos noted that a newspaper article in 1926 had recommended banning parades and processions because of the lack of respect and solemnity displayed by participants. He countered this recommendation by including in his text a report of traditional processions held in France and Belgium and concluded pointedly, "The reader will see how the people of these lands, in an irrefutable testimony to their solid character, maintain tradition."[59] Europe, held up as a universal ideal for culture, celebrated its traditions, and Silva Campos believed that Bahia could learn from its example.

The museum demonstrated a clear interest in this decidedly nonelite subject matter as it published another collection by Silva Campos, one that chronicled folktales and traditional stories from the area surrounding Salvador. The same issue also dedicated considerable space to transcribing the memorial from Silva Campos's recent funeral. As a tribute to his work—cited by Valladares as expressive of the museum's mission—a gallery was renamed in his honor and a newly commissioned portrait was inaugurated by the museum.[60] The actions proved a telling contrast to those of the Museu Histórico

Nacional in Rio de Janeiro, where galleries were named after not folklorists and storytellers but war heroes, presidents, and the elite. The contrast is all the more remarkable when we consider that Silva Campos was black.[61]

The next issues of the museum journal would emphasize not only popular traditions but also the multiethnic roots of Bahia. The prominent U.S. anthropologist Melville Herskovits detailed the African contribution to Bahian culture in the third issue of the journal, titled "Pesquisas etnológicas na Bahia" (Ethnological research in Bahia).[62] Herskovits, one of the most prominent ethnologists of the time, focused on Africans and the African diaspora in the New World. Already he had authored a controversial book about African influences in the United States, *The Myth of the Negro Past*, finding significant continuities with African practices in African American habits and lives.[63] He had submitted papers on African culture to both the first and the second Afro-Brazilian congresses, and his essay published in the museum journal was based on a formal presentation given in 1942 to inaugurate the Faculdade de Filosofia, which offered Bahia's first advanced degree program in the humanities. Having chosen Bahia as an ideal site to study the survival of African cultural forms, Herskovits outlined in his essay his overall approach, then turned to the impact of African culture in Afro-Bahian life, and especially in the practice of Candomblé.

Valladares was anxious to include this contribution, and his preface indicated the impact he hoped it would make in Bahia's intellectual life. He began by introducing Herskovits in superlative terms, citing praise from Brazil's most famous anthropologist, Arthur Ramos. Valladares presented Herskovits as one of the leading specialists in "Afro-American problems" and stressed that it had been a lucky opportunity for the museum journal to edit a work by such an esteemed scholar. After his enthusiastic introduction Valladares expressed disappointment, however, that Bahians had not given Afro-Brazilian topics as much attention as they deserved: "Nonetheless, not all of the readers of the journal show the interest in the study of Afro-American questions that is to be desired in every man of science, or history, or of national letters. If some readers are ignorant of the importance of Professor Herskovits's work, this is not surprising. The present publication will have accomplished its mission most satisfactorily if it leads a small portion of these readers to seek out the national books that address the arrival, accommodation, and assimilation of the actual state of Africans on this side of the Atlantic."[64] In emphasizing the unassailable academic pedigree of Herskovits, Valladares sought not just to demonstrate the importance of the issue but to endorse the topic as a whole. Valladares envisioned an ambitious role for his museum journal: its objective was not simply to preserve academic knowledge but to reshape Bahia and its intellectual elite.

Herskovits and Valladares would develop a friendship and a correspondence that spanned decades. Valladares had first contacted him in 1934; as secretary of the First Afro-Brazilian Congress he was charged with issuing invitations to scholars abroad. Their later exchange of letters upon Herskovits's return to the United States reveals that Herskovits used Valladares as his principal connection to the world of Candomblé in Bahia, depending on him for updates on religious leaders and even for copyright permissions for the sound recordings of Candomblé ceremonies that Herskovits wished to publish in the United States.[65] Indeed, Valladares had served as translator for the extensive interviews that Melville Herskovits and his wife Frances conducted in Salvador. I will examine Herskovits and his study of Bahian ethnology more fully in chapter 4, as he played a critical, if polarizing role, in a larger group of U.S. scholars who came to conduct research on Afro-Brazilian life in Bahia. Though Herskovits and Valladares clearly reached agreement on the importance of Afro-Brazilian culture, particularly for Bahia, their shared views were broader than that: Herskovits's essay, despite its focus on the present-day population of Bahia, reflected Valladares's interest in the past and in tradition.

Indigenous culture also commanded attention from the museum journal, as shown by the publication of an issue by Carlos Ott in 1945 titled "Vestígios de cultura indígena no sertão da Bahia" (Vestiges of indigenous culture in the Bahian sertão).[66] Valladares stressed that the essay simultaneously accomplished "two things of importance." First, it filled a need for local archaeology highlighted two years earlier by the director of Rio de Janeiro's national museum, Heloisa Torres. Second, Valladares pronounced proudly, "It proves in a concrete manner—and it is only necessary to read the monograph to verify this—that currently, contrary to what many have imprudently dared to think and say, culture in Bahia is giving proof of hearty vitality, perhaps now more than ever."[67] Showcasing the extensive list of publications by Ott, printed at the beginning of the issue, Valladares remarked approvingly that the author had already dedicated himself admirably to Bahian questions with "impassioned dedication."[68] The study of indigenous culture was continued by Frederico Edelweiss in 1947 and balanced the following year by an Afro-Brazilian focus.[69] Edison Carneiro's study of Bahian Candomblé in 1948 would mark one of the most influential publications in the series and one of the most important works of Carneiro's career.[70]

Through his thematic selections and his own impassioned prefaces,

Valladares made the objective of the museum journal clear: to foster a sense of Bahian pride, to consolidate a sense of Bahian identity, and to embrace the many contributions to its culture, whether they be popular, African, or indigenous. Valladares believed that just as his readers uncovered the true impact of Bahia's significance, the rest of the nation would also come to realize Bahia's centrality, both in its role as a producer of culture and in its culture itself. Yet while the museum journal continued to focus on popular and ethnic culture through the 1940s, changes were under way in the museum itself at the early part of the decade. A dramatic turnaround began in the museum, corresponding with both an extended trip abroad by Valladares and a change in the location of the museum.

Valladares Goes to the United States, 1943

In the midst of the frenzy that must have inevitably accompanied the museum reorganization and the start of a new publication series, Valladares applied for and received a Rockefeller Fellowship in 1943 for a year of study in the Americas, with an extended stay in the United States. Valladares's application proposed "an expanded program" for the Bahia museum. It appeared that this new program aimed to move his museum more toward the social sciences than the fine arts as his plan of study spanned not only "museum techniques" but also archeology and anthropology.[71] This focus changed over the course of his studies, however, possibly through the influence of his advisers, Robert C. Smith and Melville Herskovits.

In his final report, Valladares dedicated little time to his original interests, anthropology and archeology, and instead focused on explaining the newest thinking in museum theory and organization. He spoke in emphatic terms on a variety of topics critical to museum management: lighting, display, and the need to attract a wider public. As indicated by the title of his final report, "Museus para o povo" (Museums for the people), published as an issue of the museum journal, he was particularly preoccupied with the latter concern. He divided his report into three sections: "The Museum and Popular Education," "Conditions for Educational Efforts," and "The Museum at Service for the Community." Clearly the museum was to be a new educational tool and a link between the government and its citizens. Valladares prepared his report for the Rockefeller Foundation, presented it to a group in Bahia's new Faculty of Philosophy, and then published it in the museum journal series.

The report displayed considerable ambivalence about the role to be played by regional collections like his own. Valladares struggled repeatedly in his text to define the ideal museum and vacillated in his view of the role for smaller, younger collections. In a striking rejection of his own earlier efforts, he dismissed local concerns as irrelevant or worse: "Museums organized with the criteria of only giving distinction to the local, whether it be local archeology, local ethnography, or fine arts or history, condemn themselves to be destined only for specialized study or for tourists in search of the exotic. The former destiny is not the objective of the museum, which is becoming, more each day, a place of learning for the people in general. The latter, more than anything, is unpatriotic."[72] The ideal audience for a museum, then, was a general public, and local exhibits threatened to derail this purpose and pander to outside tourists. The charge of deficient patriotism was fierce indeed, particularly in the period's atmosphere of heightened nationalism. Yet this was a confusing statement from someone who only a few years earlier had proclaimed the purpose of his own museum to be the preservation of "local history." Either Valladares had long felt frustration with this approach, or he was signaling a new turn in his own thinking and the direction for the museum.

Valladares continued that the objective of the modern museum was not to appeal only to those with existing interest in the arts or in history but to attract new viewers to the museum and seduce them into learning with attractive displays and carefully crafted exhibits. This learning, then, should be of the broadest sort, to appeal to the broadest sectors of society—the "people." Local history fell short of this goal of education and left citizens in a painful state of backwardness. Without a larger context to situate their knowledge, they remained ignorant of wider trends and their own place within them. Museums should avoid at all costs the "deification of local works" and draw instead on a comparative framework.[73]

Valladares seemed to contradict himself in the same section, however, arguing that attention to the universal by no means signified hostility to local tradition. Citing an article on regional museums written by the Brazilian Herman Lima, he argued that local traditions should be favored as much as possible and that museums represented some of the best sites to cultivate these traditions. The key, he noted, was to ensure that the museum not limit itself to "local traditions while crossing its arms with respect to past and present events in the rest of the world."[74] In some ways Valladares had not strayed far from his idea of a local museum celebrating regional heritage, but he now advocated a wider understanding of the national and international context.

Although "Museus para o povo" raises many questions about Valladares and his new ambivalence toward local history, it seems that the museum did shift after his return to Bahia. In part, this shift corresponded with a change of location and a substantial addition to the museum's collections. In 1943 the Bahian government had determined to purchase the house and holdings of the Góes Calmon family, an old political clan in Bahia. While it is uncertain whether the acquisition was a strategic effort to bring renewed attention to the Calmon name, it seems clear that José Valladares was not involved in the negotiations: the purchase of the collection was completed by early 1944 and coincided with his museum studies in the United States.

The negotiations for the collection remain mysterious, but they may have gotten some help from the then-mayor, Elysio de Carvalho Lisboa. Lisboa, after all, had been a significant critic of Valladares's original framework for the museum, and the Góes Calmon acquisitions certainly pushed the museum's collections further toward the elite vision of Bahia that Lisboa had hoped to highlight and display.[75] Valladares nonetheless appeared pleased with the results, writing to his friend Melville J. Herskovits in 1944: "I am half convinced that I could become a useful man for Bahia."[76] He noted approvingly: "After the purchase of the Calmon collection, the government appears interested [*parece empenhado*] in endowing the city with a worthy [*condigno*] museum."[77]

What is certain about the purchase of the collection is that it aimed in part to get Salvador ready for the four hundredth anniversary of its founding in 1949. Immediately upon his return to Bahia in 1944, Valladares wrote back to his friends from the Brooklyn Museum that his work for the event was already being planned. "People in Bahia have been very nice to me," he wrote. "They believe that I have important suggestions to make and, in what the museum is conceived [*sic*] the Government wants to install a good one for the Centennary [*sic*] (1949)." The museum's shape, he proposed, would be very much along the lines of the Brooklyn Museum where he had conducted a three-month internship.[78] The move to the new location nonetheless took some time, and the museum reopened in early 1946.[79] Despite such delays Valladares remained optimistic about the museum's potential. As he wrote to Herskovits in 1947, the museum would have a tremendous opportunity with the coming of the centenary celebrations of Bahia's birth.[80] Indeed, he seemed satisfied with the celebrations and the occasion to show off the art from the Góes Calmon collection.[81]

From other sources, however, it appears that Valladares may have had significant misgivings about the new museum location. His correspondence with Rodrigo Melo de Andrade, director of the newly created Serviço do Patrimônio Histórico e Artístico Nacional (National Historic and Artistic Heritage Service, or SPHAN), indicated that he hoped the museum's move was only temporary. Valladares had been consulting with federal cultural authorities from the start of his tenure; the first letter directed to Andrade dates from 10 October 1939, and by that point Valladares was already in weekly contact with SPHAN's regional representative, Godofredo Filho. His correspondence with Andrade, which indicated a close friendship as well as intellectual agreement, suggested that both believed the move to the Góes Calmon house was temporary. As Valladares wrote in 1945, in the midst of moving the museum to the Góes Calmon house, the museum's future relocation to Fort São Pedro seemed assured. He only hoped that politicians would not upset such ideal plans.[82]

Unveiling the New Museum, 1946

Valladares reorganized the museum completely as it moved to its new location, finishing a visitor's guide for the reopening sometime in 1946. This guide would accompany the viewer through the museum, now primarily made up of items from the Góes Calmon collection. Notably, Valladares set aside special acknowledgment in the guide for his former critic at the newspaper, the former Mayor Elysio de Carvalho Lisboa. Lisboa, named as a dedicated friend of the museum, had helped shape the new museum with his suggestions for classification and nomenclature and had also contributed items from his own family.[83]

It appeared that Lisboa had achieved what he once desired: an eclectic elite repository of the past. The museum retained an organization that reflected its original domestic use by a moneyed upper stratum. The entry hall displayed some of the earliest eras of Bahian history, with a sign for Bahia's municipal council crafted in Holland in 1615 and an oil painting of one of the most prestigious colonial Jesuits, Padre Antônio Vieira.[84] The dining room contained imported porcelain from China, shipped for the use of Bahia's most privileged families, as well as a wall of medallions.[85] The *fumoir* moved forward in time and included Chippendale and Louis XV style furniture as well as more porcelain and an assortment of teapots.[86] The first vestibule hosted furniture from the eighteenth century, two copies of Dutch paintings by Franz Hals, and several cameos and brooches.[87] The other downstairs rooms continued in similar patterns, with more antique furnishings, more imported luxury goods, more copies of European art, and curtains and lamps brought from sugar plantation and churches. There was also a music room with a piano and a series of portraits of Bahian notables decorating the staircase. On the second floor two more rooms displayed eighteenth-century furnishings, and a series of rooms displayed nineteenth-century furniture. Finally, a room was dedicated to religious paintings. There was no mention of indigenous or African objects, or any mention of popular culture. The rooms, arranged to evoke an elite home, highlighted elite furnishings of bygone eras, with an emphasis on imported luxury goods from around the world. Few of the items could be linked to particularly Bahian production or origins.

This organization appears to be the same as that detailed in an article Valladares wrote for the *Bulletin of the Pan American Union* two years later, in 1948. There he highlighted the international links of Bahian society. Beyond "the works of art they [Bahian artisans] created," he wrote, "there soon were added others imported from various parts of the globe, thanks to the expansion of Portuguese maritime trade and also to the fact that Bahia was a port strategically used as a place to stop for water and provisions on the route to the East Indies. Bahian society was a mestizo society from the beginning."[88] Valladares paid further tribute to the idea of a multiethnic Bahia by mentioning early unions between the Portuguese and Indians; "the blood of the African" was later added to the mix as well.[89] Even in elite, baroque art this "contact of cultures" had visibly altered the European form: indigenous and African artists added their own aesthetics and often their own images to buildings and decorations, and this cultural *mestiçagem* was further enriched by Jesuit international influence and exchange with the East.[90] This framework seemed to fit well with the stated aims of "Museus para o povo"—it was a local collection situated in a national and international context. Although Valladares attempted to frame Bahia's history by stressing its multiracial origins, however, this emphasis would not be reflected in the museum's collection or layout.

The rooms of the museum, Valladares said, had been "arranged according to artistic periods." Gone was the old division of five disciplines; the space was now organized according to a chronology that seemed to stop in the nineteenth century. A series of photographs accompanied the article, apparently corresponding to the highlights of the collection. One, for example, showed the Jesuit bell mentioned in the 1946 guide; Valladares described the bell as one of the most precious pieces in the collection. And, corresponding to the described strength of the museum, many of the images displayed furniture, with a few selections of religious art. In the middle of all of these fairly predictable illustrations, however, were two large, high-quality images of silver and gold *balangandans*, labeled as a "necklace and bracelets formerly used by Bahian Negresses," both from the nineteenth century.[91] Though these two images together occupied a full page of text, there was no treatment of them in the article itself. Valladares only mentioned in passing that the museum also had a "small ethnological collection."[92]

The puzzling inclusion of the *balangandans* with no mention of their location in the museum and no description of their significance seems to indicate a last struggle by Valladares: though they had little place in Bahia's new elite repository of memory, Valladares was reluctant to omit mention of them altogether. Beyond this the indigenous tools and artifacts so proudly exhibited to the tourist from the United States at the start of Valladares's tenure received no mention, nor did the collection of Baiana dresses that had struck Jack Harding's imagination. Valladares closed his article with the hope that the museum would "become the kind of institution that befits the Brazilian city with the greatest wealth of tradition," but he neglected any mention of the popular traditions trumpeted in the museum's earlier incarnation.[93] While the first issues of the museum journal had emphasized the importance of folklore to the museum, and extolled traditional processions, Valladares's account for the Pan American Union in 1948 instead played up Bahia's elite and institutional heritage, with "the richest churches and convents in Brazil, the most spacious and beautiful city mansions and country homes, and the strongest fortresses."[94]

Already by 1947 Valladares had altered his description of the institution significantly, defining it in its journal as "a regional museum, with emphasis on colonial art of Bahian origin." In the same issue, a study of indigenous culture by Frederico Edelweiss, Valladares now felt obligated to explain the inclusion of a work of ethnography, a "topic not properly within its sphere," where before he had assumed the topic to be of central importance to the museum.[95] The museum's focus had moved from ethnography and anthropology to history, and from a popular vision of the past to an elite one. Valladares's evocative groups of Baiana dress and items from popular sambas had been replaced by staid groupings of eighteenth-century furniture. Representation had shifted from the people and street life of Bahia to its material opulence and to cloistered sitting rooms. Popular culture, once displayed in innovative exhibits of samba and Afro-Bahian life, had been swept away.

The transformation of Bahia's Museu do Estado reveals that many elites remained unconvinced of the need for a more inclusive vision of the past. In its final incarnation the museum, the central repository of Bahian identity and history, combined the worst of all worlds: it both nostalgically evoked a time in which many blacks had been enslaved and wiped out all material mention of their contribution to society as a whole. Here was all the grandeur of the sugar estates and the white elite, without any hint of the black and brown laborers who provided the elite's riches and Bahia's very backbone. A transformation of the museum had occurred, but why? Had José Valladares decided that ethnology, archeology, and local history could not be developed adequately and instead tailored the museum's focus to its newly donated collections? Had he changed his thinking about the purpose of the museum? Had political pressures derailed his own passions? What accounted for the museum's shift from a center of popular and local history to a preserve of the colonial elite?

Although we cannot know for certain, it is likely that political shifts played the most important role in changing the focus of the museum. The 1942 dismissal of Secretary of Education and Health Isaías Alves, a champion of popular culture and the Estado Novo, coincided roughly with the purchase of the Góes Calmon collection and the more elite turn of the museum. In addition, the impending four-hundredth anniversary of Salvador's founding created political pressures that definitively reshaped the exhibits. Valladares himself seems to have warned of such a danger in an early letter to Rodrigo Andrade in 1939, as he was in the midst of his first reorganization of the museum. Andrade had suggested that Bahia might create an executive council for its museum, in part to stimulate donations from council members. Valladares responded that such an idea would not work in Bahia. "I should confess," he wrote, "that my intention was to safeguard the museum from the capricious wants of the ruling powers, today very well-intentioned but tomorrow possibly less enlightened and well capable of making purchases, determining publications, and promoting commemorations, all of which will only cost money and diminish the renown that the museum might come to have. . . . I would like for you to think, if possible, again about our provincial difficulties here."[96] It appears that the ruling powers of Bahia came to do precisely what Valladares had feared: negotiate purchases and determine commemorations which had much to do with political imperatives and less to do with fostering innovative views of Bahian society.

Indeed, it seems unlikely that Valladares himself lost his energy or enthusiasm for popular culture: his continued publications in the museum series and his own writings reflected an ongoing interest in questions of Afro-Brazilian culture and popular traditions.[97] And it is worth nothing that his catalog for the museum in 1946 asserted that the museum would organize rotating exhibits in the future. Though such hope may have reflected his museological studies in the United States, which advised against the display of too many items at once, it may also have been a voice of resistance against granting a permanent home to an elite-driven view of the past. Valladares still insisted, quixotically, that the museum would be malleable. For whatever reason it appears such hopes of changing exhibitions and the museum's predicted relocation were not fulfilled during his tenure: Valladares produced no future catalogs and the museum remained in its location until 1982.

Indeed the museum seemed to have changed little under his directorship during the next decade. Annual reports submitted through the 1950s by Valladares altered little from year to year and described the museum as focused on "colonial Bahian art and objects of foreign art brought over during the colonial period."[98] Much, if not all, of the ethnography collection remained unavailable to the public. And public attendance at the museum dropped dramatically in the new location, perhaps because of the static, elite displays and perhaps because the neighborhood of Nazaré attracted less traffic than the more central Campo Grande plaza where the museum had first opened.[99] The vision of Bahia's past had been constricted, and so had its audience. No more could the museum be imagined as a key transmitter of culture and values for a broad public; it was now an elite sanctuary, protected from, if not ignored by, the masses.

The museum journal series showed a corresponding shift as the 1940s came to a close, but it was more gradual. Valladares's own study of museums occupied the 1946 issue, and the following years produced some of the series's most important works—the study of indigenous culture by Edelweiss in 1947 and Edison Carneiro's study of Bahian Candomblé in 1948.[100] Yet Valladares's contributions to the journal turned increasingly to topics of the fine arts and the colonial period, and away from popular culture. His 1950 issue sketched the history of a series of oil portraits donated by a British faculty member of Bahia's medical school in the nineteenth century. And the other works produced that year, spurred by Salvador's four hundredth anniversary, included a history of the colonial founding of Bahia, as detailed by the historian Pedro Calmon, as well as a survey of colonial architecture conducted by the art historian Robert C. Smith.

While the museum series and the museum itself had become more conservative, some interest in Afro-Brazilian culture still lingered. A new museum series in the 1950s, this one with no formal association with Val-

ladares, showcased the work of the artist Carybé. A series titled "The Recôncavo Collection" emerged in ten parts, each focused on a different arena
of popular culture, with representations of the ritual washing of Bomfim,
Candomblé, and capoeira. It would be republished, first in 1962 and later,
in 1994, by Valladares's successor to mark the renewal of Salvador's historic
center.[101] By 1959, when Valladares was killed in an airplane crash, the museum's divergent directions proved to be untenable. The museum's collection was dismantled, its collection carved up into donations to other local
endeavors, including Bahia's new Modern Museum of Art. The innovative
moment of encouraging both popular and elite culture had passed, to be
resurrected in the tourist campaign of a later era. Bahia's State Museum was
renamed the Museu de Arte da Bahia, an institution now dedicated primarily to the fine arts.

Conclusion

The Estado Novo and Interventor Landulfo Alves brought some tentative
steps toward crafting plans for Bahia's economic modernization, but a
consensus was building that in terms of culture, and in terms of its larger
identity, tradition would be Bahia's claim to fame. Many Brazilians began to
assert with greater certainty that Bahia harbored the most authentic of the
nation's traditions, and they began to evoke the idea of Bahia as the cradle
or birthplace of Brazilian identity. This strategic move played to the state's
strengths. Getúlio Vargas's cultural emissaries emphasized *brasilidade* in
terms of both the modern and the traditional, but it was clear that São Paulo
would win any contest in building modernity while Bahia's economy remained agrarian and oriented toward exports.

   As the celebration of the past became an acceptable and even laudable
ideal, debates surfaced about what type of tradition Bahia best represented.
The Vargas era and especially the period of the Estado Novo show that Bahia
still struggled to define its identity, and that the aristocratic sugar clans continued to wield decisive power in the debate. Yet as we have seen, Bahia was
moving slowly, haltingly, to an identity that gave a role to multiethnic and
popular contributions, despite occasional elite opposition. The movement
gained traction with the Second Afro-Bahian Congress in 1937 and was enhanced through the actions of state officials in Bahia's State Museum in the
early 1940s. It was further consolidated with the arrival of researchers from
the United States during the same period, as the next chapter reveals.

CHAPTER 4

Debating African Roots

The U.S. sociologist Donald Pierson memorably characterized the city of Salvador in the late 1930s as "not unlike a medieval city surrounded by African villages." His adviser's introduction to his work employed much of the same language: Salvador's spatial juxtaposition permitted one to walk though "Europe on the ridges" of the city's hills and hear "the insistent boom of African drums . . . from Africa in the valleys."[1] Paradoxically, these descriptions highlight the racial divisions of the city that Pierson's book attempted to explain away, but they are also significant for their view of Salvador as a city of the past. This vision of a medieval European town and an African village coexisting side by side clearly communicated the idea of a city lost in time and space, and outside the present world. Ultimately, Pierson found this preservation of the past to be key to Bahia's stability and what he viewed as its exceptionally harmonious race relations.

Pierson himself was considerably affected by the Bahian cultural scene, and it is no accident that he found himself inclined to emphasize tradition and a preservation of the past as key to a particularly Bahian form of race relations. As the first social scientist from the United States to conduct extensive research in Bahia, Pierson validated cultural efforts under way by Bahians and brought them to a new international audience. That these same themes echoed through much of the U.S. scholarly work of the period reveals not just the lens of the Western anthropologist in viewing an exotic other but also how Pierson's example, as well as the Bahian intellectual scene, encouraged and supported such conceptions.[2]

As we have seen, a cult of tradition and the past was developing momentum in Bahia. The museum journal of José Valladares, which began at the end of Pierson's stay, similarly advocated that Salvador be considered a cultural preserve of the past. But Valladares selected authors to suit his objectives and interests, and a similar process of selection was going on in a larger arena. Bahian intellectuals began to meet foreign researchers with a variety of approaches to race: a bevy of scholars from the United States began to arrive in Bahia in the late 1930s and early 1940s, attracted by its growing reputation as a center for Afro-Brazilian culture. These foreigners were accepted or censored depending on their alignment with ideas already dominant in Bahia, ideas that stressed racial harmony and a focus on African lineage and "survivals." Though they arrived with their own cultural and theoretical baggage, they were also deeply influenced by their local guides—such as Arthur Ramos, José Valladares, and Edison Carneiro—who served as cultural filters and native authorities of a particularly Bahian reality. This chapter provides a snapshot of the dominance of Bahian ideas of tradition not only among Bahians, but also among outside observers who became influenced by the Bahian scene. Ideas of tradition figured large in conceptions of Bahian identity in the late 1940s and 1950s, and foreign observers played a powerful role in reinforcing Bahia's intellectual trends.

This chapter begins with Donald Pierson—the first U.S. social scientist in Bahia (and Brazil) to study race relations—and examines his influence and legacy. It then turns to two "failed" researchers who gained little support in Bahian circles—E. Franklin Frazier and Ruth Landes—and examines the controversies their approaches ignited. Finally, it returns to the figure of Melville Herskovits, the U.S. anthropologist whose scholarly approval was hotly contested and sought after in the Afro-Brazilian congresses. Herskovits gained a receptive audience for his ideas in Bahia because he, too, touched on themes dear to Bahians. Herskovits was viewed in reverential terms among Bahian intellectuals: later taken up as the father figure of Bahian anthropology, he inaugurated, during his stay, the new humanities faculty at the Universidade Federal da Bahia. The chapter ends by examining his inaugural speech, published in the journal of Bahia's Museu do Estado, and reveals how Herskovits's views of African survivals appealed to a particularly Bahian vision of the past.

Donald Pierson's Salvador: A City Frozen in Time

Donald Pierson was a student of sociology at the University of Chicago, and his adviser was the famed Robert Park, a leader in the Chicago school of sociology. Park and the Chicago school stressed the importance of fieldwork and firsthand ethnographic observation. Pierson had a particularly close relationship with his adviser, as well as with Park's wife, to whom he referred as "Mom."[3] Indeed, Park's influence, on Pierson and on later scholars of Bahia, cannot be underestimated: he played a primary role in encouraging Pierson to study Brazil and advised the more senior Ruth Landes in her preparations for Bahia in 1937. E. Franklin Frazier—a former student of Park's who went on to become a prominent sociologist—arrived in Bahia in 1940. Each of these visitors was shaped by Park's guidance, but even more important were Pierson's contacts, advice, and his formative study of Bahian race relations. Pierson provided his colleagues from the United States with letters of introduction to authorities such as Arthur Ramos and Edison Carneiro, as well as to many other Bahian friends. Furthermore, his *Negroes in Brazil: A Study of Race Contact at Bahia* (1942) became required reading for all later U.S. researchers; after its translation into Portuguese in 1945, its influence in Brazil was also profound. Pierson's conclusions, particularly those that stressed Bahia's exceptional racial harmony, echoed throughout later studies of Bahia and established an underestimated cornerstone for international perceptions of the region.[4]

Pierson conducted the research for *Negroes in Brazil* in Bahia from 1935 to 1937. He concluded that Bahia was a supremely well-adjusted society in terms of race relations. In December 1934, almost a year before arriving in Brazil, he described his project: "My study is to center at Bahia, the ancient port for forced African immigration and the locus of early contact of the Portuguese with the indigenous Indian. My chief concern is with white-Negro contact, accommodation, and fusion, with particular interest to the present racial adjustment."[5] This sense of accommodation and fusion, carried throughout his work, was no doubt shaped by his dismay at what he viewed as the more antagonistic model of U.S. race relations, and by a formative experience in the American South. On Park's recommendation, Pierson began his preparation for research with a stay at Fisk University in Nashville, an experience that Park would also suggest for Ruth Landes. Pierson believed that his time at a Southern black college had awakened him to the discrimination faced by blacks in the United States. The implicit comparison to the U.S. system of segregation would play a large part in shaping his work in Brazil.[6]

Arriving in Rio de Janeiro in mid-1935, Pierson rapidly made contact with Arthur Ramos, who provided him with additional letters of contact for Bahia, writing that Pierson was doing a study of "ethnic elements of African origin."[7] Whether Ramos misunderstood the project or Pierson misrepresented it (in what may have been still rudimentary Portuguese) any tendencies to study African origins were cut short by his advisers, not only Park but the other members of his dissertation committee, the anthropologists Robert Redfield and Louis Wirth. As Park reminded him in early 1936, "This is, as Redfield remarked, a study of race relations and not of the origins of such remnants of African culture as still exist in Brazil."[8]

Pierson settled into Bahia and began sending periodic reports back to his thesis committee in February 1936. Though his early statements indicated evidence of racial problems, such conceptions seem to have been modified over time. He worried in an early report that his Bahian friends who had once insisted that Brazil was free from prejudice had begun "to acknowledge that such description is theoretical only, that in reality they do not accept the Negro on a plane of complete social equality."[9] Remarkably, however, Pierson relegated this information to a footnote in his own report, an approach that he would follow in his book as well. In the end, observed prejudice in Bahia, often reported in his own ethnological detail, would be swept away by a larger theoretical focus on the concepts of class, status, and color.

Central to Pierson's approach was the idea of Bahia as a "culturally passive" society. He owed this view to Park, who proposed that life in such areas maintained itself "in the same unbroken and traditional routine. . . . [Changes occur] at an almost imperceptible pace."[10] Pierson emphasized, from the start of his book, that Bahia had not undergone any significant historical or social shifts in the recent past. The Bahian way of life, he argued, remained very much shaped by colonial structures: "The social order is still relatively stable. There has been in recent times little change. Bahia is, as we have seen, a comparatively old city, conscious of its traditions and proud of them. Conventions originally developed in response to the needs of colonial life still persist and direct life pretty much in the old familiar channels. . . . Bahia is thus a 'culturally passive' area with a stability and order reminiscent of Europe in the Middle Ages. In fact, Bahia is, in some respects at least, a medieval town."[11] Pierson found Bahia's social relations favorable compared to "cities of comparable size in industrial societies." Bahia lacked the tensions of the industrial world and instead seemed more akin to "an overgrown village." Far from viewing modernization as necessary, Pierson began his study by observing that this static society had produced an "absence of most forms of conflict." He alerted his readers in his introductory comments that "a minimum of racial conflict will be evident throughout this account."[12] In Pierson's view, though Salvador was a deeply divided city, it had avoided racial tensions because of its tenacity in maintaining tradition and avoiding change. Its static, medieval position in the midst of the modern industrialized world held the secret to its present harmony.

Despite his repeated assertions of harmony, indications of stark racial inequalities exist in Pierson's account. He stressed that the lower class was principally black and dark mulatto, and that whites dominated the elite. He noted that the elite lived along the ridges of the city, where: "the five newspapers circulate almost exclusively. . . . Here are to be found the owners of virtually all of the city's 3,855 telephones, its 1,028 automobiles, its radios and private libraries. Here live most of the 20,524 voters who cast ballots in the municipal election of 1936. Here attachment to the Candomblé, or Afro-Brazilian fetish cult, is minimal and Catholic belief is least modified by elements from the more primitive religions. Here live[s] that portion of the population which *o povo* ('the people') call the *ricos*, or the rich." There existed, he explained, a wide "social gulf" between rich and poor that was difficult to cross. A visitor to the city would note "that this segregation by economic and educational classes conforms in a general way, although with certain important exceptions, to the differences in color in the population." Pierson believed that this "ethnic segregation is largely due to the circumstance that color and class, as we shall soon see in detail, tend to coincide." In his view this was understandable given the recent experience with slavery, but "the important consideration is that there is in Bahia, it seems, no deliberate attempt to segregate the races as a means of maintaining caste or class distinctions."[13] Pierson struggled to come to terms with a society that offered none of the explicit discrimination based on race that he had known in the United States. As he observed, however, there was not yet a full acceptance of African elements of culture, nor was there social equality between people he labeled as nonwhite and the elite.

Pierson trod carefully. He reported what he observed, which included statements of an undeniably racist nature. Such language was always dismissed, however, as of limited real importance. His appendix, for example, which recorded "common sayings regarding the negro" mediated the shock of racist statements by insisting that they were mostly a thing of the past and in any case "always said with a smile."[14] Pierson's arguments, if not his evidence, downplayed the significance of racial barriers in Bahian society, hypothesizing instead that the dominant divide was one of status. His conclusions backed away from racism to insist on the importance of color hierarchies, but he emphasized the permeability of such categories and the potential for upward mobility. This argument reinforced many of Freyre's more seductive theories of racial harmony, and, as I show in chapter 5, received ample attention in the UNESCO project on race in the 1950s.

During this period, however, Pierson was remarkable because he was the first to study race relations, rather than African survivals, in Bahia. This was made explicit by Arthur Ramos in the 1945 translation of *Negroes in Brazil* into Portuguese; Ramos noted the book's departure from the more anthropological focus of the Nina Rodrigues school. Pierson's study of "race contact" walked a fine line, however; although undoubtedly assimilationist, it also discussed the role of African culture, and particularly Candomblé, in Bahia. "If he now too [like the Bahian school] studies Africanisms," Ramos noted, "it is more as a point of reference for the evaluation of how the phenomena can influence race relations."[15] Although Pierson claimed to be examining a dynamic process of "race contact," his work paid tribute to static traditions more than to social change: his focus on cultural passivity, combined with attention to African culture, gave his work much more in common with the study of Africanisms than he cared to admit. Perhaps it was this attention to African roots and to Bahia's traditions that allowed Pierson to continue his relationship with Bahian scholars and the Bahian school, which stressed African continuities. Pierson escaped with a laudatory review of his work by Freyre and an extended preface by Ramos. Despite his stated deviation from the Bahian school—whose methodology lay principally in exploring Africanisms and origins—Pierson never incurred their wrath.

Ruth Landes and E. Franklin Frazier, the two researchers who most emphasized departure from African survivals in Bahia, would not be so lucky. Frazier also observed color prejudice in Bahia, and for this he was critiqued directly in Ramos's preface to Pierson's book, as an example of a "visitor" from the United States whose conclusions on race were not nearly so credible.[16] More significant, Frazier denied Africa a role in Bahian family structure, which turned the full wrath of Herskovits against him in a printed exchange. Ramos would attack Ruth Landes in the basest of ways, casting long-lasting doubt on her personal and scholarly reputation. Both Frazier and Landes were extensively criticized by Bahians disturbed at their disregard for the Bahian framework of tradition. And both weathered direct, public attacks by Herskovits, the most aggressive supporter of the Bahian school and its focus on an unchanged past.

The Controversy of Cultural Change: Ruth Landes and E. Franklin Frazier

Ruth Landes trained in anthropology at Columbia University under Franz Boas and Ruth Benedict, completing her degree in 1935. Benedict's encouragement inspired much of Landes's dissertation and early research, which focused on the structure of Native American life in Canada and the United States.[17] Though several scholars from Columbia would go on to study indigenous culture in Brazil (including Charles Wagley, whom I discuss in chapter 5), Landes turned her attention to blacks in Brazil.[18] In preparation for her research she received advice from Pierson's mentor, Robert Park, who suggested, as he had for Pierson, that she spend a term studying and teaching at Fisk University. Fisk offered the advantage of one of the best libraries on race in Brazil, and, as Landes remembers, she was further advised that it was an ideal location "to 'get used to Negroes'" before leaving for her trip. As she wrote later, "I got used to Negroes, as I was supposed to, but in a strained new way." The arrival of Landes, as well as several other scholars from Columbia, seemed to only heighten racial tensions on the campus, and Landes reported considerable anger by black students about their position in U.S. society.[19]

Landes finally arrived in Brazil in May 1938 and drew early explicit contrasts between the position afforded to blacks there and in the United States. Although she spent the first months in Rio de Janeiro, she was already convinced that her chief research would be in Bahia, having met and consulted with Donald Pierson in the United States. Her contact in Rio with Arthur Ramos further reinforced her choice to study Bahia. Landes had wished to do a project that would look not only at Salvador but at surrounding towns such as Santo Amaro; Ramos convinced her otherwise. He argued that she should restrict her focus to Salvador, since it was "known as a norm of reference" and because, there, "Negro life is far more vigorous and intense, and more varied."[20] Although Landes would follow his counsel on this matter, her later analysis of matriarchy and homosexuality in Bahian Candomblé contradicted Ramos's findings and earned his fierce retribution.

Pierson also provided connections for Landes in Bahia, writing to friends in 1937 to inform them of her arrival, as he would do for Frazier.[21] Landes did echo some of Pierson's tropes. Her introduction to her resulting study, *City of Women*, specified that "this book about Brazil does not discuss race problems there because there were none."[22] Not only did she reinforce Pierson's conclusions on race, she also drew on similar notions of a culture lost in time. Writing in a personal style that merged her anthropological observations with her own experience, she opened her book with her own memories of her first steps off the boat in the port of Salvador: "I felt completely suspended in space, in thoughts, in time."[23] Though her book itself presented a vibrant view of Bahian culture, she would end with this same sense of Bahia as immutable. On the final page of her book she mused, "There are no solemn conclusions I can draw from my observations in Bahia. In retrospect, the life there seems remote and timeless."[24]

In fact, Landes drew extensive conclusions throughout her book, and she used her unique voice to reflect on them. Landes inserted herself into the narrative, rather than using the omniscient scholarly authority to which most academics of the time were accustomed. Although her conclusions, which stressed the creative adaptation of Candomblé to Bahian life, were later validated, at the time they struck a sour note. Candomblé was not, for her, simply a continuation of an African past. Pierson had implied much the same thing, and Edison Carneiro stressed adaptation as part of Candomblé, but Landes integrated herself less ably into Bahian and Brazilian circles and thus found herself censured. In the United States and beyond, she suffered from the scathing refutation of her conclusions published by Herskovits, the foremost international authority on African survivals.

Landes's innovation was not only her subject matter, the gendered nature of leadership in Candomblé, but her approach. As the anthropologist Sally Cole argues, Landes rejected a "rigid opposition between 'tradition' and 'modernity.' She did not catalogue 'African survivals' and 'Catholic' elements. She describes Candomblé practices as imaginative and innovative. . . . Landes understood that Candomblé represented a new religion in a changing sociocultural universe."[25] As Landes herself wrote upon her arrival in Salvador, "I knew I could not study Bahia as I would an art gallery."[26] This focus on exploring cultural dynamism, rather than tracing static survivals, broke with the approach of Ramos and Herskovits. Yet the historian Mark Healey has argued that despite such efforts, Landes remained mired in an anthropological framework that saw Bahian society as a premodern, exotic other. In fact, Landes alternated between these two approaches: her early scholarly work on homosexuality stressed cultural adaptation in certain "upstart" houses of Candomblé; but her later book, produced almost a decade after her field research, seems to have been written with nostalgia, reserving greatest praise for the preservation of "traditional" Yoruba Candomblés and viewing African-based culture, and Bahian culture more broadly, as stopped in time. Like Pierson, she lamented what she saw as ongoing modern corruptions of a more idyllic way of life grounded in the past.[27]

Although *City of Women* would not be published until 1947, Landes's early articles had already disseminated some of her most controversial views. Her article of 1940 gave details of her most remarkable conclusions: that homosexual men had taken new positions of power in offshoot Candomblé houses. Throughout she stressed cultural dynamism, concluding "it is clear also that Candomblé has been radically changed by their [homosexuals'] assumption of such roles."[28] Landes contributed her own exoticized portraits of Bahia, describing the streets as surging with people ever swaying to music.[29] But her findings broke with this romanticism by arguing that homosexuals, though accepted in the world of Candomblé for their feminine qualities, came primarily from the lowest echelons of society: they were most often, she described, "outcastes and vagrants." The ones that she had known, she commented, came "from the ranks of the street prostitutes and boy delinquents, and from the town's ruffians."[30] In this early article Landes showed little sympathy for these men and for the *caboclo* (Amerindian and Euro-Brazilian mestizo) Candomblés that they joined, portraying instead a world of degenerates who used religion for their own debased purposes. Though she praised more traditional houses, she noted change in outlier Candomblés that broke with the framework of continued Africanisms.[31] With these conclusions, and with her later *City of Women*, Landes fundamentally changed the study of Candomblé.

Landes's most controversial assertion, however, was the role she saw for women in the Candomblé community. There, surrounded by the patriarchal relations of modern Bahia, she found that the female heads of *terreiros* had carved out independence and prestige for themselves, inverting many of the gendered hierarchies of the everyday world. In her book, she described a conversation about this with Carneiro: "'I know by now that women are the chosen sex,' I said to Edison. 'I take it for granted just as I know in our world that men are the chosen sex.'"[32]

Landes felt these gender hierarchies vividly in her own research endeavors: as a single woman she was continually advised of her need for a male escort in Salvador. Her partnership with Carneiro was built out of mutual respect, but it also stemmed from considerable restrictions on her ability to move through the city and conduct her research alone.[33] Certainly, her views on the gendered freedom of Candomblé resonated with her personally, and she held up Bahia as a potential model of female power to be used across the West. In the last line of her book, she promised her Brazilian host to disabuse the West of its stereotypes of Brazil. Her host joked that she could finally show that Brazil was not a tropical wilderness, with tigers in the streets, but she saw her exposé in different terms, replying, "'I'll tell them also about the women. I think they help make Brazil great. Will Americans believe that there is a country where women like men, feel secure and at ease with them, and do not fear them?'"[34]

In fact Landes echoed many of Carneiro's findings. Carneiro also noted that Candomblé had long been the business of women, and that there was a new role for men in recent times. In his view, however, these men "took" to homosexuality, ostensibly as a result of their new position.[35] Carneiro shared the disdain shown by Landes, saying that such men were all "celebrated drunkards, homosexuals and magicians of Bahia."[36] Though Landes developed the idea of a matriarchy much further than Carneiro, parallel descriptions in their work are explained by the fact that Landes conducted her fieldwork with Carneiro as her guide. Their scholarly agreement may have been further developed by the translation that each did for the other's publications. It also may have had roots in the romance that developed between them in Bahia. Landes's relationship with Carneiro would further fuel the dramatic controversy involving her, Ramos, and Herskovits.

Landes's attention to gender was revolutionary for her time. Indeed, scholars such as Ramos rejected her focus on women and sexuality largely because they viewed such questions as extraneous to serious scholarship. According to anthropologist J. Lorand Matory, Landes earned the wrath of Ramos for "embarrassing" Brazil with her public discussion of homosexuality in front of an international audience. For all the new trails she blazed in some respects, however, Landes trod well-worn paths in others, particularly in her views of Bahian Candomblé as a premodern enclave steeped in tradition. At a party where the men and women of a Candomblé *terreiro* had gathered to dance to popular music, Landes felt disapproval and discomfort as she watched her "traditional" friends move to the secular foxtrot of the outside world: "I discovered that I had become African in my prejudices, as African as Martiniano, as Menininha, as Luzía [the heads of traditional Candomblés]. I felt that the people had lost themselves when they put on heels for the ballroom and abandoned the patterns that they usually stamped with naked feet on floors of dirt."[37] Although Landes allowed that religion itself might still be dynamic, she still imagined it as functioning beyond the limits of a modern society and expressed dismay when the two came together.[38] She hoped, in her words, that the women of Candomblé would continue to "keep those near them from joining the modern world."[39] As Healey argues elsewhere, Landes's scholarly innovation came from her gendered analysis, but she remained grounded in ideas of primitivism that had long marked western anthropology.[40] Like Pierson, Landes saw the beauty of Bahia's world in its timelessness and its preservation of an older way of life. Pierson viewed Bahia's race relations as medieval; Landes tied the power of the Bahian matriarchs to a vanishing landscape of a primitive past. In both views, modernity was a threat.

E. Franklin Frazier was the next scholar from the United States to arrive in Bahia with Park and Pierson as references. At the time of his travels in Brazil he headed the Sociology Department at Howard University, and in 1948 he would become the first black president of the American Sociological Association. A scholar of exceptional stature, Frazier already had developed a well-established, if controversial name in U.S. race studies. Though he dedicated himself to denouncing the race relations of the United States, he directed much of his critique to the black community itself, which he believed had floundered under the "pathological" culture created by the "evils of segregation."[41] Vividly and personally aware of the struggles for black equality in the United States, Frazier joined many other African Americans in praising the comparative racial harmony of Brazil, and especially Bahia, titling a 1942 popular article "Brazil Has No Race Problem."[42]

As David Hellwig notes, however, Frazier gave a much more positive portrait of the situation in his works for the popular press than he did in his scholarly assessments.[43] A closer examination of his scholarly work published the same year reveals that although Frazier agreed with Pierson that there was no racial prejudice in Brazil, he also insisted that "when the situation is studied closely, it is found that there are distinctions based upon color."[44] Frazier's subtle analysis picked up all of the ambiguities of Brazilian race relations, making points that would be drawn out by later generations of scholars. Yet this was only part of what made his work on Brazil and Bahia controversial. More important was his analysis of black family formation in Salvador. His research in black culture in the United States found little to no importance for African continuities, and these conclusions were largely replicated in his writing on Bahia.[45]

Frazier arrived in Rio de Janeiro in September 1940 and soon made contact with Pierson, who provided letters of introduction to scholars in Bahia as well as to Gilberto Freyre and Arthur Ramos.[46] He continued on to Bahia in late 1940 and conducted five and a half months of fieldwork in Salvador, often working in concert with another African American scholar researching there, Lorenzo Turner. Frazier's trip was part of a larger research program; he intended to travel to Haiti, Jamaica, and Brazil "to gather through field studies original data on the family in these areas."[47] His effort to study New World cultures in a comparative context was similar to Herskovits's proposal to trace levels of African influence across the Americas, but Frazier's analysis of Bahian family structures found that African culture had little bearing on the contemporary lives of blacks.

Frazier introduced his own Brazilian findings in a 1942 article by citing Ramos's conclusion "that African culture survived only in his folklore." In agreement with Ramos, he concluded: "That this has been true specifically in regard to the Negro family was borne out in the data which were collected on the families studied." Frazier was struck by the disorganization of Afro-Bahian family life, finding proof in that disorder that no one system of culture prevailed: "African patterns of family life have tended to disappear. . . . so far as family relationships are concerned, there are no rigid, consistent patterns of behavior that can be traced to African culture."[48] Frazier emphasized that Afro-Bahians showed flexible reactions to the social context rather than a strong connection to their past. His evidence, he believed, revealed an eclectic cultural adaptation, shaped by local surroundings: "we find no consistent culture pattern but rather an accommodation to Brazilian conditions."[49]

One of the conclusions that would prove controversial was Frazier's analysis of the low rates of marriage among Afro-Bahians. Frazier believed that social factors such as the fees for church marriage explained some of the reluctance; but most couples, he believed, were committed to a form of common-law union. When male infidelity occurred, Frazier saw it as part of a patriarchal system of male privilege. Afro-Bahian families were shaped by poverty, and by the gendered structure of Brazilian society, but persevered in forming lasting unions nonetheless. Herskovits, who argued instead that men in Bahia followed an African system of polygamy, would disagree, and publicly. His research in Bahia began a year later.

Melville J. Herskovits: Charting African Survivals

Melville Herskovits arrived in Brazil with his wife and coresearcher, Frances Herskovits, in August 1941 for a year of field research with six months dedicated to Bahia alone.[50] It is likely that Arthur Ramos had some role in this decision; he and Herskovits had corresponded for almost a decade and had become better acquainted during Ramos's stay in Chicago on a scholar exchange program in the spring of 1941. Indeed, Ramos served as an intellectual gatekeeper of sorts for most scholars of Afro-Brazilian culture during this era. For many researchers from the United States, visiting Ramos in Rio de Janeiro was a critical first stop in their research program; with his extensive contacts, he gave numerous letters of introduction to scholars traveling to Bahia.[51]

When he arrived in Brazil, Herskovits had just published *The Myth of the Negro Past*, a book that would arouse considerable controversy in the United States.[52] The debate encapsulated the principal divide in Afro-American studies at the time. Herskovits argued that considerable continuities with Africa could be seen in African American communities, and he outlined a methodology that aimed at "charting the intensity of Africanisms in the various areas of the New World," and in Brazil in particular.[53] The foreword, written by members of the Carnegie Foundation, hinted at the debate that would rage over the book, warning that "cultural differences are so important in the social adjustment of different peoples to each other that the retention even of cultural fragments from Africa may introduce serious problems into Negro-white relations. On the positive side, the origin of the distinctive cultural contributions of the Negro to American life must not be overlooked."[54] Herskovits argued that his book attended to the latter concern and felt that he was working to valorize a culture which had long been denigrated. His conclusions, he argued, pointed to the fact that "African culture, instead of being weak under contact, is strong but resilient."[55]

As W. E. B. Du Bois correctly predicted in his review the next year, the work was "epoch making in the sense that no one hereafter writing on the cultural accomplishments of the American Negro can afford to be ignorant of its content and conclusions."[56] Though he approved the valorization of African culture, Du Bois anticipated that Herskovits's claims of African cultural continuities would foster the most disagreement among readers. He expressed significant reservations about Herskovits's methodology: "Of course there is little here that is actually measurable. One sees a trait among American Negroes and discerns a somewhat similar trait among Africans. How far this is actual cultural inheritance and how far accident, is difficult to say. Herskovits probably errs on the side of credence; but if the careful study and comparison which he lays out are followed, future study will do much to make clear the fact."[57]

For other African American scholars, not only was the methodology faulty, but Herskovits's approach threatened to undermine, rather than improve, the position of blacks in the United States. E. Franklin Frazier worried that the emphasis on African culture threatened to alienate African Americans further in U.S. society, and that differences between blacks and whites would soon be seen as unalterable and rooted in culture rather than in discrimination or in economic and social opportunities. The dispute between Frazier and Herskovits was well established by the 1930s and the two scholars had a long history of trading barbs over each other's work.[58] In 1928 Frazier's biting review of Herskovits's book *The American Negro: A Study in Racial Crossing* concluded that it "throws no light on the sociological aspects of the Negro population. . . . [These data] have no significance."[59] As both men undertook research on Bahia these tensions would become only more marked, leading to very public disagreement on the nature of African influence in Bahia.

Bahian intellectuals may not have been familiar with all of Herskovits's work on the United States, but many certainly would have been aware of his focus on Africa. This reputation preceded him by 1943, when his work was published by Bahia's Museu do Estado. As José Valladares noted in his introduction, for those in Brazil interested "in the questions relative to the role played by the African in the New World, it is not necessary to say who Professor Melville Herskovits is." Valladares emphasized that none other than Arthur Ramos had referred to Herskovits as the "greatest North American scholar of the problems of the Negro" and the "great Africanist of Northwestern University" at Bahia's Afro-Brazilian Congress and in the second edition of *O negro brasileiro*.[60] Herskovits had submitted papers to both Afro-Brazilian congresses and thus was probably well known among scholars of African culture in Brazil. For Recife's congress of 1934 Herskovits submitted a short survey of art in Dahomey (today the Republic of Benin), as well as a study of the African origins of blacks in the New World.[61] For the Salvador congress, Herskovits sent a paper examining African and Catholic influence in the religious beliefs of blacks in the Americas.[62]

Herskovits's stay in Bahia in 1941 came at an important juncture in his attitude toward African culture. On the one hand, he was beginning to advocate a move away from a strict African "survival" approach, and a reorientation of the study of African American culture around the concept of acculturation. On the other hand, Herskovits had not fully embraced this change himself. His research in Bahia represented a transitional period in his thought. Herskovits proposed acculturation theory as an ideal, but his own research still searched for untouched African practices.[63]

A closer look at Herskovits's work published by the journal of Bahia's Museu do Estado demonstrates this methodological contradiction, one all the more ironic as Herskovits was himself attempting to give a lesson in the principles of the "new" ethnology.[64] The publication itself was not a formal paper but rather a lecture delivered to inaugurate Bahia's new Faculdade de Filosofia in May 1942, an invitation that gives some sense of the prestige Herskovits enjoyed in Bahia.[65] The tone, then, was informal but often pedantic. Herskovits began with an overview of recent evolutions in the field of ethnology, emphasizing that ethnologists had abandoned their focus on "primitive" cultures and instead recognized that all cultures had similar types of structures. Cultural relativism had gained ground, as had a recognition cultures were not superior or inferior; as Herskovits emphasized, the science of ethnology now "attempt[ed] to understand cultures, and not to bring them under judgment."[66] Herskovits took care to stress that he was not in Bahia to study the "primitive" and did not believe that African cultures should be treated as such.

After asserting the equality of all societies, Herskovits moved to the central emphasis of his talk: describing the study of acculturation, or "cultural contacts." The idea of cultural contact was indirectly counterposed to an older approach, which Herskovits insisted was no longer useful: the study of African survivals. While Herskovits used and praised earlier work on Afro-Bahians by Brazilian scholars, he faulted it for seeking out the exotic with its focus on Candomblé: "Those who devote themselves to problems of African survivals in Bahia naturally have turned to the customs that differ most from their own practices." In addition, he classified the existing research as primarily descriptive and most useful as a foundation for later, more sophisticated and scientific studies. "*In terms of the problem of description*," he said, "Afro-Bahian culture has received a considerable attention—ever since the publication of the much-cited critique of Sílvio Romero—from all who worked to furnish the necessary information. The names of the pioneers Nina Rodrigues and Manuel Querino are too well known here to need more than a mere mention. Those who came later—Ramos. . . . Edison Carneiro and Donald Pierson, and others who contributed to the two Afro-Brazilian Congresses have completed a worthy task, moving this initial work forward."[67] Though his criticism was subtle, to be sure, Herskovits drew an unmistakable contrast between his own scientific study of "contacts and change" and earlier, more simplistic portraits of Afro-Bahian life, particularly those searching for the exotic in Candomblé.

Instead of mere description, the concept of acculturation promised a more dynamic vision of a society, one with universal application since "no matter where or in what circumstances, peoples with different traditions have met, exchanged ideas and behaviors."[68] Herskovits clearly imagined himself as the ambassador of this methodology, and he meticulously explained the research process for such a study. The first step consisted of gathering a description of a society or culture; then one attempted to understand its historical development and its contacts with other cultures; and finally, one sought to understand how individuals interacted with these norms.[69] This was the framework, claimed Herskovits, that he and his wife, Frances, had attempted to use in their research in Bahia.[70] For such a study, Bahia boasted "material of the first order."[71]

In the same paragraph, however, and as he moved into his own analysis, Herskovits reverted back to the paradigm of African survivals, saying that in Bahia "numerous African institutions and modes of conduct were conserved" and that African artistic woodworking and metal traditions "had been preserved."[72] It was this framework of preservation rather than of dynamism and contact that Herskovits used for his observations, which, though he excused them as preliminary, can be seen as surprisingly out of line with his own new methodology. For example, the first finding he highlighted concerned the Baianas who sold prepared food, sometimes with the help of associates. This, he pronounced, "is easily recognizable as a survival of the African economy." Without further elaboration he moved on to his second finding: "Certain attitudes of cooperation in the work of fishermen and others, and the tradition in which every group of workers must have a leader, reflects well-defined African traditions that were assimilated into the routines of the present day."[73] Finally, in a topic with which Frazier would take issue, Herskovits argued that the often informal unions of men and women in Afro-Bahian society were reminiscent of African practices of polygamy.[74]

All of these examples presented ample opportunity to discuss questions of acculturation, and how Portuguese contacts and Brazilian culture might have shaped these practices. Instead Herskovits engaged in a sweeping analysis that grouped any type of informal economic practice or communal effort into the category of African and classified those who strayed from monogamous unions not as adulterers but polygamists.[75] Herskovits here revealed his true interest and focus to be in cultural origins, rather than in a more dynamic process of cultural contacts. Despite his professed methodological interest in acculturation, Herskovits engaged in an analysis of Bahian society that examined Bahian culture in static terms and with almost exclusive interest in untainted authentic preserves of African culture. This focus on timelessness, rather than social change, fit well in Bahia's Museu do Estado.

This approach, and particularly Herskovits's conclusions on the nature of family life, differed considerably from those of Frazier, whose methods and conclusions would be minutely dissected and refuted by Herskovits in an article in 1943. In a rejoinder published in the same journal, however, Frazier held firm to his original findings, claiming that, "in the case of Candomblé it is easy to observe and record African survivals, whereas Professor Herskovits's statement concerning African family survivals are chiefly inferences based on speculation."[76]

Landes would face similar opposition from Herskovits, who was particularly ruthless in writing of her work. In a 1948 review of her *City of Women*, he scoffed that she was "ill prepared" for the research and that "she knew so little of the African background of the material she was to study that she had no perspective."[77] The review was not just critical but sometimes petty; Herskovits mocked, for instance, Landes's complaints about the heat. He adopted a particularly condescending tone when he used her as a counterexample of how "we" should prepare "our students" to go out into the field; though Landes was in the early stages of her career, she qualified to be treated as a peer rather than as a student. Herskovits went further, however, in writing his ally José Valladares and encouraging him to review *City of Women*. He then recommended his name to a U.S. journal looking for a Bahian expert to review the book.[78]

Valladares opened his review in the *Journal of American Folklore* by saying that Bahians, "proud of their city," could thank Landes for bringing further attention to their home. As he wrote: "Natural beauty, colonial art, colorful people and well preserved African traditions, side by side with modern life, deserve attention." Valladares noted that while much had changed since Landes's original research ten years earlier, some of her points were still valid. Candomblé retained its "bewildering ritual dances and ritual drumming." He critiqued Landes, however, for a more general romanticization, faulting her for exaggerating the number of churches in the city and for depicting singing bands in the street marching to work. He objected tartly to the idea that Bahia had a "Candomblé museum" and attacked her descriptions of bracelets bearing the images of African deities as items that he had never encountered in his eight years of museum experience. Perhaps Candomblé items might be found in the museum of the Nina Rodrigues Institute, he allowed, and perhaps Landes was thinking of similar bracelets that displayed the heads of the emperors of Brazil, but Valladares nonetheless denounced Landes for the number of similar errors in her work. While some might forgive such seemingly "unimportant historical mistakes," Valladares saw in them a larger pattern of avoidable "absurdities." He feared, he said, that tourists arriving in Bahia would have altogether the wrong impression. And as he wrote suggestively, though he could not comment on the anthropological element of her work, "when one sees so many mistakes, of the type noted above, one cannot help questioning the accuracy of much of her ethnographic information."[79]

His fiercest accusation was still to come: "Moreover, it is difficult to believe that she was taken very seriously by her informants." Valladares concluded that Landes offered "no clear picture of the life of the colored people of Bahia" and that her narrative instead paid more attention to the amorous dramas of the small community of U.S. expatriates and her own personal "shocks she received in witnessing customs different from her own." Dismissing all scholarly significance for her work, Valladares suggested with biting condescension that her effort instead be relegated to the genre of "popular non-fiction, travel book or autobiographical essay." As for her title *City of Women*, which referred to her principal findings of matriarchal patterns in Candomblé, he could find no reason for it. No matter, he wrote: "painters, sculptors and poets" always found some justification for the titles of their (fictionalized) works.[80]

Landes's Bahian defamation was complete, but in fact it had been in the works for some time. Ramos and Herskovits had together made earlier, even more destructive efforts to censor and punish Landes. Most shocking among these was the charge that Ramos began to disseminate in the field of Afro-Brazilian studies that Landes had paid her informants with sexual services. As Landes remembered later, an anthropologist in Africa had written to a friend about "the funny story of 'Landes running a brothel' in Brazil. I did not think it funny. And it traveled the literate world."[81] In finally exposing the role of Herskovits in the story in the 1980s, Landes also wondered what Robert Park would have said, as "his student Pierson joined the two sinners [Ramos and Herskovits]."[82] Prompted in 1986 by the anthropologist Mariza Côrrea to meditate on the reasons for such attacks, Landes mused that Pierson had begun his "slander" even before that of the "two sinners," while her research was still under way, an effort that Landes attributed to academic rivalry and insecurity.[83] Ramos, she believed, was threatened by her approach to fieldwork, as he "never went into the field to observe or talk but called informants into his office." And his student Luiz Costa Pinto had further told her that Ramos "was furious that I had written about the male homosexual priests." As for Herskovits, Landes believed he also was angry that Landes had stepped into the study of Candomblé, for he had wanted to be chosen as her adviser and also wanted to claim the topic for himself.[84]

That Frazier and Landes differed from Herskovits in their approach to Afro-Bahian culture was evident. In addition, they occupied social positions—an African American and a female Jew, respectively—that compromised their ability to maneuver in Brazilian academic circles. Partly as a result, both failed to establish an academic following in Brazil.[85] And the hostility of powerful "patrons" such as Ramos and Herskovits certainly damaged the reputations of both scholars in Brazil.[86] Livio Sansone has asked whether the relative lack of prestige of scholars such as Frazier and Landes in Brazil can be seen as one result of "a struggle for power in the field of Afro-Brazilian studies," and I argue that this was indeed at the heart of the problem.[87] Brazilians themselves, however, played a considerable role in determining these successes and failures, particularly in the case of Bahia; Bahian intellectuals had ample opportunity to engage with Landes and Frazier and almost certainly knew of their research and findings, yet they chose to discard them, choosing instead Herskovits as the foreign authority on Afro-Bahian culture.[88] And it is no coincidence that Herskovits was the scholar who most clearly agreed with his Bahian colleagues on the importance of the African past.

Ramos, for example, was surely familiar with Frazier's work but had little, if any, contact with him and seemed unconcerned to meet him when he found out about his impending arrival in Brazil. Pierson wrote to Ramos repeatedly about Frazier's arrival in Brazil, praising his methodology and sending excerpts of his work on the family in the United States. As Corrêa notes, Pierson was critical of Herskovits and must have been disappointed when he learned that Ramos would miss meeting Frazier in Brazil because Ramos had accepted an invitation from Herskovits to Northwestern University. It would be a shame, Pierson wrote, since Frazier's interest "is not limited, as in the case of other of our fellow countrymen, to the mere cataloguing of African cultural survivals and the search for their origin and diffusion."[89] Ramos and others were aware of the methodological divides in the field, yet they chose to valorize the work of Herskovits and enshrine work that stressed African continuities. Herskovits's influence in Bahia arose not only from his stature but from his agreement with Bahian trends. As one

Bahian account put it over a decade after his departure, "the teaching of anthropology began in Bahia with Prof. Melville J. Herskovits at the great hall [*aula magna*] of the solemn inauguration of the Faculdade de Filosofia" in 1942.[90] The anointing of Herskovits as the doyen of Bahian anthropology was a particular victory in the larger struggle over the importance of African lineages.

Conclusion

> As a matter of fact the attitude of the Brazilian people to the race problem so far as concerns the Negro seems, on the whole, to be academic rather than pragmatic and actual. There is a certain ethnological and archeological interest in the survival of the African fetish cults, the so-called Candomblés. . . . Since most of these Candomblés are living and functioning forms of African religious practices, although obviously in process of assimilation to the ritual and mythology of local Catholicism, perhaps they should not be classed as survivals. —DONALD PIERSON, *Negroes in Brazil*, 1942

In his book Pierson noted that Afro-Brazilian culture, particularly the institutions of Candomblé, had a long history of study in Salvador but that its racial relations had escaped similar scrutiny.[91] It was its "past" (as represented by "primitive" African and colonial-era traditions) not its "present" that interested anthropologists. Candomblé in Bahia had been viewed primarily as a static institution, one that preserved the integrity of African traditions. Pierson could apparently make this judgment without incurring the censorship of Arthur Ramos, who had reviewed the manuscript,[92] but Ruth Landes was not so fortunate. Though she engaged in the same rhetoric of preservation as many Bahians, her attention to the innovative actions of Bahia's less "traditional" Candomblés brought into relief the central, conflictual question for Bahia: Was Bahia an unaltered product of the past, or was it a site of still dynamic change? As I have argued in this chapter, scholars who viewed Bahia in static terms and stressed African continuities had a sympathetic audience. Those who stressed social dynamism and change were censored or defamed. In the end, Pierson succeeded only by walking a tightrope between these two views. Although he was more interested in the Bahian present than the African past, he highlighted the static nature of Bahian society; tradition and the past held the secret for Bahian stability and for its exceptional racial harmony. Such views echoed throughout the work of later U.S. scholars in Bahia, and they proved dominant in the UNESCO studies of the 1950s, as I will show in the next chapter.

CHAPTER 5

Embattled Modernization and the Retrenchment of Tradition

The forced resignation of Getúlio Vargas in 1945 brought the start of re-
democratization and a sense of national renewal and hope. Brazil would
start again to build its future, and the policies of the late 1940s and 1950s
were imbued with an optimistic push toward modernization.[1] President
Juscelino Kubitschek, elected in 1956, reflected the euphoria of the period,
promising the progress of "fifty years in five." Bahians in the postwar era
saw their world rapidly changing. The discovery of petroleum in Bahia (uncovered during the Estado Novo) brought hopes of a revival as the Northeast
recorded the highest levels of economic growth in the country from years
1955 to 1960.[2] Migrants from the countryside transformed Salvador from
a sleepy capital of 290,433 in 1940 to a bustling metropolis of 649,453 by
1960.[3] Bahia witnessed immense social and economic change during this
time, changes echoed on the national scene as modernization and progress
became a national mantra, and Brasília rose as a symbol deep in the country's interior.

Yet many Bahians were left with the sense that their culture was under attack, and that change was progressing so fast that it threatened to veer out of control. Modernization, they worried, threatened to corrode the very essence of Bahia, and they proposed instead that the past offered the key to Bahia's future.[4] Select members of the elite and governing class turned aggressively to a celebration of Bahia's traditions and an insistence on a return to a simpler, more harmonious era. The mayor of Salvador expressed such sentiments in dramatic terms in 1955, prefacing a prize-winning history of the city's origins: "Our Bahia, the Bahia of today, will not be able to face the future serenely if it does not prepare itself to examine its solid roots, which are the very roots of the Brazilian fatherland. . . . [Our best men] should return their sights to the times of past centuries, and search there for the teachings they contain and the confidence and assurance of force needed to feel themselves capable of conquering the crisis which affects us in the present, forging, in the crucible of history, the tools which will construct the future of the fatherland."[5]

This historical guidepost for the future was one of many written in the years around 1949, the four hundredth anniversary of Salvador's founding. As I noted in chapter 3, the quadricentennial may have played a role in altering the mission of Bahia's Museu do Estado. It not only brought all manner of official celebration across the city but also inspired the First Congress of Bahian History. The proceedings of the congress, published in five volumes, give some indication of the interest and enthusiasm with which local Bahian scholars embraced the study of their past, as did a further five volumes for the second congress three years later. During the period interest in Bahia's history and exaltation of the past rose to a fever pitch.[6]

Bahia's cultural renaissance was not completely immune to modern cultural movements. Indeed, José Valladares, so critical an advocate for tradition, was also instrumental in organizing the first major exhibition of modern art in Bahia in 1949.[7] Despite tentative new acceptance of modern art, however, the modern artists who did best in Bahia, such as Mario Cravo, or Carybé, used Bahia's African-based traditions as material. As Carybé explained his work for a modern art exhibition in 1957 in São Paulo, "We are here to show the *paulistas* [the residents of São Paulo] our art, which looks to tradition and the people."[8] And although Bahia's governor, Octávio Mangabeira (1947–51), advocated many modernizing projects, his family was a mainstay of Bahian politics, thereby minimizing his threat to the traditional elite. Furthermore, Mangabeira appointed José Wanderly Pinho, a member of one of Bahia's most prominent sugar families, as mayor of Salvador. Pinho, himself a historian who focused on the plantation era, played a significant role in fostering enthusiasm for Bahia's glorious past and in orchestrating the extensive celebrations of Salvador's anniversary.[9]

Thus, while the optimism of the era had most Brazilians fantasizing about futuristic projects, Bahians dreamed of regaining their lost national status by celebrating their past. Increasingly, this claim for status was made in cultural terms. Bahia would no longer hope to compete as the most powerful political or economic state, but promoters turned toward the idea that Bahia preserved what was authentic about Brazil and maintained traditions that had been lost elsewhere. This idea had gained momentum in state-sponsored culture during the Estado Novo, as we saw in studying José Valladares's museum journal. It had gained added legitimacy from diverse participants in Bahia's Afro-Brazilian Congress and from the narratives of foreign anthropologists as well. Tourist literature, a growing genre in the late 1940s and 1950s, ushered this conception into the realm of conventional wisdom.

Native intellectuals were central figures in this flurry of promotion: Jorge Amado was joined by José Valladares in inviting outsiders to experience Bahia's splendid preserve for themselves.[10] But similar ideas of authenticity and tradition echoed in the writings of foreign observers as well. As a Danish guide explained in 1948: "When Walt Disney wanted Brazilian motives and music for a film he went to Bahia for both; when a Brazilian composer wants words for his latest samba he asks his lyric writer to try once more to get the word 'Bahia' into the title and refrain. . . . [My Brazilian friend in Rio de Janeiro advised that] it was in Bahia and only there that I found the true, uncounterfeited, unspoilt Brazil. If I had not known Bahia I would have had no qualification to write about the rest of the country, for Bahia has been the cradle of it all, and there the true Brazilian spirit still exists."[11]

Indeed, Disney's animated and live action film *The Three Caballeros* had granted star status to Bahian culture in 1944. Zé Carioca, a jaunty and excitable parrot from Rio de Janeiro, opens the Brazilian segment by insisting that Donald Duck visit Bahia. Ironically, however, Zé Carioca finally admits—when pressed—that although he has sung Bahia's praises extensively, he himself has never been there. This irony had been hinted at by the tourist guide: Brazilians were convinced by this point that Bahia represented the "true Brazil," but they had often little direct knowledge of the region themselves. In fact the dig at Zé Carioca may have been a coy nod to Ary Barroso, the Brazilian composer who composed the film's headliner songs: "Bahia" and "Os quindins de Iaiá." Barroso, as I noted in chapter 2, penned some of samba's most effusive lyrical homage to Bahia but had only marginal knowledge of the state. Bahia's claim to authenticity and tradition became so accepted during this time that the region became an archetype, not only for Disney writers, but for Brazilians themselves.

Indeed, this was precisely what many Bahia boosters had been working toward. Though ideals of modernization and tradition coexisted uneasily in the early 1950s, tradition finally triumphed in official representations of Bahia. The final blow was struck from abroad by UNESCO researchers who assembled in the state at the start of the decade. These scholars came in search of Brazil's fabled racial democracy, convinced that Bahia best maintained this legacy. The researchers embraced the dichotomy between modernity and tradition but came down firmly on the side of the latter. This chapter begins by examining the local context in which these studies developed and situates them in the larger modernizing agenda of Bahia's secretary of education, Anísio Teixeira. It then moves to the framing of tradition in the studies and concludes by showing the findings' dramatic difference from those put forward by researchers outside Bahia. UNESCO's observers further reinforced the idea of Bahia's race relations as exceptional within Brazil and portrayed the state as a cultural treasure that should not be disturbed. Like the travel guide, UNESCO anthropologists emphasized that Bahia was the "true, uncounterfeited, unspoilt Brazil."

Community Studies in Premodern Bahia

The UNESCO studies in Brazil had their origins in a modernization plan first developed by Bahia's education minister, Anísio Teixeira, in 1948. The studies were much shaped by a Bahian political and social context largely neglected by scholars.[12] Understanding Teixeira's early ideas and their relation to this turbulent moment in Bahian society is critical. Some of the controversy and spirit of the era can be seen in the first outline of Teixeira's modernizing project published in a somewhat mismatched outlet: Bahia's museum journal.

The museum journal produced two issues in 1950 that seemed to contradict each other in their intent. Both proved popular and attracted some attention, selling out within the year. One, written by Antônio Vianna, was a collection of chronicles, musings on Vianna's childhood growing up in Bahia in the years leading up to World War I. As Valladares remarked pointedly in the introduction, the era was seemingly carefree, "one of the happy chapters of our history. . . . [when] the Bahian lived interested in the continuation of his traditions and customs."[13] The topic of the second issue, conceived by the modernizing Anísio Teixeira, took a decidedly different approach to the past. The issue, "Uma pesquisa sobre a vida social no estado da Bahia" (Research on social life in the state of Bahia), described a new collaboration between U.S. anthropologists and the Bahian state.[14]

Teixeira, as minister of education, had determined that the state needed to study Bahia's regional differences in order to fit schools to their varied environments. For this effort, he enlisted social scientists as key members of his modernizing reform. He had approached Gizella Valladares, the wife of José Valladares, about the potential for a series of community studies in Bahia in 1948, and she in turn wrote to Donald Pierson in São Paulo to gauge his interest.[15] Gizella herself may have had some role in conceiving of the project; she had a master's degree in anthropology from Columbia University, and her own research dealt with Bahian folklore, a project for which she received much advice from her husband's friend, Melville Herskovits.[16] She worked as an anthropologist at Bahia's Museu do Estado, and when Pierson was unable to come immediately to organize the studies, she contacted the U.S. anthropologist Charles Wagley, with whom she had studied at Columbia.[17] Wagley agreed to the idea, and the project began in 1949. Teixeira invited Wagley to bring his doctoral students to assist with a series of community studies in Bahia, promising partial funding and all the state support and cooperation he could offer. Bahia would gain information about the poorly understood regions beyond its capital, and the students would gain the field research they needed to complete their degrees.

It is worth turning some attention to Teixeira's larger program for education reform to understand the tensions occupying Bahia at this time and the ideas that shaped the community studies. Anísio Teixeira was not new to Bahian politics: a native Bahian, he had served as state minister of education in the 1920s under the modernizing governor Francisco Marques de Góes Calmon. After a self-imposed political exile during the Estado Novo, Teixeira returned to play a decisive role in determining the shape of Bahia's 1947 state constitution. In the same year, the newly elected governor Octávio Mangabeira invited him to oversee the state's education system once again. Teixeira became one of Brazil's most famous educators, remembered for his writings about education and democracy, and for his role in bringing the theories of John Dewey to Brazil.[18] He attracted national attention for a series of wide-ranging reforms that sought to remake and modernize Bahian society. Yet his ideas of modernization contained a racial undercurrent that has been little examined. These ideas of race are relevant to the context of the UNESCO studies and to the larger tensions that erupted between Bahians who sought to modernize their state and those who sought to maintain links to tradition and the past.

Modernizing the "Primitive"

Teixeira initiated the fifth overhaul of the state's education system since the end of the empire in 1889.[19] His 1949 report to the governor outlined the context which had shaped his reforms. Deploring the situation he encountered in Bahia at the start of his post, he suggested that the state was inherently disadvantaged by its historical and geographical situation. In his prologue, titled "General Considerations," Teixeira wrote: "We must not forget that civilization signifies a struggle against the environment and this struggle is even more vigorous when this environment is less adapted to the precepts and standards of civilization. If to this hostile environment, such as our tropical geography, we add the indigenous populations which we found here and the Africans we imported, and to all of this, we add the Portuguese tendency toward more passive, rather than creative adaptation, the mass of force necessary for the implementation of modern standards is evident."[20] The idea of how to bring "modern standards" into this racialized environment was the central struggle Teixeira saw for education in Bahia. Teixeira returned to this contrast between the modern and the primitive countless times in his report: education, for him, provided a modernizing force whose greatest impact was not literacy for the students per se but a broader improvement for society at large and a heightened level of "civilization." This idea of socialization pervaded Texeira's strategies for remaking Bahia's education system; he wanted to turn away from a humanistic vision of learning for the sake of learning and, "most of all, [to] substitute for the school of letters a school of work and social adjustment."[21]

Teixeira focused his energies on a spectacularly ambitious new model of schools, his *escola parque* (literally, a school-park, a term of his own invention). Tellingly, Teixeira's first modernizing school would target one of Salvador's densest neighborhoods of Afro-Brazilians, Liberdade. Teixeira inaugurated the first *escola parque* in 1950 with a speech that revealed his vision of the school and its black students:

> We want to give them [the students] their complete program of reading, arithmetic, and writing, as well as physical and social sciences,

industrial arts, design, music, dance, and physical education. In addition, we want the school to educate them, form habits, form attitudes, cultivate aspirations, truly prepare the child for his civilization, one that is difficult because it is technical and industrial, and even more complicated because it is constantly mutating. In addition, we want the school to give health and nourishment to the child, seeing that it is impossible to educate him in the circumstances of malnutrition and abandonment in which he lives. . . . Whether we like it or not, we are in the midst of transforming ourselves from a primitive society into a modern and technical society. The inhabitants of this neighborhood [Liberdade] will leave behind a prebiblical stage of agriculture and primitive life to immerse themselves in the twentieth century. Either we organize institutions capable of preparing their children for our time, or their intrusion into the actual order will take the form of geological intrusions that subvert and tear apart the existing order.[22]

Neutralizing the threat of social disruption—described in geological terms that recalled turn-of-the-century essayist Euclides da Cunha—was a central rationale for the school. Children would gain reading, writing, and math skills, but transmitting these was far from the only priority of the program, which also aimed to cultivate a wide array of social and practical skills. The objectives of the school, then, fell into three categories: learning, socialization, and physical health—that is, the education of the mind, soul, and body. The school's central purpose was social, however, and Teixeira made this point exceptionally clear when he considered the alternatives to the school: immense, reverberating waves of social disruption that threatened the bedrock of society itself. Teixeira based his bid for education on its modernizing, civilizing influence and promised social upheaval should his modern project be postponed any further.

Though Teixeira never referred to race in the opening of the school, its very location and its objectives suggested that this "urban" program was tailored not to the city as a whole, but to its urban problem—the Afro-Bahian poor. Teixeira emphasized the abandonment of the children, and even classified the neighborhood parents as primitive. The Liberdade neighborhood, despite its location in the supposedly "civilized" city, presented much the same problems as Teixeira would diagnose in Bahia's *sertão*: its population was abandoned, primitive, and even prebiblical in its level of advancement. The racial concerns in the program were clear. Afro-Brazilians here were seen as representing tradition, but a cultural tradition that threatened the future.

In 1928 Teixeira had written to a friend, expressing his frustration that Bahia "today seems to me like one of the most backward places that presently exists on the face of this earth."[23] What is remarkable is how little had changed for Teixeira by the 1950s as he continued his battle for progress and advocated a radical break from the past. As he asserted at the 1947 constitutional convention, Bahia in particular had a dangerous tendency to cling to the past and to tradition: "I hear, constantly, that we must persist in our obedience to our traditions, and I am, I should declare, profoundly sensitive to the legitimate and good Brazilian traditions. But among these traditions I distinguish some that seem to me profoundly pernicious and bad, although [nonetheless] alive and vibrant."[24]

Teixeira viewed traditions in a broad sense, and one of the traditions under attack in his programs was the Afro-Bahian cultural tradition, a culture he deemed inferior. Yet while one of Bahia's premiere social thinkers developed a critique of Bahia's traditions, others were developing an idea of Bahia that celebrated its tradition and relished its past, believing that Bahia's uniqueness rested in its ability to maintain an older way of life. The French anthropologist Roger Bastide, a scholar of Afro-Brazilian religion, was one of those who turned his research to Bahia as it developed its reputation as a preserve of Afro-Brazilian traditions. As he wrote in 1953: "I remember that Anísio Teixeira, with the lucid intelligence that characterizes him, one day reprimanded me [*censurou-me*], as well as Ramos, Herskovits, Pierson, and Edison Carneiro, for having fortified the survival of the Candomblés and thus impeded or slowed the work of assimilation of the black of the Northeast to Western culture. He was in part correct. The '*pais de santo*' use our work to take themselves back to Africa. I accept this responsibility with a clear mind, however."[25] That Teixeira viewed these researchers—all of whom conducted the core of their research on Afro-Brazilian culture in Bahia—as detrimental to his cause only reveals how embattled Bahia had become by the 1950s. The tension between anthropologists and modernizers became increasingly evident. Teixeira's discourse on the modern not only insulted and denigrated the population he hoped to educate but eventually alienated him from the Bahian intellectual climate of the times. In the end Teixeira's program of a modernizing education became untenable as anthropologists stressed that "premodern" populations needed to be studied and protected rather than changed.[26] Teixeira was surely unaware of this outcome when he invited anthropologists from the United States to study the dynamic between the primitive and modern populations of the state and to analyze how best to demolish traditions while forging a new modern identity.

Bahia's Community Studies: A Contrast of Progress and Tradition

As Teixeira's community studies project developed in 1950 it brought together not only U.S. anthropologists but also several Brazilian advisers. On the North American side Charles Wagley chose three of his graduate students in anthropology to participate in the research: Benjamin Zimmerman, Marvin Harris, and Harry Hutchinson. The project also drew on experts across the nascent field of Brazilian social science: Eduardo Galvão, ethnologist at the Museu Nacional in Rio de Janeiro, helped in its planning, and Luiz A. Costa Pinto, a professor of sociology, also from Rio, helped to gather preliminary data. Locally, Gizella Valladares took an active role in the project and Thales de Azevedo, anthropologist at Salvador's newly formed Universidade da Bahia, rounded out the Bahian team.

By the time of the publication of the Museu do Estado journal issue in 1950, research was already under way. The initiative promised that administrators and field scientists would work together to solve social problems: the objective was to examine the process of social change taking place in the Bahian countryside. As the 1950 report explained, new roads, schools, and the spread of radio and television were beginning to impact Bahia's interior, and "the rural folk societies" were "undergoing sporadic but rapid and profound changes."[27] The choice of Bahia's backlands was ideal, they wrote, because "until quite recently modern cultural influences issuing from Rio de Janeiro and from abroad" had a limited diffusion beyond Bahia's coast, and particularly outside of Salvador.[28] The project envisioned a series of community studies to address these "folk" societies in three different regions of the state, each with different histories and different physical environments. The plan specified that as a counterpoint to a "traditional" community chosen in each region for study, there would also be a comparison with a more "progressive" community in the same area. Although these progressive areas would not receive the same level of analysis, their inclusion nonetheless helped to address the central questions of the study: "to understand how the 'progressive' differs from the 'traditional,' what new factors have been instrumental in bringing about 'progressive' developments, what forms of social disequilibrium have resulted . . . [and] the line of change in the adaptation of man from the 'traditional' to the more 'modern' and more 'progressive' within this same environment."[29]

As Thales de Azevedo remembered, the idea of choosing both a traditional community and a progressive one had originated with Wagley, who had then recommended it to Teixeira. As Azevedo explained in a later interview, both Wagley and Teixeira were fundamentally interested in the nature of change: "Anthropology was very concerned with social change. Anísio was a progressive person, so he wanted to contribute so that this progress was made in a truly new direction of advancement. . . . He wanted to modernize institutions. . . . He was a man against the traditional routine."[30]

Wagley and Teixeira agreed not only on the importance of studying change but also on the fundamental rankings of peoples along a scale of modernity. The anthropological notions of traditional and modern used by Wagley and his company of researchers fit very well with the framework also envisioned by Anísio Teixeira for the community studies; both sides conceived of the traditional regions as untouched by time, still very much representing a "premodern" state of existence. In fact, the very genre of community studies—the theoretical framework used by Wagley—began with the premise of wide ideological divides between urban and rural, traditional and modern.[31] Although transition between these categories was viewed as disruptive, the report portrayed such movement as a "line of development," hinting at a linear view of progress. Yet despite this agreement on the starting point for these communities, Teixeira and the anthropologists would come to fundamentally opposed conclusions about the path for the future. Teixeira's education polices labeled such areas as inferior and in need of modernization; the anthropologists prized them as relics of an earlier era and advocated preservation of precious folkways. The state reformer who had expressed the need to break with tradition came up against the authority of social scientists who proposed that these traditions represented a more authentic and harmonious way of life. Both posited the potential for social unrest and disruption with modernization: Teixeira advocated that state intervention was needed for this very reason. The anthropologists advocated avoiding disruption by limiting contact with a corrupting outside world.

Almost before the project began it took a slightly different turn, however, due to the close relationship between Charles Wagley and Alfred Métraux, anthropologist and head of the new UNESCO commission on race. Wagley wrote to the UNESCO officer in June 1950, having read of a proposed UNESCO project on race tensions in his local New York newspaper. He suggested that Bahia would make an ideal location for such a project, and that it would be easy to initiate since his researchers were already in place.[32]

From Study of the Rural "Folk" to Studies of Race Relations: Anthropologists and the UNESCO Project in Bahia

The UNESCO studies and their role in shaping racial thought in Brazil have attracted much scholarly attention; they are credited with posing some of the first challenges to Brazil's ideology of racial democracy, as well as with sparking the development of the social sciences in Brazil.[33] Yet the very regional nature of these research projects has sometimes been glossed over by scholars who have seen them as national studies.[34] In fact, UNESCO at first focused its attention solely on Bahia; a comparison with Rio de Janeiro and São Paulo emerged only as the project developed. Furthermore, the findings themselves reflected significant regional variation. Ideas of racial democracy were not disrupted in Bahia, where they only gained strength and scholarly authority. Although scholars such as Florestan Fernandes and Roger Bastide amply documented racial discrimination in São Paulo, images of Bahia as a site of unique racial harmony nonetheless remained largely unchallenged and even further entrenched. The UNESCO studies in Bahia reinforced an idea of Bahian exceptionalism, and the idea that Bahia somehow preserved a more idyllic past, with fewer social tensions. This was an idea that had been steadily developed by diverse sectors across Bahia, as well as by foreign observers. Though the implications of this difference are often regarded as a footnote to the studies today, this current of thought had significant impact in Bahia at the time and can be seen from the very early moments of the effort.[35]

UNESCO director and anthropologist Alfred Métraux announced in 1950 that Brazil had been chosen as the site of a major research project for what was termed "the race problem." Stunned by the atrocities of the Holocaust and determined to "lead the campaign against race prejudice and to extirpate this most dangerous of doctrines," UNESCO had decided that documenting alternatives was an important path to change.[36] Métraux emphasized that Latin America could stand as an important model for the rest of the world: "What better argument can be opposed to race prejudice than a demonstration that harmonious race relations are possible?"[37] Even before the field research began to arrive, Métraux enthusiastically proclaimed that Bahia represented an ideal, an exceptional site even within Brazil. In fact it was the exceptional nature of Bahia that led him to propose a comparison: "The region of Bahia lends itself admirably to the study of the racial question in Brazil, for the percentage of Negroes is high. Nevertheless, the enquiry could well be pursued in other parts of Brazil, which, from our point of view, show appreciable differences."[38]

Here Métraux voiced his own opinions, as well as echoing advice from other scholars of Brazil. He may well have been influenced by Arthur Ramos, who was appointed head of the Department of Social Sciences for UNESCO in 1949. Or he may have been influenced by E. Franklin Frazier, invited by Ramos to be part of the drafting of a UNESCO statement on race.[39] Otto Klineberg, an U.S. scholar who held the position before Ramos arrived, also felt that the situation of São Paulo seemed significantly different; he urged in 1950 "strongly, once again, that the study be not restricted to the situation in and around Bahia."[40] A few months later Charles Wagley himself admitted that Bahia might be an exceptional case, writing in a letter to UNESCO, "I wonder if Salvador is not rather special and if studies in São Paulo or Rio de Janeiro would not show different aspects of the general Brazilian picture of race relations."[41] The idea that Bahia offered a unique preserve of racial harmony, even within Brazil, developed early in the UNESCO research project.

By 1952, Métraux was fully convinced that Bahia occupied an exceptional space in Brazilian race relations. Chiding an author charged with summarizing the state of race relations for another UNESCO publication, he wrote: "The pages you devote to Brazil are based mostly on Pierson's good, but dull book [*Negroes in Brazil*, published in 1942]. Our whole investigation would have been pointless if it were to repeat what Pierson had already said and which is true only for Bahia. Race relations in Brazil as a whole are not as harmonious as Pierson presents them. The Portuguese edition specifies in the title that the book deals exclusively with Bahia."[42] The idea of Bahian exceptionalism continued as the research unfolded, and indeed the findings of the Bahia research crew did not challenge these assertions. Their work overall revealed significant contradictions, however. As a group, the U.S. researchers in Bahia clung to Pierson's assertion that Bahia was predominantly a society divided by class; nonetheless, the ethnographic detail in their work documented repeated cases of discrimination and prejudices toward the Afro-Bahian.[43] Despite this reality buried in the works, the broader conclusions of the studies continued to reinforce the idea of Bahia as uniquely harmonious. UNESCO authors admitted that other regions such as São Paulo had prejudice, and even racial problems, but this blame was placed squarely on the forces of modernization and industrialization. In contrast, their portrayals of Bahia emphasized that by resisting (or having been passed over by) modernization, Bahia had also sidestepped the corruption that came with modern society.[44]

Such a vision of corruption stemming from modernity would have amused many Bahians, who were well accustomed to a long trajectory of voting fraud and personalistic bossism that owed more to traditional politics and rural isolation than to modern intrusions.[45] The most extreme example of this idealized portrait of the past can be seen in Harry Hutchinson's study of a Bahian sugar-mill town.[46] Despite his description of highly racialized and hierarchal relations in the town and on the surrounding sugar plantations, Hutchinson's analysis summarized social relations as free of tension, guided more by family and affection than by motives of profit. His picture of one plantation emphasized, above all, the benevolence of the owner: "the former master is now the patron. It is she who arbitrates any differences between workers, or between a worker and Seu Paulo [the overseer]. It is her task to protect the worker against injustices, to provide medical care, to aid at weddings and baptisms, in short to do all the things the worker is unable to do through ignorance, fear, or poverty."[47]

Yet a closer look exposes that this "preserve" had also retained blacks in positions very close to those held under slavery. His report revealed that an aristocratic white elite still controlled all of the plantations, intermarrying only with one another and occupying the top of the social ladder. Black fieldworkers, "considered servile and cheerful," occupied the bottom rungs of society.[48] As Hutchinson acknowledged, "classification by race is one of the most important aspects of local culture" and "derogatory racial criteria are used to deride competitors who would like to rise out of the lower class groups."[49] These classifications and prejudice combined so that "traditionally the *preto* [black] is linked with ignorance and superstition."[50]

It is slightly jarring after such descriptions, then, to read in Hutchinson's conclusions that "there is no race problem." This, in his view, was because "the essential hierarchy has changed little since colonial times; and the relationship between these aristocratic whites and their negro and mixed workmen is still a highly personal one lacking in social tensions, since each knows his proper position and each knows his rights, duties and obligations toward the other." As Hutchinson noted, the absence of social tensions came with an understanding that everyone knew his or her place. Hutchinson remarked mournfully that other communities in the area had lost the "personal element" and instead faced a class society based in part on "racial type." Contrasting the area with more "depersonalized" settings where labor conflicts had erupted, Hutchinson gave his highest praise to social stability rather than social change. As he wrote approvingly, the plantation zone remained "sufficiently isolated to preserve much of the tradition of the past, of easy-going personal relations between people of all classes and racial types."[51] Having returned to the village five years later and found it changed, he mourned the passing of a traditional way of life and lamented the intrusion of a cold and foreign capitalism. "What was formerly a peaceful, 'all in the family,' almost preservelike area," he wrote wistfully, "has become an area of tensions and of poor business, and social, relations."[52] In this portrayal, the erosion of the paternalistic plantation system was a tragedy for all involved.

This difficulty in reconciling distressing descriptions with optimistic conclusions can be further seen in the contribution of Marvin Harris, perhaps the most critical of the Bahian observers. Harris, who examined an old mining town in Bahia's interior, documented extensive stereotypes of Afro-Bahians as well as a consensus by the six village teachers that white superiority was a scientific fact. Harris nevertheless never saw race as the principal factor in shaping social relations and hierarchies and ascribed discrimination to class differences.[53] These discrepancies surely presented a challenge to Charles Wagley, who was charged with summarizing the racial situation uncovered by his students. Wagley expressed some significant reservations but highlighted that Pierson's findings for Salvador had largely been replicated for the surrounding areas.[54] This was in fact a concise way to put it, for these studies displayed the same uneasy balance of descriptions of prejudice and curiously optimistic assessments of race relations that Pierson had pioneered.

Thales de Azevedo, the only Bahian contributor to the UNESCO project, also struggled to reconcile seemingly irrefutable evidence of racism with his assertions that "active racial prejudices do not really exist in Brazil," and that Bahia was "undoubtedly the most typical" site of Brazil's harmonious race relations. Azevedo argued that a high degree of social mobility existed in Salvador for nonwhites, although he admitted that "the great majority of darker skinned colored people and mulattos are concentrated in the lower levels of society, and in the lowest, humblest occupations." Although the ethnographic detail embedded in his account pointed to high levels of discrimination and racial disparities, his conclusions for the UNESCO *Courier* stressed that "the people of Bahia finally are very proud of their traditions of tolerance and of the absence among them of any 'racialism.'"[55]

Azevedo built into his analysis an idea of Bahian exceptionalism that delineated between "authentic" Bahian practices and "foreign" practices that originated outside the region. In this way, Azevedo explained away the presence of racist practices in Bahia without challenging his idealization of Bahia; racism might exist, but it was usually attributed to another source: "In accord with *local* custom, shown by Pierson, Bahians group and distance themselves much more as a function of their status than of their color or race. *Mestiçagem* is not prohibited by law, nor is it socially disapproved of, except to the extent that it is affected by the class structure firmly in place in Brazil [*o país*], one in which the upper strata are made up almost exclusively of whites."[56] Bahia's benevolent local traditions suffered from their exposure to Brazil's larger stratified environment, but they nonetheless remained a preserve of more harmonious relations.

In later work, Azevedo would emend his conclusions to allow for the existence of racial prejudice, but he again would build an idea of Bahian exceptionalism into his conclusions. In a 1955 study he surveyed Bahians on the nature of racial stereotypes in Salvador. Shockingly, given all of Azevedo's denials of prejudice in Bahia, not one positive characteristic was selected for blacks. The top six adjectives chosen were (in order of frequency): "superstitious," "not very intelligent" (*pouco inteligente*), "submissive," "sad," "untrustworthy," and "lazy."[57] Azevedo performed some contortions to rescue the idea of a more moderate Bahia. He allowed that stereotypes of blacks existed as part of a universal legacy of slavery, but he asserted that their relative importance in society might vary. In his view, for Bahia, negative portrayals of blacks should be seen as a largely verbal phenomenon with little repercussions in Bahian life. Stereotypes, historically inevitable, therefore existed, but the Bahian environment had mediated their effect: they were a universal racist aberration in an otherwise tolerant local society.

Thales de Azevedo had stressed that Bahian tradition was key to its racial harmony even before the UNESCO studies. His 1949 history of Salvador worried that a loss of tradition and the onset of industrialization could integrate Afro-Bahians more rapidly into society but could also exacerbate racial tensions.[58] As Marcos Chor Maio argues, this warning expressed the belief that "capitalist modernization and the structure of a class society would create competition between whites and nonwhites, translating into an increased visibility for color prejudice and threatening the traditional Bahian ethos. It was not without meaning that Thales would later resume his preoccupation with preserving Bahian identity, an identity that, in Roger Bastide's words, faced a changing world."[59] Let us turn now to Bastide, who studied São Paulo as part of the UNESCO project and who came to very different conclusions on the role to be played by tradition in ameliorating racial divisions.

São Paulo: The Promise and Danger of Modernization

In contrast to the findings in Bahia, researchers in São Paulo viewed tradition as a negative force to be overcome. The French sociologist Roger Bastide, for example, viewed tradition in terms that almost directly contradicted those of Harry Hutchinson. He wrote disapprovingly for the *UNESCO Courier* in 1952, "In the old traditional families, which are accustomed to submissive affection from the Negroes under their protection, there is a reaction . . . a desire to maintain the old patriarchal control and to compel the Negro to 'keep his place.'" As he concluded, São Paulo was a "transition society" in a difficult process of upheaval, but nevertheless industrialization was working to eliminate these older patriarchal ways and "helping to improve the position of the colored people as a whole."[60] Florestan Fernandes, a Brazilian sociologist who conducted research in São Paulo as well, went even further in his glorification of industry, insisting that capitalism and industrialism would eventually eliminate all racial strife and difference, as Brazil moved to a society marked only by class.[61] Notably, although these researchers acknowledged the existence of racism to a much greater degree and thus tore apart the notion of Brazil's "racial democracy," they held a hopeful view that São Paulo's racial problems would be solved through further development of industry.[62]

While the São Paulo researchers documented significant levels of racial discrimination in the South, they frequently contrasted it to the exceptional nature of race relations in Bahia. Bastide, for instance, recalled Pierson's earlier conclusions in Bahia. Bastide claimed that "if Pierson's phrase still applies to many regions of Brazil, it is no longer applicable to São Paulo, where the facility in access to education, the opportunities of industrialization, [and] the weakening of white control due to the dispersion of traditional families in an immense city permitted the ascension of blacks no longer as isolated individuals, but as a social group."[63] Blacks in São Paulo had increased opportunity to gain status in a modernizing economy, and the "dispersion of traditional families" meant a lessening of white control. Yet this larger process of industrialization and loss of tradition had also resulted in racial strife. The conclusion to be drawn was clear: Bahia would face similar racial strife to the extent that it became industrialized and lost its emphasis on tradition.

Was tradition—and a lack of social change—responsible for Bahia's racial harmony? Charles Wagley, charged with summarizing the findings of his three doctoral researchers in Bahia, felt it necessary to conclude: "Both

Brazilians and foreign observers have the impression that Western attitudes and concepts of racism are entering Brazil along with industrial and technological improvements. But there is no inherent relationship between Western industrialism and technology and Western racism, no necessary connection between the widespread improvement of social conditions and the development, through competition, of tensions and discrimination between racial and minority groups."[64] Wagley's conclusion was lost, however, in a larger and repeated focus on idyllic traditions portrayed throughout Bahia's UNESCO studies.[65] The intellectual climate of Bahia fostered a privileged view of the past in the 1950s, and the UNESCO researchers there found themselves immersed in a culture where many viewed modernization and industrialization with trepidation, a view that surely influenced their findings, and which corresponded nicely with their own focus on preserving authentic folk traditions from the threat of modern life.

An assessment of Bahia's growing petroleum industry some years later by Thales de Azevedo encapsulates much of this ambivalence about modernization and change. In a 1959 roundtable, he cautiously acknowledged to his Bahian audience that economic development and the introduction of industry had the potential to create many benefits. This was tempered, however, by repeated documentation of the "crisis" in Bahia introduced by "the shock between securely established traditional economies and societies and oil-related development." From rising levels of prostitution to "psychological and social tensions," Azevedo believed that the situation needed significant monitoring and intervention to prevent further upheaval.[66] Azevedo was surely right about the rapid and sometimes negative change introduced by the rise of petroleum. The language that marked his vision, however, as well as that of many others talking about Bahia, was a Manichaean view of modern chaos and uncertainty opposed to stable traditions. This language had a long history, but it had gained further power with the UNESCO project at the start of the decade.

Conclusion

Bahians in the 1950s and 1960s had reason to feel a new pride. Their state still could not compete with the economic growth and industrial development of the South, but such status, previously deemed "backward" by those anxious for modernization, now became the core of a new view that praised the region as a sanctuary from modernity. The UNESCO researchers helped promote the idea that Bahia preserved an exceptional racial harmony precisely because of its traditions and its distance from the troubles of the modern world. These ideas had been building in Bahia for some time, and they were familiar to Bahian intellectuals from other contexts, such as the Bahian museum journal. This framework did offer a privileged place to Bahia's black community, who became further valued as the repository of traditional folkways. It was complicated, however, by a tendency to see these same populations as representative of a primitive—and outdated—way of life. And it was further marked by a tendency to dismiss contemporary discrimination as insignificant to the dynamics of Bahian society. This esteem for Bahia's "folk" in many ways saw preservation as more essential than social reforms. Unfortunately, those who prioritized reform, such as Anísio Teixeira, though they wished to expand social services, viewed these same "traditional" qualities as problems to be demolished through modernization. The folk culture of Bahia's underclass was a menace to progress. Bahia failed, at a critical point in its history, to find a compromise where black and folk culture might be valued, even while the state extended the benefits of social services such as literacy and the vote. The UNESCO researchers did much to influence both social policy and the wider intellectual sphere in Bahia at this juncture: their work helped to consolidate a consensus that Bahian traditions should be protected, and that social change might be disruptive and dangerous.

The folklorization of Afro-Brazilian religious cults still forms part of the strategies of the apparatus of domination. Those who insist on this practice in order to favor the cash register of tourism insist on presenting us as followers of a canned, outdated religion.... Blacks have been marginalized from the political and productive process.
—Bahian Candomblé initiate
MARIA JOSÉ DO ESPÍRITO
SANTO FRANÇA,
"Candomblé and Community," 1993

Conclusion

In 1950 the newly constructed Hotel of Bahia unveiled a fresh mural for its "typical restaurant." As José Valladares described it for the newspaper *A Tarde*, the mural presented scenes from "historic and picturesque Bahia," with the Candomblé deity Iemanjá joining Baianas in the ritual washing of the church of Bomfim. Yet in his phrasing Valladares revealed one of the central tensions in Salvador and Bahia as a whole: the traditions described as "historic" were still alive, occupying a space in the present dynamic of the city.[1] Two years earlier he had similarly conflated past and present in promoting Salvador to a foreign audience in the *Pan American Union Bulletin*. There he elaborated the offerings of the Museu do Estado in the larger context of the city itself. He wrote: "The visitor to Bahia, after seeing the old section of the city, a veritable architectural museum—churches, convents, mansions, winding and narrow streets along which walk the famous Bahianas in their picturesque dress—will find in the State Museum a fair representation of the wealth of the city's past."[2] The city was an architectural museum, but Valladares casually placed living people there as part of the city's past.

Meanwhile, Bahia's inhabitants suffered the continual neglect of state authorities in terms of welfare, social mobility, and basic democratic access to education and to the vote.[3] Today, Afro-Bahian culture, viewed as "canned" or static, still wins attention from Bahian officials, but the political and economic incorporation of blacks remains neglected. While the past has been privileged, contemporary opportunity has not. Although Valladares was surely sympathetic to an image of a multicultural Bahia, his comments reveal the early tensions that developed as tourism officials began to promote Bahia as traditional, picturesque, and static. In concluding our tour of Bahia as living museum, let us turn to how its contradictions have played out since the 1950s.

Touring Tradition: Bahia's Living Museum

Bahia's first state-sponsored tourism initiatives emerged in the late 1930s, sponsored by the Estado Novo regime and Interventor Landulfo Alves.[4] Guided by the goal of preserving Bahia's traditions, the program set the tone for subsequent efforts. Though state-led plans stalled after Alves was dismissed in 1942, the municipality of Salvador took up the project in the early 1950s, with a municipal tax to support tourism efforts for the capital in 1951 and the creation of a council of tourism in 1953. In 1954, a publicity firm provided a program for the promotion of Salvador, which was put into practice the following year.[5]

The new priority given to tourism continued into the 1960s as part of an ambitious plan of economic development led by Governor Juracy Magalhães (1959–63). A new economic planning commission created a separate division for tourism and consolidated an early link between the promotion of Afro-Brazilian culture and the promotion of Bahia itself. The commission explicitly promoted Afro-Brazilian and popular culture as part of the state's attractions.[6] A state planning report in 1966 noted with approval that Salvador's municipal authorities had led the way by privileging "the primitive and ornamental arts of the *povo* [and the] . . . recuperation of popular and traditional festivities of the city."[7] This focus was embraced by heightened state-wide efforts as well.

"Recuperating" tradition became a mantra under the paternalistic rule of Antônio Carlos Magalhães, who served first as Salvador's mayor (1967–70) and later three terms as governor (1971–75, 1979–83, 1991–94). Magalhães established tourist promotion offices in Rio de Janeiro and São Paulo that advertised cultural attractions as the heart of Bahia's offerings.[8] An official retrospective of Bahia's tourist board, first created in 1968, wrote that Magalhães had supported "dying" festivals and worked to resuscitate them as part of Bahia's tourist offerings.[9] This rhetoric of revitalizing the past culminated in what would be one of Magalhães's biggest and most controversial efforts—the restoration of the historic downtown neighborhood of Pelourinho. Named for the post where chained slaves were once whipped, the area was characterized by crumbling colonial townhouses, abandoned by their owners, that had become crowded tenements for residents lacking better options.

Despite an inauspicious start, the project moved forward after Pelourinho was designated a UNESCO World Heritage site in 1985.[10] Led by Magalhães in the 1990s, the effort commanded a forty-million-dollar budget, but it allocated only minimal amounts for the relocation of residents. The revitalization effort crystallized officials' simultaneous valorization of an Afro-Bahian culture and disregard for the conditions and lives of Afro-Bahians as the city undertook a massive and often violent rezoning effort. Pelourinho residents who refused to sell at the given price were driven from their homes at gunpoint: black inhabitants were moved out so that black history could be turned into a commodity.[11] Valued as part of Bahia's past, living Afro-Bahians in Pelourinho proved an inconvenient obstacle to future development.

It is somewhat ironic, given this history, that Pelourinho today is the ultimate destination for "roots" tourism by African descendants from around the world, and especially from the United States.[12] This market began to be cultivated by Bahian state officials in the 1970s and has been revived as a priority since the 1990s. As the scholar Patricia Pinho documents, efforts to create an authentic tourist experience for such visitors led to a municipal law in 1998 that required Salvador's urban street vendors to wear traditional Baiana dress or pay a fine. Such regulations imposed a significant financial burden; to ensure compliance the city resorted to financing the dress for Afro-Bahians who could not afford to look "authentic."[13] The contrast between cultural valorization and economic deprivation for black Bahians could not be more stark. In perhaps the most bizarre instance of catering to tourists, a resort hotel on the Bahian coast offers their guests contact with Baianas within the safety of its gates. Manicured hotel grounds, modeled to evoke the street scenery of historic Salvador, provide a private setting for tourists to observe black employees dressed in Baiana costume. Tourists thus are able to experience a sanitized, Disneyesque version of black culture but without any uncomfortable exposure to black poverty and the realities of Salvador.

African Traditions and Bahia's Black Movement

Already in the early 1950s Edison Carneiro had predicted some of this dynamic. In a scathing article, he critiqued scholars' focus on the "African" on the grounds that it cast blacks as exotic foreigners in their own countries rather than as equal citizens.[14] Radical critics such as the sociologist Guerreiro Ramos and the activist Abdias de Nascimento joined him to charge that an approach that looked only at African-based culture failed to capture the political realities of exclusion and discrimination.[15] Carneiro identified the Afro-Brazilian congresses in particular as chief culprits in the process of alienating blacks in Brazil. He also blamed Brazilian intellectuals more broadly for never attempting "to see the *black* in his *present* reality, or how he assumed a Brazilian way of life [but rather saw only] the *African*, a strange and foreign element with unfamiliar ideas, appearance, and habits. . . . The search for Africa turned into something more pernicious and prejudicial over the long term."[16]

Carneiro's condemnation, however, glosses his own role as organizer of Salvador's Afro-Brazilian Congress, and ignores popular black efforts to counter discrimination by reclaiming Africa as central to an empowered black identity. In fact, the black community in Bahia often managed to reconcile privileging African heritage and fighting for contemporary change. This was certainly clear for those who participated in Bahian Candomblé and who protested against religious oppression just as passionately as they sought to privilege (sometimes invented) African traditions. And while Carneiro spoke at a nationalistic moment when African roots still seemed too exotic to fit into a broader national identity, this dynamic changed as African independence efforts in the 1960s and 1970s renewed black interest in African cultural movements and African roots.

Foreign policy under Brazil's military dictatorship further encouraged links to Africa. Brazil's military regime (1964–88) energetically pursued diplomatic relations and trade agreements with the continent, often using Brazil's claim of racial harmony to gain proximity to African leaders.[17] Bahia in particular welcomed closer contacts with Africa through a variety of new cultural initiatives.[18] In 1959 the Centro de Estudos Afro-Orientais was founded to support Bahian scholars studying Africa and to encourage broader interest in African culture.[19] A new Bahian museum, the Museu Afro-Brasileiro, opened with displays of primarily African origin in 1982.[20] Yet while the Afro-Bahian community surely benefited from high-level initiatives celebrating African heritage, they wielded little control in these arenas. Autonomy came instead in the realm of carnival, where Afro-Bahians expressed pride in Africa and blackness on their own terms. *Afoxé* groups drummed Candomblé rhythms in their annual parades, while the *blocos afro* took their inspiration from African themes. The formation of the *afoxé* Filhos de Gandhy (Sons of Ghandi) in 1949, and the *blocos afro* Ilê Aiyê (1974) and Olodum (1979) revealed that carnival would provide the setting for a new articulation of Bahian black identity.[21]

In this process Bahia's black community drew not only from freedom struggles in India, but also from reggae protests in Jamaica, and black power and soul movements in the United States. These diverse international influences combined with a larger sense of African pride that arose with decolonization and negritude movements in Africa itself. And nationally, Brazil witnessed its own black power movement, as well as the growth of a counterculture that formed the backdrop for Tropicália music in Bahia in the late 1960s.[22] This rich cultural scene, perhaps inevitably, produced very different local approaches and revealed a divide in black politics in Bahia. Ilê Aiyê insisted on an African ethnic focus and limited its membership to blacks, working especially to cultivate a new sense of black pride. Olodum took inspiration from Africa as well as from Jamaican reggae, and urged cooperation across all races for social change.[23] Though Olodum gained wider international recognition than Ilê Aiyê (playing with such luminaries as Paul Simon and Michael Jackson), both had a striking impact on the "re-Africanization" of Bahian culture.[24]

Beyond the realm of carnival, however, efforts to build an active black political movement gained little support in Bahia. A brief experiment with the Frente Negra in the 1930s attracted few supporters and quickly withered, never gaining the momentum that the organization gathered in the South. Another effort by Brazil's Movimento Negro Unificado (Unified Black Movement) in 1978 fared no better. Although Salvador joined other cities in supporting the founding of the organization, membership remained limited to a black intellectual elite.[25] More recently, leaders who gain a popular following at carnival have been unable to win followers with a black political platform. The president of Ilê Aiyê ran for city council in 1988 and received only 781 votes: the number represented just a quarter of those he was able to lead through the streets during carnival, or a quarter of the membership of

Ilê Aiyê itself.[26] And Bahia, the blackest state in Brazil, has still never elected a black governor, no matter what the platform. Even the city of Salvador, with Afro-Bahians making up roughly 80 percent of the city's population, has yet to elect a black mayor.[27] As a *New York Times* article quipped about Bahia in 1991, "If It's 'Black Brazil,' Why Is the Elite So White?"[28]

This dynamic of a vibrant black culture combined with a stagnant, paternalistic, and white political elite defines Bahia and remains to some extent inexplicable. Although the lack of enthusiasm for race-based politics is noticeable all across Brazil, it remains puzzling in Bahia, where a black majority could prove a major force in politics, where blacks espouse a strong sense of black pride, and where Africa is valued as a motherland. Further deepening the mystery is the fact that black political movements have fared comparatively worse in Bahia than in the rest of Brazil. As the *New York Times* journalist remarked, an observer faced a strange juxtaposition of a black cultural renaissance and an exclusive white political system "frozen in amber," a contrast that continues to puzzle observers today.[29] Similarly, African diplomats arriving in Bahia, Brazil's self-proclaimed racial paradise and the heartland of African culture, often expressed surprise at the marginal political and social gains enjoyed by the black community.[30] While Bahians exalted the glories of Africa, Africans deplored the position of Bahia's blacks.

The Afrocentric identity supported by Bahian cultural politics may have shifted with the advent of the new millennium. According to the sociologist Livio Sansone, the youth culture of the 1990s cultivated a modern black identity based on a globalized worldview, with less interest in African roots and cultural traditions such as Candomblé.[31] Such an identity must find itself increasingly at odds with the state initiatives for tourism in Bahia, aimed precisely at highlighting tradition. This push to link Bahia with African-based traditions for the purpose of tourism is especially jarring when contrasted with the modern industrial development that has sprung up in the state since the 1950s.

Oil is a major industry in Bahia; petrochemicals and derivatives today make up a large portion of the state's annual exports. The first national discovery of oil, found in Bahia in 1939, spurred the construction of the Landulfo Alves refinery in the state a decade later. While petroleum production in Brazil as a whole increased with the nationalization of the industry under Petrobras in 1953, the biggest industrial growth for Bahia came in the 1970s and 1980s. Salvador's suburb of Camaçari inaugurated an industrial complex in 1978 that now ranks as the largest in all of South America; growth continued to expand with the arrival of a new Ford automobile manufacturing plant in 2000. In recent years, the automobile and petrochemical industries have come to account for more than 50 percent of annual exports.[32] Ironically, Bahia billed itself as the land of tradition during the very period when it has become, perhaps more accurately, the land of refineries and manufacturing. The static medieval village that Donald Pierson described in the 1930s has been transformed into a "traditional" metropolitan city of roughly 3.5 million.

Despite the expansion of industry and its role in driving economic growth in recent decades, poverty rates have fallen more rapidly for Brazil than for Bahia, where blacks made up roughly 80 percent of those living below the poverty line in 2003. And because poverty in Bahia is so widespread, this figure includes well over 6 million Afro-Bahians. Furthermore, while educational rates in 2003 had improved to an average of six years of school for blacks and seven years for whites, even this meager amount of schooling is recent: averages for blacks and whites in 1980 in Bahia were 2.2 and 3.5 years, respectively.[33] Such educational improvements are important, to be sure, but wage improvements have been slow to follow. And these low averages further conceal striking inequalities between a tiny, wealthy, and educated elite and the overwhelming majority of the population.

Economic growth accompanied by persistent inequality defines Brazil as a whole. According to the World Bank, Brazil was the second-most unequal country in the world in 1989, exceeded only by Sierra Leone. Brazil had made some improvements by 2004, when it ranked tenth in the world, but statistics still attest to massive gaps between rich and poor.[34] Bahia clearly has proven no more successful than the nation as a whole in solving problems of poverty and inequality. The question remains whether Bahia has proven worse. The social problems in Bahia remain intimately tied up with the ideas of tradition and race I have illustrated in this book. The simultaneous development of a tourist industry that privileges tradition and the neglect of present-day welfare are representative of this dynamic. The two engines of economic growth in Bahia, its industrial complex and its culturally based tourism, have left Afro-Brazilians with the disturbing juxtaposition of modern factories and derelict schools, well-financed refineries but antiquated, incomplete sewers. It is surely too cynical to say that it benefits Bahia's officials to keep Afro-Bahians "traditional" by depriving them of material improvements and failing to address poverty.[35] But the puzzling coexistence of privileged Afro-Brazilian traditions with black economic and political marginality remains. This book began with this dilemma, let us return to it once more in order to assess the full force of tradition in Bahia.

Tradition and Its Discontents

Tradition can be defined, or even invented, in an endless number of ways, and even as many Bahians looked to the past, they looked to different pasts and different romanticized visions of how it might be paid tribute.[36] It is worth keeping in mind that the descendants of Bahia's sugar aristocracy generally privileged the colonial past when Bahia dominated Brazilian politics, and when their ancestors dominated Bahia's economy and its slaves. As the Bahian anthropologist Thales de Azevedo remarked in 1996, "When the sugar industry collapsed, Bahia didn't know how to redirect itself to a new productive activity, and it persisted in its nostalgia [*saudade*] for the sugar mill [*engeñho*], for the farm [*fazenda*], for the sugar plantations. Someone needed to study this question of Bahian mentality."[37]

This "Bahian mentality" was a nostalgia specific to the elite. Many Afro-Bahians instead turned their own nostalgic gaze to Africa, or to a time ostensibly before slavery. In this way, different visions of different pasts enabled everyone in Bahia to speak of the need to preserve tradition. In fact, we cannot know to what extent Afro-Bahian interest in Africa was stimulated by the broader nostalgia that marked Bahian society. Certainly, no matter what their origin, ideas of pure African traditions fit well in Bahian rhetoric once ideas of black inferiority began to lose their currency.[38] Strategically, black Bahians had found a language to talk about their own history while still maintaining a place in the priorities of the state as a whole. Yet this position, too, has been limited in the extent of material and political change it has been able to mobilize. Preserving tradition has proved an ill-suited rhetoric for motivating deep social reforms. Carneiro's critique of prioritizing an often exoticized African past rather than a black present remains relevant when we remember that official interest in celebrating Bahia's African heritage has not resulted in reform that benefits blacks in Bahia.

If I have portrayed tradition and modernity in oppositional terms it is because this contrast has been used repeatedly as a framework to talk about Bahian identity and its path for the future. The problem has been to imagine a modernity that does not devalue Bahia's past and does not see assimilation to a European or white-dominated future as its goal. Modernity has often been pursued in Bahia with the explicit aim of wiping out Afro-Brazilian culture. Yet the amenities of modern social welfare, such as improved health conditions or literacy, are in no way necessarily opposed to a respect for Bahia's broader historical heritage, and its rich Afro-Bahian culture. These contrasts of tradition and modernity have often been counterposed, but there is no reason why they cannot be gracefully brought together.

As this book has shown, Bahians have struggled to define their state on their own terms. Bahia entered the twentieth century as a politically marginal state with an economy that had never truly recovered from the collapse of colonial sugar. A cultural backwater with a large and poor Afro-Brazilian population dominating its capital, Bahia strived to become relevant nationally, but its efforts repeatedly failed for most of the twentieth century. Bahians and foreigners ultimately turned to a vision of Bahia as a valued cultural preserve rather than a state that needs to address social and racial inequities. The former vision has triumphed today. Bahia has succeeded in creating an identity central to the Brazilian nation and has established itself as a premiere destination for national and international visitors in search of the "authentic" Brazil.[39] But government officials have been remarkably adept at using their support of Afro-Bahian cultural traditions (and perhaps manipulation of underlying fears of change) to sidestep demands for improvements in the quality of life for the state's black majority.

Ultimately the association of Bahia with tradition and African roots has been accepted as a natural result for the state, rather than as a result of the conscious and creative efforts of a wide cast of reformers. Unfortunately, the view of Bahia as traditional at its very essence denies an active role for Bahians and foreigners in constructing this identity and portrays the state as immune to change. Yet Bahians and outside intellectuals have engineered a dramatic transformation of Bahia's image. The conception of the state has shifted from "backward" to "authentic," and Bahia has earned national and international accolades for its preservation of tradition. Indeed, the language of tradition has been critical to the shaping of Bahian society, Bahian concepts of race, and the welfare of Bahians themselves. Paying attention to the "reinvention" of Bahia during the twentieth century, however, allows us to also consider the constructed nature of the state's striking racial inequalities. The image of Bahia and its social realities, far from being natural or inevitable outcomes, remain subject to reform and change.

NOTES

Abbreviations

AMN   Arquivo do Museu Nacional, Rio de Janeiro, Brazil
DPP   Donald Pierson Papers, Arquivo Edgard Leuenroth, Universidade Estadual
        de Campinas, Campinas, Brazil
IPHAN   Instituto do Patrimônio Histórico e Artístico Nacional, Arquivo e Biblioteca
        Noronha Santos, Rio de Janeiro, Brazil
MJHP   Melville J. Herskovits Papers, Northwestern University Archives, Evanston,
        Ill.
RSLP   Ruth Schlossberg Landes Papers, National Anthropological Archives,
        Smithsonian Institution, Washington, D.C.

Introduction

1. The question of racial and national identity in Brazil has sparked an exceptional amount of scholarship. For entry into the topic, see esp. Fry, "Politics, Nationality"; Fry, "Feijoada e *soul food*"; and Skidmore, *Black into White*. The problem, of course, is that such inclusive visions of national culture have not been realized in terms of political participation, access to social services, or standard of living. This is especially problematic in Bahia, as I show below.

2. This literature is rich and growing. See Alberto, "Terms of Inclusion"; Butler, *Freedoms Given*; Capone, *Busca da Africa*; Rachel Harding, *Refuge in Thunder*; Matory, *Black Atlantic Religion*; Parés, "Birth of the Yoruba Hegemony"; Parés, "'Nagôization' Process"; and Reis, "Candomblé."

3. It is often difficult to compare literacy rates over time in Brazil because the census frequently changed the age group under question. To account for this I developed my own estimates for literacy that allow consistent comparisons for those age five and above across the whole of the twentieth century. These numbers therefore come from Romo, "Race and Reform," 279. The racial gap in literacy is treated further below.

4. Recent studies have turned, for example, to oral histories to trace questions of identity in contemporary black Bahia. See Patricia Pinho, *Reinvenções*; and Sansone, *Blackness*. Part of the problem for historians of the modern era also stems from the nature of archival sources in Bahia. State and private institutions have prioritized archival records treating the colonial period, slavery, and especially Bahia's independence movement; much of the twentieth century documentation remains unorganized or fragmentary, a result partly of historians' interests and partly of insufficient state funding. For pioneering historical work in the study of Bahia's black community in the twentieth century, see Butler, *Freedoms Given*; and Bacelar, *Hierarquia*.

5. For important studies of this cultural perspective, see Albuquerque, *Algazarra*; Ferreira Filho, *Quem pariu*; Ickes, "'Adorned'"; and Ickes, "Salvador's Transformist Hegemony." The connection between popular Afro-Bahian culture and state tourism efforts in the 1970s and 1980s is developed in Santos, "Mixed Race Nation." The politics of Bahia in the postwar period deserve further attention. This book cannot claim to be an in-depth study of formal Bahian politics, although the matters discussed are undeniably political.

6. Schwartz, *Sugar Plantations*; Barickman, *Bahian Counterpoint*; Mahoney, "World Cacao Made"; Mattoso, *Bahia*; Tavares, *História*.

7. Klein, *Atlantic Slave Trade*; Merrick and Graham, *Population*, 66; Reis, *Slave Rebellion*.

8. Slaves were both *pardo* and *preto*. The nonwhite populations of Amazonas were of primarily indigenous heritage. Piauí had a smaller white minority than even Bahia at this point (22.5%), but this changed over time. Brazil, Directoria Geral de Estatística, *Recenseamento, 1872*. I use here the most common translation for the terms *preto* and *pardo*, but the terms themselves, as well as their relation to Brazil's reality, remain controversial. I have used the term *Afro-Brazilian* or *black* to refer to the combined categories of both *pardo* and *preto*, and *Afro-Bahian* to refer to these same populations (both *pretos* and *pardos*) specifically in Bahia. This follows the most recent trends in the Brazilian census (which has not always recorded race or color consistently) as well as the black movement. Viewed in these terms, Bahia's racial composition has remained fairly stable; it still today maintains a small white minority and a large black majority. Data from 2007 shows Bahia to be 21% white, 16% black, and 63% brown (Salvador has an even smaller white minority, with a population classified as 17% white, 29% black, and 54% brown). What has changed, obviously, over the twentieth century, is the increasing proportion of the nonwhite population that classifies itself as brown rather

than black (in addition, the term *caboclo* is no longer used by census authorities). Nonetheless, the category of black has grown in recent years (from 1996 to 2007 the black population increased from 11% to 16% in the state of Bahia generally and from 17% to 29% in Salvador). The reasons for these demographic shifts are far from straightforward, however. It is very possible that the changes are due as much to changing racial ideologies (whitening in the early part of the century and black pride in the latter part) than to any ostensibly objective difference (such as migration from other regions or intermarriage between "blacks" and "whites"). For these numbers, see IBGE, *Síntese*; and IBGE, *Indicadores*. As such discussion makes clear, I refer to race throughout this book not as a natural or biological category but as a social construct that shapes reality differently across time and space.

9. Gradualist laws for slavery's abolition were passed in 1871 and 1885, but full emancipation arrived only in 1888, making Brazil's abolition the last in the Western world. For the process in Bahia, see Graden, *From Slavery to Freedom*; and Brito, "Abolição na Bahia."

10. Racially deterministic ideas meant that whiteness was most often associated with progress and that racial mixture was assumed to create degeneracy and instability. Brazilian elites broke from total adherence to European and U.S. racial science to propose theories of whitening, or *branqueamento*, that posited a whiter and stronger—not more degenerate—population through racial mixture. See esp. Skidmore, *Black into White*; Borges, "Recognition of Afro-Brazilian Symbols"; Schwarcz, *Spectacle of the Races*; and Maio and Santos, *Raça, ciência e sociedade*.

11. Andrews, *Blacks and Whites*. State elites in early twentieth-century São Paulo deployed notions of progress and whiteness to reinforce a particularly Paulista version of modernity, as shown in Weinstein, "Racializing Regional Difference."

12. Pang, *Bahia*; Consuelo Sampaio, *Partidos políticos*.

13. Cited in Lara, *Nova Cruzada*, 21. Demosthenes was one of the greatest orators of the ancient world.

14. A sampling of classical names includes Virgílio Damásio, Bahia's first republican governor; Archimedes Pereira Guimarães, the head of Bahia's Department of Education in the 1920s; and Homero Pires, a later follower of Nina Rodrigues and member of Bahia's Academy of Letters.

15. I borrow here from Dain Borges's translation of this term, which best captures the original meaning. For this and an excellent overview of the social history of Bahia in the early twentieth century, see esp. Borges, *Family in Bahia*, 1–45.

16. The idea of racial democracy gained currency in the 1930s and received its first major scholarly critique in the UNESCO studies of the 1950s. Statistical studies that revealed dramatic inequalities based on race demolished the idea's validity in the 1980s, but such evidence has not destroyed its power in popular culture. For excellent recent scholarly appraisals of the idea of racial democracy, see Antônio Sérgio Guimarães, "Misadventures of Nonracialism"; and Telles, *Race in Another America*. For a succinct overview of the idea's trajectory, see Costa, *Brazilian Empire*. As Costa remarks, the exposure of the idea as "myth" and statistical proof of racial inequalities fail to address why the idea has proven so durable among not only whites but also people of all racial

backgrounds. Recent scholarship has addressed this question by turning attention to popular understandings of race with the use of ethnographies. See Goldstein, *Laughter Out of Place*; Sheriff, *Dreaming Equality*; and Twine, *Racism in a Racial Democracy*.

17. Euclides da Cunha, *Rebellion in the Backlands*. See the modern historical account in Levine, *Vale of Tears*.

18. Fry, Carrara, and Martins-Costa, "Negros e brancos."

19. Butler, *Freedoms Given*; Bacelar, *Hierarquia*; Albuquerque, "Esperanças de Boaventuras"; Patricia Pinho, *Reinvenções*; Matory, "English Professors"; Dantas, *Vovó Nagô*. For the African influence on nineteenth-century Afro-Bahian culture, see esp. Rachel Harding, *Refuge in Thunder*; Reis, "Candomble"; and Reis, "Batuque."

20. Risério, *Carnaval Ijexá*. For the question of a distinctly Bahian identity, see esp. Osmundo Pinho, "Bahia no fundamental"; and Risério, "Bahia com 'H.'"

21. Patricia Pinho, "African-American Roots Tourism."

22. Literacy rates here are for the population age five and older. It should be noted that, although Bahia's overall literacy rate is significantly worse than that of Brazil as a whole (76%), the racial gap is marginally less pronounced. In 1991 the literacy rates for racial groups throughout Brazil were 84% for *brancos*, 67% for *pardos*, and 65% for *pretos*. See IGBE, *Censo demográfico 1991*, no. 1: 184; no. 17: 95–100. For analysis of Brazil's educational inequalities, see Silva and Hasenbalg, "Tendências." For comparative study of racial inequalities in the United States and Brazil, see Andrews, "Brazilian Racial Democracy."

23. Telles, *Race in Another America*, 6. For a similar framework, see Hasenbalg and Silva, "Notes," 167.

24. Peard, *Race, Place, and Medicine*.

25. This has been the focus of more recent work in Latin America, represented in the excellent collection, Appelbaum, Macpherson, and Rosenblatt, *Race and Nation*.

26. Reis, "Introdução," 9. Important work in this vein has been undertaken since this time, as this introduction has highlighted, but see esp. Albuquerque, *Algazarra*; Bacelar, *Hierarquia*; Butler, *Freedoms Given*; Kraay, *Afro-Brazilian Culture*; Patricia Pinho, *Reinvenções*; and Sansone, "Desigualdades."

Chapter 1

1. João José Reis shows how Bahian doctors in the 1830s also initially failed when taking on the church in their campaign to replace church burials with outdoor cemeteries. Then, as at the end of that century, medical professionals in Bahia and Rio portrayed themselves as critical agents of modernization and civilization and occupied significant positions of political influence. See Reis, *Death Is a Festival*. For the modernizing tensions of the era in Bahia, see esp. Mário Santos, *República*; and Albuquerque, *Algazarra*. For parallel anxieties concerning public hygiene in Argentina in the 1890s (and a similar study of the danger of saliva-coated religious icons in 1906), see Ruggiero, *Modernity in the Flesh*, 91.

2. Holloway, *Immigrants on the Land*. Select planters began this effort even earlier, in the 1840s. See, e.g., Dean, *Rio Claro*, chap. 4. The incomplete transition of black work-

ers into São Paulo's industrial sector after abolition is treated in Andrews, *Blacks and Whites*.

3. The development of Brazilian racial thought is surveyed in Stepan, *"Hour of Eugenics"*; Schwarcz, *Spectacle of the Races*; Skidmore, *Black into White*; and Maio and Santos, *Raça, ciência e sociedade*.

4. Before the advent of the republic, Doctor José Luis de Almeida Couto, a graduate of Bahia's medical school and a Tropicalista, held the position of provincial president, or governor. The exception to this pattern is José Gonçalves da Silva, Bahia's governor from November 1890 to November 1891, who graduated from São Paulo's school of law.

5. Historian Luiz Castro Santos provides an important exception to this trend; his work portrays an active public health movement in Bahia in the early twentieth century that unfortunately coincided with a particularly ineffective period of Bahian politics derailed by *coronelismo*, or local bossism. His expert political analysis does not, however, directly address Bahia's racial context or how the theories of Nina Rodrigues and a public health movement might have emerged and influenced one another at the same time. Castro Santos, "Power, Ideology, and Public Health"; Castro Santos, "Origens da reforma sanitária." Lilia Moritz Schwarcz also takes up the analysis of Bahian medical thought after 1890 but leaves aside the Tropicalista legacy and the public health reformers. Though Schwarcz tabulates the subjects of the articles published in the *Gazeta Médica da Bahia* from 1870 to 1930 and finds topics in public hygiene to be the most numerous (36% of 1,742 articles), she instead concludes that racial mixing was the dominant concern for Bahian doctors. Although undoubtedly racial mixing did come to be a worry, viewing the period as a cohesive whole underplays the dynamic contests in the field, particularly at the turn of the century, and her focus on racial mixing fails to give the public health movement due attention. Schwarcz, *Spectacle of the Races*, 253–71. Julyan Peard provides excellent treatment of the reformist efforts of Bahian medical circles in the nineteenth century. Peard ends her story in the 1890s, however, with what she terms the decline of the Tropicalistas, thus leaving the ascendance of the public health movement unexamined and the connections between the movement and Nina Rodrigues still largely untouched. Peard, *Race, Place, and Medicine*.

6. The Portuguese term *escola* (like the English *school*) is frequently used to indicate a current of thought. Antônio Coni established the groundwork for the contribution of the Tropicalistas, but Julyan Peard provides the most insightful analysis of them. Coni, *Escola tropicalista*; Peard, *Race, Place, and Medicine*.

7. Damásio, "Introducção," 1.

8. Cited in Coni, *Escola tropicalista*, 76.

9. At the end of the empire in 1889 Brazil had two law schools, two medical schools, one engineering school, and one school of mines. For the expansion of these schools and the final formation of Brazil's universities, see Fernando de Azevedo, *Brazilian Culture*.

10. Peard estimates that until 1889 the Tropicalistas probably consisted of twelve core members with perhaps two dozen associated members. For a fuller biographical portrait of the founders and the movement, see Peard, *Race, Place, and Medicine*, 21–26.

11. For the evolution of racial science more broadly, see esp. Gould, *Mismeasure*

of *Man*; and Stocking, *Race, Culture, and Evolution*. Nancy Stepan points out that French scientists preferred less deterministic models and were greatly influenced by Lamarckian trends. This French approach proved exceptionally influential for scientists across Latin America, especially for those in Brazil. See Stepan, *"Hour of Eugenics,"* 72–76; and Stepan, "Eugenics in Brazil," 120. For currents particular to Latin America in this era, see esp. Graham et al., *Idea of Race*; Rodriguez, *Civilizing Argentina*; and Bronfman, *Measures of Equality*.

12. For epidemic disease in Brazil, see Cooper, "Brazil's Long Fight." For a broader history, see Winslow, *Conquest of Epidemic Disease*. At the turn of the century São Paulo took a leading role in developing an effective state system of public health, while Rio developed what would become the most important research center for epidemic disease, the Oswaldo Cruz Institute. For São Paulo, see Castro Santos, "Power, Ideology, and Public Health." Rio's reforms ushered in urban renewal projects that focused especially on clearing out the downtown's lower-class residents and resulted in clashes between the state and angry citizens. See Meade, *"Civilizing" Rio*; and Needell, *"Revolta contra Vacina."* Health initiatives in Pernambuco generally skirted questions of race; see Blake, "Medicalization of Nordestinos."

13. Peard, *Race, Place, and Medicine*, 107–8. Miasmatic theory changed in Rio de Janeiro over the nineteenth century depending on different racial concerns; see Chalhoub, "Politics of Disease Control." For the early dominance of miasmatic theory in Bahia, see Reis, *Death Is a Festival*.

14. "Decreto de 18 de janeiro de 1890," 341.

15. Though Bahian politicians received cabled word of the republican coup in Rio almost immediately, they chose to reject the new regime and uphold the empire. For Bahian politics in the republic, see Tavares, *História*; Consuelo Sampaio, *Partidos políticos*; and Pang, *Bahia*.

16. Vitorino also proposed a centralization of state politics, thereby upsetting regional *coroneis*, or local bosses. See Pang, *Bahia*.

17. There has been little work on the Pereira brothers. For Manuel Vitorino's collected writings, see Manuel Vitorino Pereira, *Idéias políticas*. The history of Bahia's vocational school, a project dear to his heart as well, is traced in Leal, *Arte de ter um ofício*.

18. Antônio Pereira, "Hygiene das escolas," 193.

19. Ibid., 196–97.

20. Ibid., 198.

21. For a study of the dominance of Lamarckian views in Latin America, see Stepan, *"Hour of Eugenics."*

22. Antônio Pereira, "Hygiene das escolas," 201.

23. Ibid., 346. The Mackinnel theories of ventilation, popular in the late nineteenth century, aimed to transport stale air out of a space and replace it with fresh air from outdoors.

24. Ibid., 434.

25. Ibid., 435.

26. Ibid., 448.

27. Romo, "Race and Reform," 49.

28. Antonietta Nunes and Luis Tavares both briefly chronicle these reforms. Neither, however, examine questions of race; nor do they focus on Vitorino and his influences. Nunes, "Política educacional"; Tavares, *Duas reformas*.

29. Manuel Vitorino Pereira, "Ato de 10 de janeiro de 1890," 95.

30. Health regulations for the schools occupied thirteen pages, while the reform of education as a whole was sketched in only five. Both are reprinted in Manuel Vitorino Pereira, *Idéias políticas*.

31. Manuel Vitorino Pereira, "Ato de 31 de dezembro de 1889," 79.

32. Brinton, "Nomenclature and Teaching," 264.

33. Manuel Vitorino Pereira, "Regulamento de hygiene escholar," 93. Note that in its published form the law specified "somotological exam," which was later replaced in the *Gazeta Médica* by "sanatological exam."

34. According to a founder of the field of physical anthropology, anthropologist Paul Topinard, physical measurements or anthropometry provided valuable data in two principle areas: tracking growth development and distinguishing among the races. And as Topinard noted, school populations were an ideal data mine for such studies. Topinard, "Observations," 212.

35. Questions of race in Rio de Janeiro's public schools in the Vargas era are treated in Dávila, *Diploma of Whiteness*. Brazil's national education congress of 1935 dedicated its entire meeting to questions of physical education. Congresso Nacional de Educação, *Anais*.

36. Nina Rodrigues expressed great disappointment that the study was to be canceled along with the rest of Manuel Vitorino's reforms; see Nina Rodrigues, "Anthropologia: Collecção anthropologica."

37. Cited in Tavares, *Duas reformas*, 40. Dias had first begun his service as director of public instruction in Bahia under the Tropicalista governor José Luís de Almeida Couto in 1888, the last year of the empire. Born in Bahia in 1844, Dias had attended Bahia's medical school and was friendly with Virgílio Damásio and Manuel Vitorino. Though his friendship with Vitorino may have ensured his stay in power through the new republican regime, it did not prevent him from speaking vehemently against the reforms once Vitorino had been ousted from power.

38. Cited in Nunes, "Reforma," 81.

39. Romo, "Race and Reform," 43-49.

40. "Terceiro Congresso Brasileiro," 437. Congressional rules specified that the organizing committee held exclusive control over the shape of the program.

41. Silva Lima, "Terceiro Congresso Brazileiro," 151-52.

42. For the development of legal medicine in Bahia, see Corrêa, *Ilusões*. For policies of criminal identification in Rio de Janeiro that intersected with racialized theories of criminality, see Olívia Gomes da Cunha, *Intenção e gesto*. For criminal identification and legal medicine in Argentina and Cuba, see Rodriguez, *Civilizing Argentina*; Ruggiero, *Modernity in the Flesh*; and Bronfman, *Measures of Equality*.

43. "Terceiro Congresso Brasileiro," 439. Hygiene was also included as part of this category, which was defined as "Legal medicine, hygiene, medical geography, and professional ethics." Marcos Chor Maio views the attempts of Nina Rodrigues to assert the

legitimacy of legal medicine as an academic struggle to define the field of medicine and its scope; he attributes Nina Rodrigues's unpopularity to this struggle for power. Maio, "Medicina."

44. "Quarto Congresso Brasileiro," 43.

45. Unfortunately there is no way to determine actual circulation or readership in Bahia, but it was undoubtedly one of the foremost medical journals in Brazil. The existing issues have been scanned and compiled; the introductory essays for this collection give some overview of the journal as a whole. See Bastianelli, *Gazeta Médica*.

46. "Terceiro Congresso Brasileiro," 443.

47. Ibid., 443–44.

48. Ibid., 444.

49. Ibid., 443–44.

50. In 1897 the then-doctor-governor of Bahia, Luís Vianna, would sign a contract to bring twenty-five thousand European immigrants to settle in Bahia, and three thousand Asian immigrants. Bahia, *Mensagem*, 13. His predecessor, Rodrigues Lima (1892–96), had initiated the contracts.

51. The studies by Nina Rodrigues are still critical sources for scholars of Candomblé.

52. The most complete survey of Nina Rodrigues and the intellectual context of his time is provided by Corrêa, *Ilusões*.

53. Peard, *Race, Place, and Medicine*, 102; Corrêa, *Ilusões*, 269–72. Gilberto Freyre also stresses his activism; see Freyre, "Nina Rodrigues."

54. The publications of Nina Rodrigues are complicated as they most often emerged first as articles and were later compiled into books. This work was published in book form in French in 1900 but issued as a book in Portuguese only in 1935, under the editorship of Arthur Ramos. Nina Rodrigues, *Animismo fetichista*, 13. Mariza Corrêa provides a valuable bibliography of his scholarship in *Ilusões*.

55. Nina Rodrigues, *Africanos no Brasil*, 277.

56. An example of the embarrassment caused by Nina Rodrigues can be seen in a 1946 laudatory history of the medical school, written by one of its own; Nina Rodrigues receives only passing mention. See Octávio Torres, *Esboço histórico*.

57. "Professor Nina Rodrigues," 59, 60.

58. For traditional treatment of Nina Rodrigues as a strict adherent of racial determinism, see, e.g., Peard, *Race, Place, and Medicine*, 103–6; Skidmore, *Black into White*, 57–62; and Corrêa, *Ilusões*.

59. Nina Rodrigues, "Contribuição," 446.

60. Nina Rodrigues, "Assistencia medico-legal," 165.

61. Nina Rodrigues, "Contribuição," 453.

62. When a colleague objected that lepers were not really sick and thus did not want to be isolated in a hospital, Nina Rodrigues dismissed his objection as irrelevant. The purpose of a new hospital, which he saw as critical, was to prevent contagion; protecting the common good therefore justified isolating the lepers. Ibid., 451.

63. Ibid., 363.

64. Ibid., 358.

65. Ibid., 363.

66. Ibid., 362.

67. Ibid.

68. Dain Borges perceptively situates Nina Rodrigues's fears of "turning black" in terms of pollution and contamination. Borges, "Recognition of Afro-Brazilian Symbols."

69. Nina Rodrigues, "Contribuição," 363.

70. Nina Rodrigues, "Anthropologia pathologica."

71. Skidmore, *Black into White*, 73. Another prominent proponent was the director of the Museu Nacional of Rio de Janeiro, João Batista de Lacerda. See Seyferth, "Antropologia e teoria."

72. Nina Rodrigues, "Contribuição," 450.

73. Nina Rodrigues, "Craneo do salteador Lucas," 137.

74. Ibid.

75. Nina Rodrigues, "Reforma dos exames medico-legaes," 14.

76. See, e.g., Nina Rodrigues, "Craneo do salteador Lucas." Historian Robert Levine makes this point as well for Nina Rodrigues's analysis of the religious rebels in the Canudos revolt. See Levine, *Vale of Tears*.

77. Nina Rodrigues, *Raças humanas*; Corrêa, *Ilusões*, 269–72.

78. Nina Rodrigues, *Alienado*. His efforts in politics are traced in Corrêa, *Ilusões*, 269–75.

79. Nina Rodrigues, *Africanos*, 18.

80. Ibid.

81. Ibid., 21.

82. Ibid., 300–301.

83. Ibid., 16.

84. It should be noted that Nina Rodrigues was not alone in his uncertainty about the *mestiço*. For the approach taken in Brazil, see Stepan, *"Hour of Eugenics"*; Schwarcz, *Spectacle of the Races*; and Skidmore, *Black into White*. As Nina Rodrigues himself was *mestiço*, we may well wonder whether his search to define the *mestiço* and ultimately to uncover African roots was not also a more personal (and deeply ambivalent) search for identity.

85. Cited in McNeely, *"Medicine on a Grand Scale,"* 5; see also Ackerknecht, *Rudolf Virchow*.

86. Bahian doctors devoted an entire issue of *Gazeta Médica da Bahia* to Virchow's work in 1901. See, e.g., Moreira, "Rudolf Virchow." For descriptions of his birthday celebrations in Bahia, see "Celebration"; and "Scientific Notes and News."

87. Stepan, *"Hour of Eugenics."*

88. Cited in Lima and Hochman, "Condenado pela raça," 24. See also Hochman, *Era do saneamento*.

89. Castro Santos, "Origens da reforma sanitária."

90. Ibid.

91. Novaes, "Bahia Azul." Despite ambitious programs initiated in 1995, by 2004 only 68% of the population had access to sewers.

92. These reforms were important for restoring state control of primary education and have often been deemed successful. Such assessments seem to neglect the failure to improve literacy rates. I argue elsewhere that Teixera's efforts revealed racialized views of education that limited the efficacy of his reforms. See Romo, "Race and Reform," chap. 2. For analysis of race in Teixera's later reforms in Rio de Janeiro, see Dávila, *Diploma of Whiteness*.

93. Gilberto Hochman makes a similar point, as does Charles-Edward Winslow in his survey of epidemic history. The latter points out that while early sanitary reforms may have misjudged the importance of miasmas, they still targeted dirt and thus ultimately helped reduce disease. Hochman, *Era do saneamento*; Winslow, *Conquest of Epidemic Disease*, xi.

94. Indeed, it appears that medical activism declined significantly in the 1920s. Bahia's *Gazeta Médica* turned away from its fervent petitions for change and moved toward a fairly staid acceptance of the status quo. The reasons for this shift are unclear, but they may be traced in part to the rise of eugenics, which put less emphasis on the environment, and to the development of bacteriology, which became able to target disease trajectories in individuals rather than seeing the causes of disease in poor city sanitation and miasmas. A 1918 study of tuberculosis in the *Gazeta* gives one illustration of this trend. The author concluded that prevention of the disease was easier at the individual level, and that social preventative measures were difficult to implement. Certainly, these conclusions were true, as instructing people to stay home was easier than far-reaching public disinfections and improvements in public sanitation and water provision ("Luta anti-tuberculosa," vi.) They ignored, however, the social realities that had been the concern of the earlier generations. How, after all, could the poor afford to quarantine themselves, and how effective might this be given the city's public health priorities?

Chapter 2

1. For a political history of the Vargas era, see Skidmore, *Politics in Brazil*. Bahian politics during this time are treated in Juracy Magalhães, *Minhas memórias provisórias*; Silva, *Ancoras*; Consuelo Sampaio, *Poder e representação*; Tavares, *História*; and Romo, "Race and Reform," chap. 3.

2. The cultural developments of the Vargas era and its nationalist programs are traced in Borges, "Recognition of Afro-Brazilian Symbols"; Martins, *Modernist Idea*; Williams, *Culture Wars*; Oliveira, Velloso, and Gomes, *Estado Novo*; and Nava and Lauerhass, *Brazil in the Making*.

3. Vargas, "Instrução profissional," 114.

4. Moura, *Tia Ciata*; Vianna, *Mystery of Samba*. Recent work has challenged this idea of Bahian hegemony in samba's roots and instead points to a more diverse group of influences. See Gomes, "Para além da casa da Tia Ciata."

5. Shaw, *Social History*, 148.

6. McCann, *Hello, Hello Brazil*, 107. See also Risério, *Caymmi*.

7. For the ways in which comparative nature of studies of race in Brazil and the United States have influenced the resulting findings, see Seigel, *Uneven Encounters*; and Seigel, "Beyond Compare."

8. Pierson, *Negroes in Brazil*, 338.

9. Pierson, "Raça e classe," 164.

10. Pierson, *Negroes in Brazil*, 178–81.

11. Ibid., 130.

12. Ibid., 183, 186, 195.

13. Ibid., 148.

14. For this transformation across Latin America, see esp. Andrews, *Afro-Latin America*; Graham et al., *Idea of Race*; and Appelbaum, Macpherson, and Rosenblatt, *Race and Nation*.

15. This tension resulted in a national arts program that encouraged modern art and traditional art forms simultaneously. Williams, *Culture Wars*.

16. Both congresses have been curiously understudied. For the first congress, see Romo, "Rethinking Race"; and Levine, "First Afro-Brazilian Congress." Beatriz Góis Dantas cites the congress in Recife, as well as the Afro-Brazilian Congress of 1937 in Salvador, as critical events in the process of idealizing and reifying "pure" African traditions in Brazil; Dantas, *Vovó Nagô*, 192–201. Mariza Corrêa has a more recent, albeit brief, appraisal of the congress; Corrêa, *Antropólogas*, 167; Corrêa, *Ilusões*, 223–29. Livio Sansone marks the congress of 1934 and its successor in Bahia in 1937 as the initiation of a contentious field of race studies, but does not analyze the congresses themselves. See Sansone, "Campo," 7.

17. Bastide, "Present Status," 112.

18. José Valladares to Melville J. Herskovits, 20 September 1934, MJHP, series 35/36.

19. Freyre, *Masters and the Slaves*. I do not address here Freye's larger contribution; for his controversial role in Brazilian racial thought, see Burke and Pallares-Burke, *Gilberto Freyre*; Costa, *Brazilian Empire*; Skidmore, *Black into White*; and Lund and McNee, *Gilberto Freyre*. For an analysis of *Casa-grande*, see esp. Araújo, *Guerra e paz*; and Skidmore, "Raízes de Gilberto Freyre." Despite this cultural focus, Freyre attempted to discriminate among African cultures to argue that some were superior to others. See Araújo, *Guerra e paz*; and Romo, "Rethinking Race."

20. Freyre, *Masters and the Slaves*, 278. In quoting from *Casa-grande* I have used the English-language edition but reconciled its translations with the original 1933 edition in Portuguese. I retain in this citation the phrasing of the first 1933 edition; it was changed in later versions. I translate, here and elsewhere, *negro* as "black" and *branco* as "white" but retain other terminology in its original Portuguese.

21. It is important to note that while some of Freyre's arguments repudiated whitening, the ideas of Portuguese survival were certainly paramount for him.

22. Freyre, *Masters and the Slaves*, xi–xiii. *Culture* at this time was broadly defined, encompassing notions of environment and social setting. I use the term throughout this chapter in this wider sense. For studies of Boas, see Stocking, *Race, Culture, and Evolution*; and Stocking, *Shaping of American Anthropology*.

23. Meticulous research by Maria Pallares-Burke reveals that Freyre's break from racially determinist ideas dated only from the late 1920s. See Burke and Pallares-Burke, *Gilberto Freyre*, 269–327.

24. For the evolution of Brazilian racial thought in this era, see Borges, "Recognition of Afro-Brazilian Symbols"; Maio and Santos, *Raça, ciência e sociedade*; Schwarcz, *Spectacle of the Races*; and Skidmore, *Black into White*.

25. For treatment of some of these alternate views and a fuller discussion of the congress, see Romo, "Rethinking Race."

26. The invitation highlighted the participation of Arthur Ramos, Gilberto Freyre, Edison Carneiro, Mario Marroquim, Ulysses Pernambucano, and Renato Mendonça; see José Valladares to Melville J. Herskovits, 20 September 1934, MJHP, series 35/36. José Valladares was the secretary for the event and he, rather than Freyre, issued the invitation to Herskovits.

27. Andrade, "Nota anthropologica," 262.

28. See, e.g., his tribute to the Tropicalistas in Moreira and Autran, "Silva Lima."

29. Widow Juliano Moreira, "Juliano Moreira," 150.

30. Freyre, "Deformações de corpo." This essay was expanded and published much later in Freyre, *Escravo nos anúncios*.

31. Freyre also used this article's medical arguments in *Casa-grande*. They helped support his view that the problems of Brazilian blacks might ultimately be cured, or changed. For the influence of the public health movement on *Casa-grande*, see Luiz Teixeira, "Da raça à doença."

32. Freyre, "Deformações de corpo," 248.

33. For the importance of neo-Lamarckian thought in Latin America, see Stepan, *"Hour of Eugenics."*

34. Freyre, "Deformações de corpo," 250.

35. This effort drew on the earlier effort by Nina Rodrigues, who made the same argument. For the ranking of African civilizations in Freyre, see also Araújo, *Guerra e paz*; and Romo, "Rethinking Race."

36. Carneiro has not been studied sufficiently. An exceedingly brief outline of his life may be found in the prefaces to Carneiro, *Cartas*; and Carneiro, *Religões negras*.

37. This activity by Edison's father became controversial when the senior Carneiro published a volume of folklore that was harshly criticized by Arthur Ramos in 1937; see Barros, *Arthur Ramos*, 189–92.

38. Nina Rodrigues was also important in the forging of this path, as traced in chapter 1. The figure of Manuel Querino is provocative and deserves further attention. See Burns, "Bibliographical Essay"; Leal, "Manuel Querino"; and Butler, *Freedoms Given*. Butler raises especially interesting questions about Querino's relationship with Bahia's black community.

39. Carneiro, "Xangô," 139.

40. For studies of Arthur Ramos, see Olívia Gomes da Cunha, "Sua alma em sua palma." Campos, *Arthur Ramos*; Corrêa, *Ilusões*.

41. Ramos, *Negro brasileiro*.

42. For further discussion of Ramos's role in the congress, see Romo, "Rethinking

Race." Although he is best classified as a psychiatrist at this point in his career, he moved easily between disciplines and later became known for his role in the field of anthropology.

43. Carneiro, "Situação do negro," 237, 238.

·44. Ibid., 239.

45. Ibid., 239–40.

46. For Carneiro's ambivalent position toward black scholars such as Manuel Querino, see Ari Lima, "Blacks as Study Objects and Intellectuals," 91–95; and Carneiro, *Cartas*, 97.

47. Lee Baker places E. Franklin Frazier in a wider circle of black intellectuals at Howard University, all of whom emphasized a rejection of African influences and a focus on the incomplete assimilation of "legitimate culture." Baker, *From Savage to Negro*, 176–79. I discuss Frazier in more detail in chapter 4.

48. It is intriguing that the text of Carneiro's paper is punctuated by three ellipsis points in its published form. It is not clear if these represent cuts from the original version.

49. Ramos, *Negro in Brazil*, 179. Ramos often reused portions of his writings, and this statement is repeated that same year in his introduction to the republished work of Nina Rodrigues.

50. Pierson, *Negroes in Brazil*, 297.

51. Aninha headed the Candomblé of Opô Afonjá. Vivaldo da Costa Lima provides an early and important study of the two figures and their mutual reinforcement of concepts of tradition and authenticity in Bahian Candomblé. See Lima, "Candomblé da Bahia." I refer to Aninha and Martiniano by their first names as that is how they were known in the community and how later scholars have referred to them.

52. Pierson, *Negroes in Brazil*, 294–95.

53. His importance in defining Bahian Candomblé and narratives of tradition in the religion has been highlighted by many scholars. See Vivaldo da Costa Lima, "Candomblé da Bahia"; Dantas, *Vovó Nagô*; Braga, *Na gamela do feitiço*; and Matory, *Black Atlantic Religion*.

54. Turner, "Some Contacts," 63.

55. See the note by Vivaldo da Costa Lima in Carneiro, *Cartas*, 86.

56. Landes, *City of Women*, 23.

57. Matory, *Black Atlantic Religion*.

58. Kim Butler makes this point as well and argues that Salvador's Afro-Brazilian Congress marked the consolidation of this view of Candomblé. See Butler, "Africa," 146–47. The early work of Beatriz Dantas provides the framework for much of the idea of invented traditions in Candomblé. See Dantas, *Vovó Nagô*.

59. Capone, *Busca da África*; Parés, *Formação do Candomblé*; Parés, "Birth of the Yoruba Hegemony"; Parés, "'Nagôization' Process." Both Capone and Parés call attention especially to the process in which the Yoruba-Nagô *terreiros* became accepted as the true guardians of tradition and portrayed their competitors as corrupted or impure. Both agree that scholars ultimately reinforced these hierarchies. Dantas originally called attention to the invented traditions in Candomblé, although she has been

criticized for attributing much of the invention and agency to scholars rather than to the Candomblé community itself. Dantas, *Vovó Nagô*.

60. See Matory, *Black Atlantic Religion*, chap. 3.

61. Vivaldo da Costa Lima, "Candomblé da Bahia," 52; Matory, *Black Atlantic Religion*, 100, 118–19.

62. Pierson, *Negroes in Brazil*, 293–94.

63. Ibid., 292–93.

64. This creative adaptation was noted first by Vivaldo da Costa Lima, "Obás de Xangô"; it has been stressed also by Braga, *Na gamela do feitiço*; Capone, *Busca da Africa*; and Parés, "Birth of the Yoruba Hegemony."

65. Landes, *City of Women*, 28.

66. Carneiro, "Aninha," 207.

67. Matory, *Black Atlantic Religion*, 139–45.

68. This claim was cited in Salvador's Afro-Brazilian Congress of 1937, as I will discuss later.

69. Pierson, *Negroes in Brazil*, 219.

70. Parés and Capone emphasize the competitive advantage that could be gained in terms of clients, prestige, and the attention of researchers for those *terreiros* who claimed to be most authentically African. See Capone, *Busca da Africa*; Parés, "Birth of the Yoruba Hegemony"; and Parés, "'Nagôization' Process."

71. Lühning, "Acabe com este santo."

72. Cited in Pierson, *Negroes in Brazil*, 219.

73. Vivaldo da Costa Lima, "Candomblé da Bahia," 41.

74. Deoscóredes dos Santos, *Axé Opô Afonjá*, 23.

75. Landes, *City of Women*, 60. Oliveira, "Estudos africanistas," 32.

76. Carneiro to Ramos, 27 January 1936, in Carneiro, *Cartas*, 90. The change of date appears to have been the result of delayed submissions for many papers.

77. See, e.g., Maio, "Tempo controverso."

78. Illegible in the English original, it is not clear if Freyre wrote "were" or "are."

79. Freyre to Herskovits, 19 December 1936, MJHP, series 35/36.

80. The text of Freyre's interview granted to the *Diário de Pernambuco* and reprinted in *O Estado da Bahia* is excerpted by the editors in Carneiro, *Cartas*, 128–29.

81. Freyre, cited in ibid., 129.

82. Freyre served as personal secretary to Pernambuco Governor Estácio Coimbra (1926–30), the husband of one of his cousins. The two were forced into exile with the disruption of the revolution of 1930. Maria Pallares-Burke provides the best biography of Freyre's early years; see Burke and Pallares-Burke, *Gilberto Freyre*.

83. Freyre, cited in Carneiro, *Cartas*, 129. See his claims in Freyre, "O que foi," 349. Such insistence on this point suggests that his original summary of the first congress was indeed written with knowledge of the upcoming second congress.

84. Levine, "First Afro-Brazilian Congress."

85. Freyre, cited in Carneiro, *Cartas*, 129.

86. This is not to say that Freyre was uninterested in politics; after his 1920s involvement in the oligarchic politics of Pernambuco, his most notorious stances included

support of the military coup of 1964 and his support of the Portuguese colonial regimes in Africa.

87. Freyre to Herskovits, 28 November 1934; Herskovits to Freyre, 17 January 1935, MJHP, series 35/36.

88. The second volume's publication in a series edited by Ramos may indicate why Ramos was asked to write the preface. On the one hand, it is possible that Ramos stepped into what otherwise was a difficult publishing situation for Freyre, and that Freyre, out of gratitude, asked him to write a preface. On the other hand, it is possible that Freyre felt obligated to ask the editor of the series to preface the work as a matter of form. It is not clear why the two volumes of proceedings from the congress were not published by the same press.

89. Freyre, "O que foi," 351.

90. Ibid., 348.

91. Ibid. Quotation marks in the original. "Scientificism" is not an ideal translation, but the word in Portuguese is *scientificista*. I translate *cultivam* as "[they] promote."

92. Ibid., 352.

93. Emphasis added. See the unpaginated insert in *Novos estudos*.

94. While it is not clear when the plans for the Salvador congress became public, Arthur Ramos and Edison Carneiro, its chief organizer, had been discussing the idea at least since January 1936. (See Carneiro, *Cartas*, 80.) In early November 1936 Freyre claimed in his interview with the Pernambucan press that he had only learned of the congress a few days earlier. Unfortunately Freyre's essay does not have a date, but since Ramos wrote his introduction and dated it December 1936, it seems likely that Freyre had written his own essay close to this time. Although it is impossible to say definitely when Freyre learned of the second congress and when he wrote the essay, the tenor of his essay indicates that it was crafted with knowledge of the upcoming congress.

95. Ramos, "Prefácio," n.p.

96. Ibid.

97. Ibid.

98. Ramos, "Nina Rodrigues," 337–38.

99. Carneiro and Ferraz, "Congresso Afro-Brasileiro," 8. The essay was written after the congress but not dated. The differences in ideology between Freyre and Carneiro could be called generational only to a limited extent: Freyre was at this time thirty-seven, and Carneiro would have been twenty-six. The third member of the organizing party was the secretary of the congress, Reginaldo Guimarães.

100. Carneiro and Ferraz, "Congresso Afro-Brasileiro," 9.

101. This collection came in large part from police confiscations, as did most collections of the time.

102. Carneiro, *Cartas*, 131.

103. Ibid., 135, 137. This sponsorship was, of course, a further benefit to paying homage to Nina Rodrigues in the congress.

104. Ibid., 131. This represented the first transmission of the sacred music of Candomblé.

105. Freyre, "O que foi," 350.

106. Carneiro did clarify later in an essay in 1940 that the grant was not from the governor personally, as Freyre had alleged. See Carneiro, "Congresso Afro-Brasileiro."

107. It would be interesting to know why Magalhães decided to grant this support. As I note later, there were rumors that he had a close friendship with some Candomblé leaders, but his ultimate decision to privilege the event with his endorsement remains unclear.

108. They especially highlighted their satisfaction at attracting a submission by Melville Herskovits to the proceedings. The importance given to a foreign presence is most likely due to the still nascent development of the social sciences in Brazil. Miceli, *História das ciências sociais*. See also Thales de Azevedo, *Ciências sociais*.

109. Carneiro and Ferraz, "Congresso Afro-Brasileiro," 8.

110. Ibid., 9.

111. Carneiro et al., "Palavras inauguraes," 15; emphasis added.

112. Carneiro, "Congresso Afro-Brasileiro," 99.

113. Carneiro, "Estudos brasileiros," 115.

114. Carneiro and Ferraz, "Congresso Afro-Brasileiro," 10.

115. Carneiro et al., "Palavras inauguraes," 16. This address was most likely written by Carneiro and Ferraz, but Martiniano do Bomfim is also listed at the end of the address as a member of the congress's executive committee, along with Azevedo Marques and Reginaldo Guimarães, the congress secretary.

116. This depiction provoked significant controversy and polemic with the true Jubiabá, as traced in Braga, *Na gamela do feitiço*.

117. Amado, "Elogio," 327.

118. Landes, *City of Women*, 78–79.

119. Carneiro and Ferraz, "Congresso Afro-Brasileiro," 7.

120. Carneiro et al., "Palavras inauguraes," 15.

121. Carneiro, "Aninha," 208.

122. Ibid.

123. Vivaldo da Costa Lima, "Candomblé da Bahia," 60.

124. See "Nota sobre comestíveis africanos" in the appendix of Congresso Afro-Brasileiro (Bahia), *Negro no Brasil*.

125. Pierson, *Negroes in Brazil*, 222. Such a view may have been a minority, however, considering the poor support shown for the Frente Negra (Black Front) formed in Bahia in 1932. The black movement in the 1930s attracted few adherents and dissolved shortly afterward, leaving little historical record. Bacelar, *Hierarquia*; Butler, *Freedoms Given*.

126. Carneiro, "Revisão," 64.

127. Bonfim, "Ministros de Xangô," 236. For unknown reasons this paper was not presented at the congress but rather published first in the newspaper *Estado da Bahia* and then in the proceedings. See Parés, "Shango," 34 (n. 49).

128. Ramos, "Nina Rodrigues," 337–38.

129. Carneiro, "Homenagem a Nina Rodrigues," 331.

130. Ibid., 333–34.

131. Carneiro, *Cartas*, 132.

132. Carneiro to Ramos, 12 December 1936, in ibid., 131.

133. Carneiro to Ramos, 15 July 1937, in ibid., 150.

134. Carneiro and Ferraz, "Congresso Afro-Brasileiro," 11.

135. Cited in Braga, *Na gamela do feitiço*, 166–67.

136. Bittencourt, "Liberdade religiosa."

137. Interview of 7 August 1936, cited in Braga, *Na gamela do feitiço*, 82.

138. Carneiro to Ramos, 19 July 1937, in Carneiro, *Cartas*, 152.

139. See editorial note in ibid., 153.

140. Carneiro to Ramos, 19 July 1937, in ibid., 152.

141. Carneiro to Ramos, 22 September 1937, and 27 September 1937, in ibid., 160–61.

142. Reprinted in ibid., 165.

143. The appointment of Martiniano testified to his prestige in Bahia, for he was widely acknowledged to be a diviner and did not actually head or participate regularly in any Candomblé *terreiro*.

144. This is mentioned obliquely by Carneiro but highlighted by the editors of his letters. See Carneiro, *Cartas*, 132–33, 151.

145. Carneiro, "Congresso Afro-Brasileiro," 99.

146. Ibid., 100.

147. Landes, *City of Women*, 74; Pierson, *Negroes in Brazil*, 17, 19.

148. Pierson, *Negroes in Brazil*, 293.

149. Ickes identifies 1936 as a turning point in Bahia and argues that intellectuals such as Carneiro had a significant role in these events. Ickes, "'Adorned.'"

Chapter 3

1. Letter signed by Heloisa Torres, 22 September 1939, BR MN MN DRCO RA 106/144, AMN. Torres specified that Carneiro's work in the states of Bahia, Sergipe, and Alagoas was at the service of the National Museum, but it is not clear if this indicated employment or simply protection.

2. See esp. Oliveira, Velloso, and Gomes, *Estado Novo*; Pandolfi, *Repensando o Estado Novo*. For Bahia, see Paulo Silva, *Âncoras*; and Tavares, *História*.

3. Landes, *City of Women*, 13. Landes noted that most faculty members at Bahian academic institutions had been exiled or jailed for opposing Vargas, although she does not note the extent to which this opposition existed (*City of Women*, 12).

4. Edison Carneiro to Ruth Landes, 28 May 1946, RSLP.

5. Ofício 566, 24 November 1939, BR MN MN DR CO RA 107/131, AMN.

6. Ofício 583, 2 December 1939, BR MN MN DR CO RA 107/131, AMN.

7. Carneiro wrote to Landes of the failed delivery, expressing in the same letter that he felt he had nothing in common with Torres. Edison Carneiro to Ruth Landes, 24 October 1940, RSLP.

8. Corrêa, *Antropólogas*, 151,179.

9. Certainly there is evidence of early attempts by Torres to bring representations of Afro-Brazilian culture into the museum. One explanation for the 1947 exhibition's focus on indigenous culture may have been that its opening was organized around the

"Week of the Indian." Though Torres turned the attention of the museum primarily toward indigenous cultures in future years, she remained interested in Afro-Brazilian culture, as her research on Baiana dress reveals. Indeed, in applying for the academic position left vacant by Arthur Ramos in 1950, she developed her research on Baiana dress further, in part through a new research trip to Bahia's Museu do Estado. For this trip see RA 143, Ofício 464, 17 July 1951, Relatório, 1950, AMN. For detailed description of the 1947 exhibition, see Castro Faria, *Exposições*.

10. Williams, *Culture Wars*, 146. For museums in Brazil, see Schwarcz, *Espetáculo das raças*. For broader treatments of the topic, see Bennett, *Birth of the Museum*; and Stocking, *Objects*.

11. Bahia, *Educação e saúde*, 125–26.

12. Ibid., 125.

13. For historic preservation at the federal level, see esp. Williams, *Culture Wars*, chap. 4; and Gonçalves, *Retórica da perda*.

14. Bahia, *Educação e saúde*, 124.

15. Bahia, "Nossa capa," 16.

16. Bahia, *Educação e saúde*, 128.

17. Ibid.

18. Lühning, "Acabe com este santo"; Braga, *Na gamela do feitiço*.

19. Albuquerque, "Santos, deuses, e heróis." See also Albuquerque, *Algazarra*; Fry, Carrara, and Martins-Costa, "Negros e brancos."

20. Bahia, *Educação e saúde*, 127–28.

21. Sparse biographical information on Valladares can be found in José do Prado Valladares cards, record group 10, series: "Fellowship Recorder Cards," collection RF, at the Rockefeller Archive Center, Sleepy Hollow, N.Y.; and in the obituaries by fellow art critic Robert C. Smith and by the Instituto Geográfico e Histórico da Bahia. See Smith, "José Antônio do Prado Valladares," 435; and "José do Prado Valladares."

22. The letter of invitation to U.S. anthropologist Melville Herskovits specified that the artists would include Cicero Dias, Luís Jardim, Santa Rosa, Noêmia, Di Cavalcanti, Manuel Bandeira, and the photographer Francisco Rebelle. José Valladares to Melville J. Herskovits, 20 September 1934, MJHP, series 35/36. Freyre notes the role of Clarival Valladares in Freyre, "O que foi," 350. After an early career in medicine Clarival do Prado Valladares would become one of the foremost critics of Northeastern art, although he took this career path only after José's death in an airplane crash in 1959.

23. Bahia, *Educação e saúde*, 124.

24. It is also likely that his lack of political and bureaucratic experience may have been seen in positive terms. The Estado Novo in Bahia, headed at this time by the similarly inexperienced political outsider Landulfo Alves, sought to break from traditional oligarchic politics and recruit idealistic newcomers into government service.

25. Though the 1918 law was exceptionally vague in shaping the institution itself, it was exquisitely precise in dictating the inscription for the museum's inauguration, with a prominent place of honor for the then-governor of Bahia, Antônio Ferrão Moniz de Aragão. This may have been one of the few actions possible in these early years, as the law declared the museum a new entity but without any dedicated personnel or funding,

all of which would ostensibly come from its association with the state archives. Bahia, Archivo Público, "Untitled."

26. Valladares, "Resumo histórico."

27. Bahia, *Regulamento.*

28. Ibid., arts. 3–5.

29. Such a division was not unusual in museums; the creation of France's Musée de l'Homme in 1938 posited places of equality for all humans but in typical ethnographic fashion displayed only cultures and peoples outside of France. See Conklin, "Civil Society, Science, and Empire."

30. Bahia, *Educação e saúde*, 123–24.

31. Ibid., 36.

32. Weinstein, *For Social Peace.*

33. Valladares, "Resumo histórico."

34. Holanda, *Recursos educativos*, 67–77. This description of the holdings for the Nelson de Oliveira museum is from 1958, but presumably the eclectic character of the museum had not changed significantly over the years. The collection also included fragments of a meteorite and "'souvenirs,' etc" (ibid., 67). The city had two other museums: the museum of medical anthropology organized by the Nina Rodrigues Institute and the collection of Bahia's Geographic and Historic Institute. It is unclear, however, whether these museums were open to the public in the 1930s.

35. Visitation in 1935 was 18,508; authorities noted a drop in 1936, when it declined slightly to 16,550. For figures for 1931–35, see Bahia, Secretaria do Interior e Justiça do Estado, *Relatorio, 1935*, 361–68. For 1936, see Bahia, Secretaria do Interior e Justiça do Estado, *Relatorio, 1936*, 338. Unfortunately, I have not been able to find statistics for the 1940s; the next available statistics come from 1950; as I discuss later, these are considerably lower, settling around 5,500 through the rest of the decade.

36. Bahia, *Educação e saúde*, 124.

37. Museu do Estado da Bahia, "Report of Holdings for 1939." I have titled this report provisionally; it is an untitled mimeograph available only in the IPHAN archives.

38. The provenance of these items is not available, but they were most likely collected in police raids of Candomblé. Such confiscations created later debate in Bahian museums; see Sansi-Roca, "Hidden Life." The titles refer to spiritual leaders and initiates in Candomblé.

39. For historical treatments of these episodes, see Chandler, *Bandit King*; and Levine, *Vale of Tears.*

40. Museu do Estado da Bahia, "Report of Holdings for 1939."

41. Valladares, "Resumo histórico."

42. Ibid. "Azulejos" here referred to blue and white tile paintings brought with the Portuguese.

43. Jack Harding, *I Like Brazil*, 192. The book itself was actually somewhat pedantic: its message was to improve the Good Neighbor policy and increase cooperation across the Americas. Based on the book's publication date (1941), I am assuming the visit was conducted in 1940.

44. The *balangandan* was a gold or silver frame hung with gold or silver charms and

historically worn at the waist by Baianas. For the best study of their use and origin, which is still somewhat unclear, see the essays by Simone Trindade and Solange de Sampaio Godoy in Fundação Museu Carlos Costa Pinto and Pinacoteca do Estado de São Paulo, *O que é que a Bahia tem*.

45. Jack Harding, *I Like Brazil*, 209.

46. For the role of Bahia in Caymmi's work, see Risério, *Caymmi*.

47. As Caymmi himself acknowledged, the word was "little known before in the South and almost never used," but the song's success brought the word, and the item, back into circulation. He reports that they became difficult to find after the song's release because of the rush to purchase them. Caymmi, *Cancioneiro*, 150.

48. Pierson, *Negroes in Brazil*, 246.

49. Barbara Weinstein shows that race, particularly "whiteness," proved important to São Paulo's view of itself in the nation in the 1930s. See Weinstein, "Racializing Regional Difference."

50. Lisboa, "Museu da Bahia."

51. Ibid.

52. Valladares, "Introdução," v.

53. Ibid., vi.

54. Ibid.

55. Ibid., v–vi.

56. Ibid.

57. Basílio de Magalhães, *Folclore no Brasil*.

58. Silva Campos, "Procissões tradicionais," 240.

59. Ibid., 5.

60. Silva Campos, "Tempo antigo."

61. For a full list of the names of galleries, see Williams, *Culture Wars*, 144. Donald Pierson described Silva Campos as *preto*, or black; Pierson, *Negroes in Brazil*, 221.

62. Herskovits, "Pesquisas etnológicas."

63. Herskovits, *Myth of the Negro Past*.

64. Valladares, "Nota do tradutor," i. José Valladares translated the Herskovits essay from the English, which may explain why he used *afro-americano* where terms such as *negro* and *afro-brasileiro* were more common at the time.

65. For the copyrights request, see Melville J. Herskovits to José Valladares, 12 June 1944, MJHP. Valladares was a critical contact for Melville and Francis Herskovits while they conducted a year of field research in Bahia, often serving as their escort to various *terreiros* of Candomblé. For evidence of this relationship, see the Melville and Frances Herskovits Collection at the Schomburg Center for Research in Black Culture, New York.

66. Ott, "Vestígios de cultura." Ott was born in Germany in 1908 and completed his degree there before becoming a faculty member in Ethnology in Bahia's new Faculty of Philosophy. He began publishing research on a variety of Bahian topics in 1941 and would later continue to write on topics of Bahian art, ethnography, and history.

67. Valladares, "Nota da direção" (1945), v.

68. Ibid., vi.

69. Edelweiss, *Tupís e guaranís.*

70. Carneiro, "Candomblés da Bahia." Though it was later reprinted, it first appeared through the museum series.

71. Jose do Prado Valladares cards, record group 10, series: "Fellowship Recorder Cards," Collection RF, Rockefeller Archive Center, Sleepy Hollow, N.Y.

72. Valladares, "Museus para o povo," 27.

73. Ibid., 29.

74. Ibid., 28.

75. See Valladares's report that the purchase was complete: José Valladares to Melville J. Herskovits, 9 March 1944, MJHP, box 31, folder 7. The mayors of Salvador have traditionally been fairly active in the realm of culture.

76. José Valladares to Melville J. Herskovits, 9 March 1944, MJHP, box 31, folder 7. Though the mutual influence is undoubtedly deep, with extended correspondence between Valladares and Melville Herskovits, Herskovits appeared curiously uninterested in the development of the museum in their exchange of letters and never offered suggestions or even much of a response to Valladares's reports of his work at the museum. Perhaps Herskovits offered encouragement in person, as Valladares reserved the greatest praise of him for the preface to "Museus para o povo."

77. José Valladares to Melville J. Herskovits, 13 October 1944, MJHP, box 36, folder 7.

78. José Valladares to Nathalie H. Zimmern, 13 October 1944, Brooklyn Museum Archives, Records of the Department of the Arts of Africa, the Pacific Islands, and the Americas: Departmental Administration, Employment [01] (file #18), 2/1933–11/1947, Brooklyn, N.Y. Nathalie Zimmern was assistant curator of the Department of American Indian Art and Primitive Cultures.

79. His correspondence notes the museum was close to done in April of that year. José Valladares to Melville J. Herskovits, 22 April 1946, MJHP, box 36, folder 7.

80. José Valladares to Melville J. Herskovits, 18 March 1947, MJHP, box 42, folder 1.

81. José Valladares to Melville J. Herskovits, 6 June 1947, MJHP, box 42, folder 1.

82. José Valladares to Rodrigo Andrade, 7 March 1945, Arquivo Técnico e Administrativo, IPHAN.

83. Valladares, *Guia*, 1.

84. Ibid., 3. This guide can be assumed to be an accurate representation of the displays as Valladares stressed that it was designed to be read while directly in front of the exhibits and would have little use outside the museum.

85. Ibid., 4.

86. Ibid., 7.

87. Ibid., 8–9.

88. Valladares, "Bahia and Its Museum," 453. The Portuguese version is Valladares, "Bahia e seu museu." The English translation was also published the same year in *Brazil* magazine.

89. Valladares, "Bahia and Its Museum," 453.

90. Ibid., 454.

91. Ibid., 456–57. An examination of the museum catalog from 1970, the next produced after Valladares's 1946 guide, notes a *balangandan* exhibited in a larger display

of colonial silverwork, labeled at this point as a colonial piece. Thus certainly by 1970 the piece had lost its popular context and was situated as part of a larger trajectory of (primarily elite) silverwork. Although we cannot know, perhaps this was also the solution of 1948 and explains how photos of the *balangandans* might be included in the 1948 article but without any treatment of popular or Afro-Brazilian culture to frame them. For the 1970 catalog, see Bahia, Secretaria de Educação e Cultura, *Museu de Arte da Bahia*.

92. Valladares, "Bahia and Its Museum," 454.

93. Ibid., 458.

94. Ibid., 451.

95. Valladares, "Nota da direção" (1947), n.p.

96. José Valladares to Rodrigo Andrade, 5 January 1939, IPHAN.

97. See, e.g., Valladares, *Bêabá da Bahia*; and Valladares, *Torço da bahiana*. He also covered a diverse array of topics as art columnist for Salvador's *Diário de Notícias*. For excerpts from these columns, see Valladares, *Dominicais*; and Valladares, *Artes maiores e menores*. It should be noted, however, that he would never highlight popular art with the same determination; his later selection of columns covered a diverse array of topics in art and was not primarily focused on Afro-Brazilian or popular contributions.

98. Report dated 22 March 1950, pasta "Biblioteca. Projetos, informações," Arquivo do Museu de Arte da Bahia, Salvador, Bahia. This summary appears to be recycled without much alteration from the guide to Brazilian museums completed by Heloisa Torres during the same era. See Heloisa Torres, *Museums of Brazil*, 26.

99. The Góes Calmon house is located at 198 Avenida Joana Angélica and is currently the site of the Academia Baiana de Letras. The earlier location for the museum had been in Campo Grande, in the spot now occupied by the Teatro Castro Alves. Visitorship in the early 1930s in Campo Grande was generally at least double that of the 1950s, which remained relatively constant at about 5,500 visitors annually. The archive of the museum includes figures on visitation for the years 1950, 1951, 1952, and 1958.

100. Carneiro, "Candomblés da Bahia."

101. See, e.g., Carybé, *Temas*. The collection was republished in Carybé, *Sete portas*; and Rocha, *Roteiro*.

Chapter 4

1. Pierson, *Negroes in Brazil*, 20, xviii.

2. I deal here specifically with the influence of U.S. scholarship in Bahia, but there was also significant French influence on Brazilian social science, most notably represented in Bahia by Pierre Verger. Although he was important for his role in encouraging African connections in Bahia, I do not treat Verger here, particularly as his chief period of influence comes later. See Massi, "Franceses e norte americanos"; Lühning, "Pierre Fatumbi Verger"; and Alberto, "Terms of Inclusion." Pierson certainly influenced the Bahian setting as well, most notably through the work of the Bahian anthropologist Thales de Azevedo. See the latter's interview in Azevedo, "Thales de Azevedo."

3. See, e.g., Donald Pierson to Mrs. Robert Clark, 22 July 1939, DPP, pasta 62.

4. After completing his research in Bahia, Pierson accepted a professorship in São Paulo and was an active correspondent and advisor in the developing Brazilian field of sociology. Though he proved tremendously influential in shaping conceptions of Bahia and in encouraging later U.S. research interest in the region, his legacy has gone largely unexamined. For important exceptions to this trend, see esp. Antônio Sérgio Guimarães, "Cor, classes e status"; Guimarães, "Classes sociais"; Bacelar, *Hierarquia*, chap. 3; and Corrêa, *História da antropologia*.

5. Donald Pierson to Mary Wilhemine Williams, 10 December 1934, DPP, pasta 61.

6. Donald Pierson to Robert Redfield, 15 May 1935, DPP, pasta 61. For the impact of such comparisons on studies of race in Brazil, see esp. Seigel, *Uneven Encounters*; and Seigel, "Beyond Compare."

7. Pierson drew on numerous contacts to amass a substantial number of letters of introduction, including several from Anísio Teixeira and Gilberto Freyre. See the collected correspondence in DPP, pasta 62.

8. Robert Park to Donald Pierson, 11 February 1936, DPP, pasta 62.

9. Report no. 3, 19 June 1936, DPP, pasta 62.

10. Park, cited in Pierson, *Negroes in Brazil*, 13.

11. Ibid., 12–13.

12. Ibid., 14, 15.

13. Ibid., 18–21.

14. Ibid., 362–65.

15. Ramos, "Introdução," 23. See the collection of reviews printed at the start.

16. Ibid., 24.

17. Landes reflects on her experience in an essay that finally exposed the role of Herskovits in defaming her career in Landes, "Woman Anthropologist." For Carneiro's view of the attacks by Ramos, see Carneiro, "'Falseta.'" The best intellectual treatment of Landes in Brazil is found in Healey, "Desencontros"; and Healey, "'Sweet Matriarchy.'" Matory provides an alternate, and largely critical, view in *Black Atlantic Religion*, chap. 5. For a rich biography of Landes and the role of gender in shaping her position in the field of anthropology, see Cole, *Ruth Landes*; and Corrêa, *Antropólogas*, chap. 5.

18. Cole, *Ruth Landes*, 145.

19. Landes, *City of Women*, 3.

20. Cited in Cole, *Ruth Landes*, 161.

21. DPP, pasta 59. Pierson was at Fisk finishing his manuscript when Ruth Landes arrived for her stay there.

22. Landes, *City of Women*, xxxvi.

23. Ibid., 10.

24. Ibid., 248.

25. Cole, *Ruth Landes*, 215.

26. Landes, *City of Women*, 16.

27. In fact Healey limits his analysis to *City of Women* alone. Healey, "Desencontros"; Healey, "'Sweet Matriarchy.'"

28. Landes, "Cult Matriarchate," 397.

29. Ibid., 387.

30. Ibid., 396.

31. Stefania Capone calls attention to the fact that scholars have privileged only a few Yoruba Candomblé; Landes's disinterest and disdain for "less traditional" Candomblés was a fairly consistent theme in the work of most other contemporary and later scholars as well. Capone, *Busca da Africa.*

32. Landes, *City of Women*, 202. She had developed this theme earlier in Landes, "Fetish Worship."

33. Landes, "Woman Anthropologist."

34. Landes, *City of Women*, 248.

35. Carneiro, "Structure of African Cults," 273.

36. Ibid., 277. J. Lorand Matory proposes that the influence flowed primarily from Landes to Carneiro, causing Carneiro to shift his conclusions, which had previously not emphasized the role of women or homosexuals in Candomblé. In both cases, Matory argues that such findings were distorted by Landes's "feminist agenda." See Matory, *Black Atlantic Religion*, chap. 5.

37. Landes, *City of Women*, 200–201.

38. Healey, "Desencontros," 191–94.

39. Landes, *City of Women*, 247.

40. Healey, "'Sweet Matriarchy."

41. Frazier, "Brazil Has No Race Problem," 125.

42. Hellwig, "E. Franklin Frazier's Brazil"; Hellwig, *African-American Reflections.*

43. Hellwig, *African-American Reflections*, 88.

44. Frazier, "Some Aspects of Race Relations," 292. Hellwig argues that Frazier's multiple scholarly reviews of Pierson's work showed his endorsement of Pierson, but it should be noted that Frazier insisted, even with generally positive reviews, that Pierson's denial of color prejudice was an "oversimplification." See Frazier, "Review of *Negroes in Brazil*," 189.

45. Frazier, *Negro Family in the United States.*

46. Hellwig, "E. Franklin Frazier's Brazil," 88; cf. 7.

47. Quoted in ibid., 87. Hellwig notes that Turner helped Frazier get settled in Bahia and that the two often worked together.

48. Frazier, "Negro Family in Bahia," 470, 478.

49. Ibid., 475.

50. Academic treatments of Herskovits give little attention to his research in Brazil. For surveys of his career as a whole, see Jackson, "Melville Herskovits"; and Gershenhorn, *Melville J. Herskovits*. For studies of his career and influence in Latin America, see Yelvington, "Invention of Africa"; and Yelvington, "Anthropology."

51. Melville J. Herskovits to Gilberto Freyre, 4 October 1940, MJHP. Scholars Mariza Corrêa and Sally Cole have both noted the critical role played by Ramos in Afro-Brazilian studies during this time. The relationship between Ramos and Herskovits is studied in detail in Antônio Sérgio Guimarães, "Africanism and Racial Democracy."

52. The book was actually part of a now famous larger study commissioned by the Carnegie Foundation. For the study results, see Myrdal, *American Dilemma.* Myrdal solicited a wide range of studies for the monumental work, which included contributions

by Landes, Herskovits, and Frazier. Cole notes that Myrdal himself weighed in on the side of Frazier and criticized Herskovits's methodology. Cole, *Ruth Landes*, 182.

53. Herskovits, *Myth of the Negro Past*, 16. This methodology had first been detailed in Herskovits's "Negro in the New World," which he cites here. Walter Jackson argues that this 1930 essay shaped Herskovits's research agenda for the next fifteen years; see Jackson, "Melville Herskovits," 109. It is interesting to note that Herskovits retreated somewhat from this approach of "charting Africanisms" in a preface written for the Beacon 1958 edition of *Myth of the Negro Past*. There he wrote that Ramos's work, especially his idea of syncretism, had been of principal importance in reorienting and "sharpening" his analysis: "It continued, of course, to be of paramount importance . . . to utilize ethnographic field research to determine the Africanisms that were present. . . . [But new research] pointed not to the question of what Africanisms were carried over in unaltered form, but how, in the contact of Africans with Europeans and American Indians, cultural accommodation and cultural integration had been achieved" (xxxvi–xxxvii).

54. Harrison, Ogburn, and Young, "Foreword," xxiv.

55. Herskovits, *Myth of the Negro Past*, 19.

56. Du Bois, "Review of *The Myth of the Negro Past*," 226.

57. Ibid., 227.

58. The difference between the two is part of a larger division in U.S. social science, as noted by Lee Baker, who distinguishes scholars interested in Boasian ideas (such as Herskovits) from those interested in the approach of Robert Park (such as Frazier); see Baker, *From Savage to Negro*. For the continued relevance of these debates in Latin American scholarship, see Yelvington, "Anthropology."

59. Frazier, "Review of *The American Negro*," 1012.

60. Valladares, "Nota do tradutor," i.

61. Herskovits, "Arte do bronze"; Herskovits, "Procedencia dos negros."

62. Herskovits, "Deuses africanos." Published in English as Herskovits, "African Gods."

63. I cannot draw conclusions here about Herskovits's later work and whether he ever truly fulfilled this methodological agenda. His statements indicate that at least by 1958 he had not. Though he noted that he had since become less interested in tracing strict African lineages, he held that the degree of acculturation could be seen on a "continuum," an assertion very close to his previous idea of "charting the intensity of Africanisms." Herskovits, "Preface," xxiii.

64. The Herskovits trip was funded by the Rockefeller Foundation and intended both to assess the state of the social sciences in Brazil and to improve U.S. and Brazilian cooperative efforts in research. Given this purpose, it is possible to read the lecture as a blueprint for what Herskovits saw as the necessary direction for future Bahian research. The stated purpose of the lecture, however, was simply to provide preliminary thoughts on his current research in Bahia.

65. According to Thales de Azevedo, Isaías Alves was particularly determined to have Herskovits as the inaugural speaker. See Boaventura, "Isaías Alves de Almeida," 260.

66. Herskovits, "Pesquisas etnológicas," 7.

67. Ibid., 11–12; emphasis in original.

68. Ibid., 8. These ideas were certainly not foreign to Bahians in the audience—Gilberto Freyre, after all, had proposed similar theories of cultural exchange and contact in his works throughout the 1930s, emphasizing the mutual influences of indigenous, African, and Portuguese cultures in the making of Brazil. Indeed, the two thinkers' influence on each other is intriguing and deserves further exploration. As I noted earlier, however, it is Ramos, not Freyre, whom Herskovits recognized as influencing his thought.

69. Ibid., 6.

70. Ibid., 9. In fact, the study of acculturation was a sort of an academic cause for Herskovits, who in 1935 had published with other leading anthropologists a series of memoranda calling for its study and in 1938 published his own volume on the subject. See Redfield, Linton, and Herskovits, "Memorandum"; and Herskovits, *Acculturation*. For an analysis of how Herskovits's emphasis on acculturation proved fundamental for the move away from ideas of Western superiority, see Gershenhorn, *Melville J. Herskovits*.

71. Herskovits, "Pesquisas etnológicas," 9.

72. Ibid., 9–10; emphasis added.

73. Ibid., 13.

74. Furthermore, although Herskovits was somewhat critical of what he believed had been too excessive a focus on Candomblé, the rest of his essay devoted itself to this topic.

75. While I do not dispute that these practices may have been influenced by African culture, my point here is both to emphasize the impressionistic nature of Herskovits's claims and to note that these subjects would have lent themselves well to a study of acculturation; the fact that they were not analyzed in this way betrays Herskovits's true focus.

76. Frazier, "Rejoinder"; Herskovits, "Negro in Bahia," 402–5.

77. Herskovits, "Review of *City of Women*," 124. Cole notes that Landes had made Herskovits aware of her findings on matrilineage in a letter dated 30 September 1939 (*Ruth Landes*, 189). Her articles on Bahia began to be published the following year; see Cole's bibliography for a complete listing of her works and for discussion of Herskovits's further role in denouncing Landes's contribution to the Myrdal report.

78. See Melville J. Herskovits to José Valladares, 17 June 1947, MJHP, for Herskovits's initial suggestion. See the response from Valladares dated 26 August 1947 where he notes that his wife, Gizella Valladares, believes the review too negative. Valladares then encourages Herskovits to make any necessary revisions.

79. Valladares, "Review of *City of Women*," 443–44.

80. Ibid., 445.

81. Ruth Landes to George and Alice Park, 13 August 1985, RSLP.

82. Ibid.

83. In this sense, it is worth considering whether Pierson played an influential role in fostering the whole debacle, but his role is still unclear.

84. Ruth Landes to Mariza Côrrea, 6 April 1986, RSLP. The correspondence inserted a handwritten note of "discovered" rather than "written about."

85. To be fair, Herskovits was also Jewish and it obviously had little negative effect on his Brazilian reputation. Cole's biography of Landes argues that many of the complications faced by Landes came about because she was a female in the male-dominated field of anthropology. In addition, her relationship with Edison Carneiro unfairly gave her a reputation as unprofessional. See Cole, *Ruth Landes.*

86. Mariza Corrêa points out that Ramos began publishing negative reviews of her work even before her book was published and that Landes reports seeing a letter written by both Ramos and Herskovits denouncing her work. Corrêa, *Antropólogas,* 168.

87. Livio Sansone posits that Frazier was relatively forgotten in Brazil because of a power struggle; Herskovits dominated in part because he fit well with the focus of the Estado Novo, and he remains held in almost "reverential" regard. See Sansone, "Campo," 8.

88. Carneiro was the exception to this, at least in the case of Landes, since he translated and disseminated her work. The denigration of Landes by Ramos was apparently a source of immense resentment and caused considerable tension in the friendship between Ramos and Carneiro. The latter, however, said nothing about it until after Ramos's death. See Carneiro, "'Falseta.'"

89. Cited in Corrêa, *Antropólogas,* 246 (n. 35). She reports further that neither responded to comments about Herskovits made in the other's letters. The letter from Pierson was dated 11 September 1940.

90. Seminário de Antropologia, *Ensino da antropologia,* 3.

91. Pierson also noted that Candomblés, rather than contemporary race relations, formed the base of the studies produced by the Afro-Brazilian congresses.

92. Pierson, *Negroes in Brazil,* x.

Chapter 5

1. For political histories of Brazil in this period, see Skidmore, *Politics in Brazil.* For Bahian politics during this time, see Paulo Silva, "Força da tradição"; Silva, *Ancoras;* and Nelson Sampaio, "Meio século."

2. Robock, *Brazil's Developing Northeast,* 7.

3. Salvador's population in 1900 was 205,813; its average annual rate of growth remained low until after 1940. More than 50% of the city's rapid demographic growth from 1940 to 1960 came from internal migration from the countryside. See Souza, "Urbanização," 106; and Faria, "Divisão inter-regional do trabalho."

4. This effort of course had precedents. The Centro de Estudos Bahianos (Center for Bahian Studies) was formed in 1941, for example, with a mission "to promote studies concerning the cultural and material development of Bahia, [and] to produce work elucidating the Bahian past." With José Valladares as a founding member, the center drew explicit links between the study of history and the shaping of policy. See Amorim, *Bahia nos gabinetes.*

5. Machado, "Prefácio," xv–xvi.

6. Congresso de História da Bahia, *Anais do Primeiro Congresso*; Congresso de História da Bahia, *Anais do Segundo Congresso*.

7. Bahia, *Primeiro Salão Bahiano*, 53. This claim of primacy comes from Valladares himself; Sansi-Roca identifies one earlier modern exhibition in 1944 for the release of Jorge Amado's tourist guide. Sansi-Roca, *Fetishes*, 127. On the modernist movement in Bahia's intellectual circles, and particularly in its university, see Risério, *Avant-garde*.

8. Cited in Sansi-Roca, *Fetishes*, 134. The emphasis here may have been shaped by its publication in a Bahian newspaper.

9. Pinho boasted connections with some of the most prominent politicians in Bahia's history. As Paulo Silva insightfully points out, Pinho's "historiographic themes were confused with the history of his own family" (*Ancoras*, 118).

10. Amado, *Bahia de Todos os Santos*; Valladares, *Bêabá da Bahia*; Valladares, *Torço da bahiana. O torço da bahiana* (The turban of the Baiana) was published with translations in German and English alongside the Portuguese text and sketches by Carybé. An official tourist guide of the same era from Bahia's municipal government shows a very interesting and direct juxtaposition of tradition and modernity in the narrative. See Bahia, *Bahia de ontem e hoje*.

11. Mielche, *From Santos to Bahia*, 313. The chapter is titled "Você ja fué [*sic*] a Bahia?" (Have you ever been to Bahia?), which came from the title of a song by the Bahian sambista Dorival Caymmi.

12. Antônio Sérgio Guimarães provides the most important exception to this trend, raising the question of precisely why the studies of Bahia and the South (São Paulo and Rio de Janeiro) came to such divergent conclusions on race. His study of the intellectual underpinnings of the studies is essential, but his focus does not include the particularly Bahian dynamics of the process. See Guimarães, "Baianos e paulistas." Marcos Chor Maio notes that Bahia was early seen as an exceptional site of race relations, but, since his main focus is the larger UNESCO project, he does not engage in how or why this view of Bahian exceptionalism developed. Maio, "UNESCO." Edward Telles perceptively argues that varying intellectual frameworks accounted for much of the difference in regional findings. See Telles, *Race in Another America*, 6–8.

13. Valladares, "Nota."

14. Wagley, Azevedo, and Pinto, "Pesquisa."

15. Maio, "História," 79. Gizella Valladares wrote to Pierson in September 1948.

16. Gizella Valladares (née Roth) was a U.S. citizen and met José Valladares when he was conducting museum research at the Brooklyn Museum of Art.

17. Maio, "História," 79.

18. His most important book remains *Educação não é privilégio*. His work is critically assessed most effectively in Monarcha, *Anísio Teixeira*; and Smolka and Menezes, *Anísio Teixeira*.

19. Previous reforms were undertaken in 1889 (Vitorino), 1889–95 (Dias), 1924–29 (Teixeira), and 1938–42 (Alves).

20. Anísio Teixeira, *Educação, saúde e assistência*.

21. Ibid.

22. Anísio Teixeira, "Centro Educacional," 79, 84.

23. Anísio Teixeira to Archimedes Pereira Guimarães, 20 December 1928, in Archimedes Guimarães, *Dois sertanejos*, 43.

24. Teixeira, *Educação e cultura*, 6.

25. Bastide, "Carta aberta," 525.

26. Literacy rates did eventually improve over the 1950s, but these gains seem to be largely due to a federal program, initiated by the federal minister of education (and native Bahian) Clemente Mariani. The program funded the building of small basic schools across rural areas of Bahia, providing infrastructure rather than socialization. This period still needs further research to weigh the impact of Teixeira's own programs.

27. Wagley, Azevedo, and Pinto, "Pesquisa," 26.

28. Ibid., 26–27.

29. Ibid., 31.

30. Azevedo, "Thales de Azevedo," 161.

31. Wagley assessed the methodology of the community study in Wagley and Azevedo, "Sôbre métodos de campo."

32. Charles Wagley to Alfred Métraux, 18 June 1950, Race Questions and Protection of Minorities, part 1, 30/VI/50, UNESCO Archives, Paris.

33. Marcos Chor Maio ably traces the origins and path of the studies. See Maio, "História"; and Maio, "Projeto UNESCO." For insightful critiques of the legacies of UNESCO in Brazil, see esp. Antônio Sérgio Guimarães, "Cor, classes e status"; and Hasenbalg, "Entre o mito e os fatos."

34. For important exceptions, see Antônio Sérgio Guimarães, "Baianos e paulistas"; Hasenbalg, "Entre o mito e os fatos"; and Maio, "UNESCO."

35. I follow here especially Antônio Sérgio Guimarães, who points out that the differences in interpretations that arose from scholars studying São Paulo and Bahia are perhaps due as much to the scholars themselves as to any observable reality. See Guimarães, "Baianos e paulistas," 89. Here, then, the ideas of Bahian race relations have a possible relation to reality (which I do not examine here), but I use them as especially revealing of the constructions of Bahia itself.

36. Métraux, "UNESCO," 384. For an assessment of the UNESCO effort as a whole, see Brattain, "Race."

37. Métraux, "UNESCO," 388.

38. Ibid., 389.

39. Maio notes Ramos's role in appointing Frazier; see Maio, "UNESCO," 123.

40. "Comments on Memorandum Regarding Research on Race Relations in Brazil," 1 August 1950, Race Questions and Protection of Minorities, part 2 up to 31/VII/50, UNESCO Archives, Paris.

41. Charles Wagley to Ruy Coelho, 9 September 1950, Race Questions and Protection of Minorities, part 2 up to 31/VII/50, UNESCO Archives, Paris. Wagley noted that it was in part a racial conference in Rio de Janeiro that spurred the idea of difference.

42. Alfred Métraux to Kenneth L. Little, 21 January 1952, Statement on Race, part 4 from 1/I/1952 to 31/II/1953, UNESCO Archives, Paris.

43. Brazil as a whole is covered in an early series of reports published in the 1952 *UNESCO Courier*, vol. 5, no. 8–9. A sampling of the Bahian works may be found in Wagley, *Race and Class*.

44. Because of the difference between the ethnographic detail and the conclusions opinions have diverged about how much the studies discredited the idea of racial democracy. Antônio Sérgio Guimarães sums it up gracefully when he concludes that the UNESCO researchers were unanimous in finding racial prejudice in Brazil (the position taken by Maio), and that the studies of the North and Northeast were hesitant to interpret the discrimination they witnessed (the position taken by Hasenbalg in "Entre o mito e os fatos"). Guimarães, "Baianos e paulistas," 77.

45. Bahia in fact had a national reputation for its extreme forms of *coronelismo*, or bossism, especially in the early twentieth century. See, e.g., the portrait in Pang, *Bahia*.

46. Hutchinson, *Village and Plantation Life*. The book further develops ideas first put forth in the *UNESCO Courier* in 1952, as well as in the collection *Race and Class in Rural Brazil*, published in that same year, and cited below.

47. Ibid., 57. Hutchinson neglects to consider that the labor situation itself is largely responsible for these conditions.

48. Hutchinson, "Race Relations," 32.

49. Ibid., 27, 45.

50. Ibid., 41.

51. Ibid., 45–46.

52. Hutchinson, *Village and Plantation Life*, 183. Here he is remarking on the differences since his original fieldwork in 1950 and 1951 and a return visit in 1956.

53. Harris, "Race Relations," 114–18. His conclusions are found on 126–27. This was later expanded on in Harris, *Town and Country*.

54. Wagley, "From Caste to Class," 152. Wagley notes repeatedly, however, that "a mild form of race prejudice exists on all levels of society in rural Brazil" (149).

55. Thales de Azevedo, "Bahia," 14–15. His ambivalence comes out even more clearly in his larger publication for the UNESCO series, where he concluded: "It is only partially true that in Bahia there is no prejudice and discrimination based on color." Thales de Azevedo, *Elites de cor*, 163. Antônio Sérgio Guimarães has argued that Azevedo was the first Brazilian to truly think of social inequalities in terms of color inequalities, beginning after this work in the mid-1950s; see Guimarães, "Cor, classes e status," 155. See also Guimarães, "*Elites de cor*." See also the revealing interview conducted by Marcos Chor Maio: Azevedo, "Thales de Azevedo"; and the tributes in *Universitas*, no. 6/7 (1970).

56. Thales de Azevedo, *Elites de cor*, 49; emphasis added.

57. Thales de Azevedo, "Comportamento verbal," 150.

58. Thales de Azevedo, *Povoamento*. Maio highlights this work as an early outline of Azevedo's thoughts on race. Maio, "História," 239.

59. Maio, "História," 239.

60. Bastide, "Race Relations," 9.

61. Bastide and Fernandes, *Relações raciais*. See also Fernandes, *Integração*.

62. It is worth noting that for all of its revisionism and social critique, this stance ultimately also endorsed the regional status quo. São Paulo was industrial, and this was the key to its present problems and its future solutions. This makes an interesting comparison to Bahia, where the status quo was also endorsed, but in a completely opposite framework: Bahia was not industrial, and this was the secret to its present and future harmony.

63. Cited in Thales de Azevedo, "Comportamento verbal," 141.

64. Wagley, "From Caste to Class," 155.

65. Wagley had an activist vision of modernization furthered by the work of social scientists, and it may have been this shared understanding that enabled him to collaborate with Anísio Teixeira. See, e.g., Wagley's preface to his most famous community study, *Amazon Town*.

66. Thales de Azevedo, *Problemas sociais*, 14, 11.

Conclusion

1. Valladares, *Dominicais*, 189–92.

2. Valladares, "Bahia and Its Museum," 454.

3. For example, life conditions remained difficult into the 1980s, when infant mortality for the state was eighty-three per one thousand births. Bahia has certainly made important advances, and recently (2005) such rates have fallen to thirty-six. Similarly, life expectancy at birth has risen dramatically, from sixty in 1980, to seventy-one in 2005. Figures for functional illiteracy for those age fifteen and over are less encouraging: 54% of Bahians were functionally illiterate in 1995 and this has declined only to 37%. These statistics and others may be downloaded from Bahia's economic research institute, the Superintendência de Estudos Eco-nômicos e Sociais (SEI). See SEI, "Bahia em números."

4. See chap. 3. The common assumption that Bahian tourism began much later has resulted in scholarship that largely neglects these critical roots in the 1940s and especially in the 1950s.

5. Empresa de Turismo da Bahia, *Bahiatursa*, 22.

6. This was the first tourism initiative to address the state as a whole. Ibid., 70.

7. Bahia, Fundação Comissão de Planejamento Econômico, *Cidade do Salvador*.

8. Empresa de Turismo da Bahia, *Bahiatursa*, 29. Official publications credit Magalhães with increasing the number of hotel rooms from four hundred to twenty-four hundred during his first term; given the excessively laudatory tone of the source, this may be an exaggeration. Mello and Batalha, *Cartilha histórica*, 131.

9. Empresa de Turismo da Bahia, *Bahiatursa*.

10. The revitalization project received encouragement in 1967 from Michael Parent, a UNESCO consultant charged with evaluating tourism's potential in Brazil. Parent had also helped conceive of the Museu Afro-Brasileiro in 1967 (Oliveira, "Pesquisas," 134). Thus the idea of the museum for Afro-Brazilian culture and the Pelourinho reforms both were impelled by a tourism initiative imagined by this newest UNESCO representative to arrive in Bahia, one surely familiar with the UNESCO studies of race in Bahia

published less than a decade earlier. With no outside funding forthcoming, however, Bahia began the effort with state funds in the late 1960s. For these early efforts, and Parent's role, see esp. Bahia, Secretaria de Educação e Cultura do Estado da Bahia, *Levantamento*, 8.

11. In contrast to the large budget for site renovations, the budget for relocation efforts was only five hundred thousand dollars. Bahia, Fundação Cultural do Estado da Bahia, *Pelourinho*, 44. For the violence used in the removal process, see Butler, "Afterword," 170. For resistance to such efforts, see Perry, "Roots." The racial dynamic of Pelourinho is surveyed in Osmundo Pinho, "Espaço." The state's own glossy portrayal of the Pelourinho revitalization can be found in Bahia, Fundação Cultural do Estado da Bahia, *Pelourinho*. Caetano Veloso, interviewed in the same compilation, notes that Magalhães was working at this stage with a Pelourinho already revitalized by the activities of Olodum, the black organization that gathered crowds weekly for public music performances in the area (82–108). The president of Olodum insists that the organization applied ongoing pressure for the project's completion. Rodrigues, "Olodum," 49.

12. Clearly, many in Bahia have benefited from this process as well, but the opportunities for most remain in the low-paying service sector, with little opportunity for advancement. Recent figures on Bahia's tourism industry are hard to come by, but for a survey of its economic and cultural impact on the state, see the 2001 issue of *Bahia: Analise e Dados*, titled "Cultura, turismo e entretenimento."

13. Jocélio Telles dos Santos, "Mixed Race Nation." Patricia Pinho, "African-American Roots Tourism," 82.

14. Carneiro originally made this suggestion in a paper given at the first Brazilian Anthropology Association meeting. His charges may have circulated little at first, as it appears that the essay was published only in 1964 in a collected work of his early writings. See Carneiro, "Estudos brasileiros."

15. In 1950 Carneiro collaborated with Nascimento to organize another type of congress in Rio de Janeiro, the First Black Brazilian Congress. Relations between the two men later soured, and Nascimento ultimately dismissed Carneiro's work as picturesque and irrelevant (Nascimento, *Negro*, 48). Notably, Nascimento would claim a central role for Africa in his vision of Brazil's black movement. See, e.g., Nascimento, *Brazil*.

16. Carneiro, "Estudos brasileiros," 103; original emphasis. The U.S. anthropologists Sidney Mintz and Richard Price in 1990 deplored what they viewed as a disturbing "desire to polarize Afro-Americanist scholarship into a flatly 'for' or 'against' position in regard to African cultural retentions." Mintz and Price, *Birth of African-American Culture*, viii. For this same debate in Latin America, see Yelvington, "Anthropology." Of his own role in presenting at the first congress and organizing the second Carneiro remains somewhat vague, though he writes: "Even I couldn't escape the current in these early times, but I believe I destroyed the esoteric nature of black studies with my *Candomblés da Bahia*, written [in 1948] with the declared intention of serving the comprehension and fraternity among Brazilians." Carneiro, "Estudos brasileiros" 108.

17. Dzidzienyo, "Africa-Brazil."

18. Paulina Alberto traces Brazil's foreign policy toward Africa with particular atten-

tion to how those in Bahia shaped the process with their own vision of African connections. Alberto, "Para Africano Ver."

19. These efforts, however, could sometimes seem strangely distant from the interests of the black community. See, e.g., Oliveira, "Pesquisas," where the first director of the Centro de Estudos Afro-Orientais expresses frustration with the Candomblé leaders who attended African-language courses, apparently violating the "true" purposes of the program and causing him to cancel the courses.

20. The museum was originally envisioned first in the late 1960s. The initiative was not without controversy as the growing black consciousness movement, gaining momentum in Bahia through the 1970s, pushed to rename the institution the "Museu do Negro." The black movement would lose this struggle, and the museum developed a focus that privileged African roots rather than the contemporary trajectory of blacks in Bahia. For the controversy, see ibid; and Jocélio Telles dos Santos, *Poder da cultura*.

21. For some of the dynamics of Afro-Bahian carnival and its "reafricanization," see Risério, *Carnaval Ijexá*; Dunn, "Afro-Bahian Carnival"; and Rodrigues, "Olodum."

22. Dunn, *Brutality Garden*.

23. The president of Olodum in the 1990s described the policy of open membership as a response to the errors of Ilê Aiyê, of which he was formerly a member. Rodrigues, "Olodum," 47–48.

24. Olodum played with Paul Simon for the album *Rhythm of the Saints* in 1990 and appeared in the Michael Jackson video "They Don't Care about Us" in 1995.

25. For the Frente Negra in Bahia, see Bacelar, *Hierarquia*. For Bahia's later black movement, see esp. Agier, "Racism"; Gonzalez, "Unified Black Movement"; Jônatas da Silva, "História"; and Covin, "Role of Culture."

26. Brooke, "Bahia Journal." The tension between black cultural and political movements in Salvador has long been noted. Frustrated with the charge that carnival organizations were not political enough, the leader of Ilê Aiyê retorted in the early 1980s that the Movimento Negro Unificado in Bahia held endless meetings, talked constantly in obtuse academic language, and accomplished nothing. In contrast, he believed, the *blocos afro* had fundamentally changed not just the week-long celebration of carnival, but also black identity through the rest of the year. Cited in Risério, *Carnaval Ijexá*, 85.

27. In mayoral elections for 2008 four black candidates announced their candidacy, but they ended up running as vice-mayors with white candidates at the head. One of these, Edvaldo Brito, had briefly served earlier as mayor of Salvador, but he was appointed, not elected.

28. Brooke, "Bahia Journal."

29. Ibid.

30. Dzidzienyo, "Africa-Brazil," 132.

31. Sansone, *Blackness*.

32. These are the most recent figures available, from 2004. Petrochemicals and derivatives alone account for 37% of state exports. Bahia, Secretaria da Indústria, "Petrochemical Industry."

33. This is calculated from a total state population of 13,815,334 in 2005. Rates of

poverty declined from 51% to 39% from 1980 to 2003 in Brazil, whereas Bahia's rates declined from 72% to 62% in the same period. Black rates of poverty have instead stayed relatively static: in Bahia blacks made up 81% of the poor in 1980 and 83% in 2003 (the national level of poverty among blacks also remained static, at 59%). Barbosa, Barbosa, and Barbosa, "Pobreza," 771–72.

34. Ferreira, Leite, and Litchfield, "Rise and Fall."

35. And in fact, as in the case of the rising cost of Baiana dress, poverty may now prevent people from looking "traditional."

36. For the foundational work of how "traditions" can be altered to fit present needs, see Hobsbawm and Ranger, *Invention of Tradition*.

37. Thales de Azevedo, "Thales de Azevedo."

38. An idea of a pure, untarnished past in need of preservation may have come in part from colonial discourse in West Africa as Matory has proposed, but it may also have been encouraged and privileged by Bahians themselves. Matory, *Black Atlantic Religion*.

39. As Christopher Dunn perceptively notes, this idea of Bahia as representative of Brazilian traditions coexists uneasily with the conception of Bahia as an exceptional preserve of Afro-Brazilian culture. See his insightful comparison between Salvador and New Orleans, in Dunn, "Black Rome and the Chocolate City."

BIBLIOGRAPHY

Archives

Brooklyn, N.Y.
  Brooklyn Museum of Art Archive
Campinas, Brazil
  Arquivo Edgard Leuenroth, Universidade Estadual de Campinas
    Donald Pierson Papers
Evanston, Ill.
  Northwestern University Archives
    Melville J. Herskovits Papers
New York, N.Y.
  Schomburg Center for Research in Black Culture
    Melville and Frances Herskovits Collection
Rio de Janeiro, Brazil
  Arquivo do Museu Nacional
  Biblioteca Nacional
  Centro de Pesquisa e Documentação de História Contemporânea
      do Brasil, Fundação Getúlio Vargas
    Anísio Teixeira Papers

Instituto do Patrimônio Histórico e Artístico Nacional, Arquivo e
  Biblioteca Noronha Santos
Museu de Folclore Edison Carneiro, Biblioteca e Arquivo Amadeu Amaral
Salvador da Bahia, Brazil
  Arquivo Público do Estado da Bahia
  Biblioteca Pública do Estado da Bahia
  Instituto Geográfico e Histórico da Bahia
  Museu de Arte da Bahia
Sleepy Hollow, N.Y.
  Rockefeller Archive Center
Paris, France
  UNESCO Archive
Washington, D.C.
  Library of Congress
  National Anthropological Archives, Smithsonian Institution
    Ruth Schlossberg Landes Papers
  Oliveira Lima Library, Catholic University of America

Books, Articles, and Dissertations

Ackerknecht, Erwin H. *Rudolf Virchow: Doctor, Statesman, Anthropologist*. Madison: University of Wisconsin Press, 1953.

Agier, Michel. "Racism, Culture, and Black Identity in Brazil." *Bulletin of Latin American Research* 14, no. 3 (1995): 245–64.

Alberto, Paulina Laura. "Para Africano Ver: African-Bahian Exchanges in the Reinvention of Brazil's Racial Democracy, 1961–63." *Luso-Brazilian Review* 45, no. 1 (2008): 78–117.

———. "Terms of Inclusion: Black Activism and the Cultural Conditions for Citizenship in a Multi-racial Brazil, 1920–1980." Ph.D. diss., University of Pennsylvania, 2005.

Albuquerque, Wlamyra Ribeiro de. *Algazarra nas ruas: Comemorações da independência na Bahia, 1889–1923*. Campinas: Editora de Unicamp, 1999.

———. "Esperanças de Boaventuras: Construções da Africa e africanismos na Bahia (1887–1910)." *Estudos Afro-Asiáticos* 24 (2002): 214–46.

———. "Santos, deuses e heróis nas ruas da Bahia: Identidade cultural na Primeira República." *Afro-Asia* 18 (1996): 103–24.

Amado, Jorge. *Bahia de Todos os Santos: Guia das ruas e dos mistérios da cidade do Salvador*. São Paulo: Martins, 1945.

———. "Elogio de um Chefe de Seita." In *O negro no Brasil: Trabalhos apresentados ao 2. Congresso Afro-Brasileiro*, edited by Congresso Afro-Brasileiro (Bahia), 325–28. Rio de Janeiro: Civilização Brasileira, 1940.

Amorim, Deolindo. *A Bahia nos gabinetes ministeriais da monarquia*. Salvador: Centro de Estudos Bahianos, 1959.

Andrade, Geraldo de. "Nota anthropológica sobre os mulatos pernambucanos." In *Estudos afro-brasileiros*, edited by Congresso Afro-Brasileiro (Recife), 261–63. Rio de Janeiro: Ariel, 1935.

Andrews, George Reid. *Afro-Latin America, 1800–2000*. Oxford: Oxford University Press, 2004.

———. *Blacks and Whites in São Paulo, Brazil, 1888–1988*. Madison: University of Wisconsin Press, 1991.

———. "Brazilian Racial Democracy, 1900–90: An American Counterpoint." *Journal of Contemporary History* 31, no. 3 (1996): 483–507.

Appelbaum, Nancy P., Anne S. Macpherson, and Karin Alejandra Rosenblatt, eds. *Race and Nation in Modern Latin America*. Chapel Hill: University of North Carolina Press, 2003.

Araújo, Ricardo Benzaquen de. *Guerra e paz: "Casa-grande e senzala" e a obra de Gilberto Freyre nos anos 30*. Rio de Janeiro: Editora 34, 1994.

Azevedo, Fernando de. *Brazilian Culture: An Introduction to the Study of Culture in Brazil*. Translated by William Rex Crawford. New York: MacMillan, 1950.

Azevedo, Thales de. "Bahia: The Negro Metropolis." *UNESCO Courier* 5, no. 8–9 (1952): 14–15.

———. *As ciências sociais na Bahia*. 2nd rev. ed. Salvador: Fundação Cultural do Estado da Bahia, 1984.

———. "Comportamento verbal e efetivo para com os pretos." In *Ensaios de antropologia social*, edited by Thales de Azevedo, 149–56. Salvador: Publicações da Universidade da Bahia, 1959.

———. *As elites de cor numa cidade brasileira: Um estudo de ascenção social e classes sociais e grupos de prestígio*. Salvador: Empresa Gráfica da Bahia, 1996.

———. *O povoamento da cidade de Salvador*. Salvador: Beneditina, 1949.

———. *Problemas sociais da exploração do petróleo na Bahia*. Salvador: Imprensa Oficial da Bahia, 1959.

———. "Thales de Azevedo: Desaparece o último dos pioneiros dos antropológicos brasileiros de formação médica." *Manguinhos* 3, no. 1 (1996): 133–71.

Bacelar, Jeferson. *A hierarquia das raças: Negros e brancos em Salvador*. Rio de Janeiro: Pallas, 2001.

Bahia. *Bahia de ontem e de hoje*. Salvador: Diretoria de Arquivo, Divulgação e Estatística da Prefeitura do Salvador, 1953.

———. *Educação e saúde na Bahia na Interventoria Landulfo Alves, abril 1938–junho 1939*. Salvador: Bahia Gráfica, 1939.

———. *Mensagem apresentada à Assembléia Geral Legislativa*. Bahia: Imprensa Oficial do Estado, 1897.

———. "A nossa capa." *Bahia: Tradicional e Moderna* 1, no. 1 (1939).

———. *Primeiro Salão Bahiano de Belas-Artes: Catálogo*. Salvador: Secretaria de Educação e Saúde, 1949.

———. *Regulamento: Arquivo Público e do Museu Histórico do Estado da Bahia*. Salvador: Imprensa Oficial, 1922.

Bahia, Archivo Público. "Untitled." *Annaes do Archivo Público e Museu do Estado da Bahia* 10 (1923): 3–4.

Bahia, Fundação Comissão de Planejamento Econômico. *Cidade do Salvador: Informações sócio-econômicas.* Salvador, 1966.

Bahia, Fundação Cultural do Estado da Bahia. *Pelourinho, centro histórico do Salvador-Bahia: A grandeza restaurada.* 3rd ed. Salvador: Fundação Cultural do Estado da Bahia, 1995.

Bahia, Secretaria da Indústria, Comércio e Mineração. "Petrochemical Industry." <http://www.bahiaexport.com.br/ing/madein/petroquimica.asp>. 14 May 2009.

Bahia, Secretaria de Educação e Cultura. *Museu de Arte da Bahia: Guia dos visitantes.* Salvador: Imprensa Oficial da Bahia, 1970.

Bahia, Secretaria de Educação e Cultura do Estado da Bahia. *Levantamento sócio-econômico do Pelourinho.* Salvador: Fundação do Patrimônio Artístico e Cultural da Bahia, 1969.

Bahia, Secretaria do Interior e Justiça do Estado. *Relatorio, 1935.* Bahia: Imprensa Oficial do Estado, 1936.

———. *Relatorio, 1936.* Bahia: Companhia Editora e Graphica da Bahia, 1937.

Baker, Lee D. *From Savage to Negro: Anthropology and the Construction of Race, 1896–1954.* Berkeley: University of California Press, 1998.

Barbosa, César, Elisiana Rodrigues Oliveira Barbosa, and Cláudio Barbosa. "Pobreza, diferenciais raciais e educação: Um estudo para as grandes regiões brasileiras." *Bahia Análise & Dados* 17, no. 1 (2007): 769–75.

Barickman, B. J. *A Bahian Counterpoint: Sugar, Tobacco, Cassava, and Slavery in the Recôncavo, 1780–1860.* Stanford, Calif.: Stanford University Press, 1998.

Barros, Luitgarde Oliveira Cavalcanti. *Arthur Ramos e as dinâmicas sociais de seu tempo.* Maceió: EDUFAL, 2000.

Bastianelli, Luciana, ed. *Gazeta médica da Bahia, 1866–1934/1966–1976.* Salvador: Contexto, 2002.

Bastide, Roger. "Carta aberta a Guerreiro Ramos." *Anhembi* 12, no. 36 (1953): 521–28.

———. "The Present Status of Afro-American Research in Latin America." *Daedalus* 103, no. 2 (1974): 111–24.

———. "Race Relations in Brazil: São Paulo." *UNESCO Courier* 5, no. 8–9 (1952): 9.

Bastide, Roger, and Florestan Fernandes. *Relações raciais entre negros e brancos em São Paulo.* São Paulo: Anhembi, 1955.

Bennett, Tony. *The Birth of the Museum: History, Theory, Politics.* London: Routledge, 1995.

Bittencourt, Dario de. "A liberdade religiosa no Brasil: A macumba e o batúque em face da lei." In *O negro no Brasil: Trabalhos apresentados ao 2. Congresso Afro-Brasileiro*, edited by Congresso Afro-Brasileiro (Bahia), 169–99. Rio de Janeiro: Civilização Brasileira, 1940.

Blake, Stanley S. "The Medicalization of Nordestinos: Public Health and Regional Identity in Northeastern Brazil, 1889–1930." *Americas* 60, no. 2 (2003): 217–48.

Boaventura, Edivaldo Machado. "Isaías Alves de Almeida." In *Dicionário de edu-*

cadores no Brasil: Da colônia aos dias atuais, edited by Maria de Lourdes de Albuquerque Fávero and Jade de Medeiros Britto, 256–63. Rio de Janeiro: Editora UFRJ, 1990.

Bonfim, Martiniano do. "Os ministros de Xangô." In O negro no Brasil: Trabalhos apresentados ao 2. Congresso Afro-Brasileiro, edited by Congresso Afro-Brasileiro (Bahia), 233–38. Rio de Janeiro: Civilização Brasileira, 1940.

Borges, Dain. The Family in Bahia, Brazil, 1870–1945. Stanford, Calif.: Stanford University Press, 1992.

———. "The Recognition of Afro-Brazilian Symbols and Ideas, 1890–1940." Luso-Brazilian Review 32, no. 2 (1995): 59–78.

Braga, Júlio. Na gamela do feitiço: Repressão e resistência nos candomblés da Bahia. Salvador: EDUFBA/CEAO, 1995.

Brattain, Michelle. "Race, Racism, and Anti-racism: UNESCO and the Politics of Presenting Science to the Postwar Public." American Historical Review 112, no. 5 (2007): 1386–414.

Brazil, Directoria Geral de Estatística. Recenseamento da população do Império do Brazil a que se procedeu no dia 10 de agosto de 1872. Rio de Janeiro, 1873–76.

Brinton, Daniel G. "The Nomenclature and Teaching of Anthropology." American Anthropologist 5, no. 3 (1892): 263–72.

Brito, Jailton Lima. "A abolição na Bahia: Uma história política, 1870–1888." M.A. thesis, Universidade Federal da Bahia, 1996.

Bronfman, Alejandra. Measures of Equality: Social Science, Citizenship, and Race in Cuba, 1902–1940. Chapel Hill: University of North Carolina, 2004.

Brooke, James. "Bahia Journal; If It's 'Black Brazil,' Why Is the Elite So White?" New York Times, 24 September 1991.

Burke, Peter, and Maria Lúcia Pallares-Burke. Gilberto Freyre: Social Theory in the Tropics. Oxford: Peter Lang, 2008.

Burns, E. Bradford. "Bibliographical Essay: Manuel Querino's Interpretation of the African Contribution to Brazil." Journal of Negro History 59, no. 1 (1974): 78–86.

Butler, Kim. "Africa in the Reinvention of Nineteenth-Century Afro-Bahian Identity." In Rethinking the African Diaspora: The Making of a Black Atlantic World in the Bight of Benin and Brazil, edited by Kristin Mann and Edna G. Bay, 135–54. London: F. Cass, 2001.

———. "Afterword: Ginga Baiana—The Politics of Race, Class, Culture, and Power in Salvador, Bahia." In Afro-Brazilian Culture and Politics: Bahia 1790s to 1990s, edited by Hendrik Kraay, 158–76. London: M. E. Sharpe, 1998.

———. Freedoms Given, Freedoms Won: Afro-Brazilians in Post-abolition São Paulo and Salvador. New Brunswick, N.J.: Rutgers University Press, 1998.

Campos, Maria José. Arthur Ramos, luz e sombra na antropologia brasileira: Uma versão da democracia racial no Brasil nas décadas de 1930 e 1940. Rio de Janeiro: Edições Biblioteca Nacional, 2004.

Capone, Stefania. A busca da Africa no candomblé: Tradição e poder no Brasil. Rio de Janeiro: Contra Capa, 2004.

Carneiro, Edison. "Aninha." In *Ladinos e crioulos*, edited by Edison Carneiro, 207–8. Rio de Janeiro: Civilização Brasileira, 1964.

———. "Candomblés da Bahia." *Publicações do Museu do Estado*, no. 8. Edited by José Valladares. Salvador: Secretaria de Educação e Saúde, 1948.

———. *Cartas de Edison Carneiro a Artur Ramos, de 4 de janeiro de 1936 a 6 de dezembro de 1938*. Edited and with notes by Waldir Freitas Oliveira and Vivaldo da Costa Lima. São Paulo: Corrupio, 1987.

———. "O Congresso Afro-Brasileiro da Bahia." In *Ladinos e crioulos*, edited by Edison Carneiro. Rio de Janeiro: Civilização Brasileira, 1964.

———. "Os estudos brasileiros do negro." In *Ladinos e crioulos*, edited by Edison Carneiro. Rio de Janeiro: Civilização Brasileira, 1964.

———. "Uma 'falseta' de Artur Ramos." In *Ladinos e crioulos*, edited by Edison Carneiro, 223–27. Rio de Janeiro: Civilização Brasileira, 1964.

———. "Homenagem a Nina Rodrigues." In *O negro no Brasil: Trabalhos apresentados ao 2. Congresso Afro-Brasileiro*, edited by Congresso Afro-Brasileiro (Bahia), 331–34. Rio de Janeiro: Civilização Brasileira, 1940.

———. *Religões negras e negros bantos*. 2nd ed. Rio de Janeiro: Civilização Brasileira, 1981.

———. "Uma revisão na ethnographia religiosa afro-brasileira." In *O negro no Brasil: Trabalhos apresentados ao 2. Congresso Afro-Brasileiro*, edited by Congresso Afro-Brasileiro (Bahia), 61–70. Rio de Janeiro: Civilização Brasileira, 1940.

———. "Situação do negro no Brasil." In *Estudos afro-brasileiros*, edited by Congresso Afro-Brasileiro (Recife), 237–41. Rio de Janeiro: Ariel, 1935.

———. "The Structure of African Cults in Bahia." *Journal of American Folklore* 53, no. 210 (1940): 271–78.

———. "Xangô." In *Novos estudos afro-brasileiros*, edited by Congresso Afro-Brasileiro (Recife), 141–47. Rio de Janeiro: Civilização Brasileira, 1937.

Carneiro, Edison, and Aydano do Couto Ferraz. "Congresso Afro-Brasileiro da Bahia." In *O negro no Brasil: Trabalhos apresentados ao 2. Congresso Afro-Brasileiro*, edited by Congresso Afro-Brasileiro (Bahia), 7–11. Rio de Janeiro: Civilização Brasileira, 1940.

Carneiro, Edison, Martiniano do Bomfim, Aydano do Couto Ferraz, Azevedo Marques, and Reginaldo Guimarães. "Palavras inaugurais do Congresso Afro-Brasileiro da Bahia." In *O negro no Brasil: Trabalhos apresentados ao 2. Congresso Afro-Brasileiro*, edited by Congresso Afro-Brasileiro (Bahia), 15–16. Rio de Janeiro: Civilização Brasileira, 1940.

Carybé. *As sete portas da Bahia*. São Paulo: Martins, 1962.

———. *"Temas de Candomblé: 27 desenhos de Carybé."* In *Coleção Recôncavo*, edited with an introduction by Carybé. Salvador: Progresso, 1955.

Castro Faria, Luiz de. *As exposições de antropologia e arqueologia do Museu Nacional*. Publicações avulsas do Museu Nacional. Rio de Janeiro: Departamento de Imprensa Nacional, 1949.

———. "As origens da reforma sanitária e da modernização conservadora na Bahia durante a Primeira República." *Dados* 41, no. 3 (1998): 593–633.

———. "Power, Ideology, and Public Health in Brazil, 1889–1930." Ph.D. diss., Harvard University, 1987.

Caymmi, Dorival. *Cancioneiro da Bahia*. 4th ed. São Paulo: Martins, 1967.

"Celebration of Virchow's Birthday in Brazil." *Lancet* 158, no. 4085 (1901): 1689.

Chalhoub, Sidney. "The Politics of Disease Control: Yellow Fever and Race in Nineteenth-Century Rio de Janeiro." *Journal of Latin American Studies* 25, no. 3 (1993): 441–63.

Chandler, Billy Jaynes. *The Bandit King: Lampião of Brazil*. College Station: Texas A&M University Press, 1978.

Cole, Sally Cooper. *Ruth Landes: A Life in Anthropology*. Lincoln: University of Nebraska Press, 2003.

Congresso Afro-Brasileiro (Bahia), ed. *O negro no Brasil: Trabalhos apresentados ao 2. Congresso Afro-Brasileiro*. Rio de Janeiro: Civilização Brasileira, 1940.

Congresso Afro-Brasileiro (Recife), ed. *Novos estudos afro-brasileiros* (Recife). Rio de Janeiro: Civilização Brasileira, 1937.

Congresso de História da Bahia. *Anais do Primeiro Congresso de História da Bahia*. 5 vols. Salvador: Instituto Geográfico e Histórico da Bahia, 1949.

———. *Anais do Segundo Congresso de História da Bahia, 1952*. 5 vols. Salvador: Instituto Geográfico e Histórico da Bahia, 1955.

Congresso Nacional de Educação. *Anais do VII Congresso Nacional de Educação promovido pela Associação Brasileira de Educação, Rio de Janeiro, 23 de junho a 7 de julho de 1935*. Rio de Janeiro, 1935.

Coni, Antônio Caldas. *A escola tropicalista baiana: Paterson, Wücherer, Silva Lima*. Bahia: Beneditina, 1952.

Conklin, Alice L. "Civil Society, Science, and Empire in Late Republican France: The Foundation of Paris's Museum of Man." *Osiris* 17 (2002): 255–90.

Cooper, Donald B. "Brazil's Long Fight against Epidemic Disease, 1849–1957, with Special Emphasis on Yellow Fever." *Bulletin of the New York Academy of Medicine* 51 (1975): 672–96.

Corrêa, Mariza. *Antropólogas e antropologia*. Belo Horizonte: Editora UFMG, 2003.

———. *História da antropologia no Brasil (1930–1960), Testemunhos: Emílio Willems, Donald Pierson*. São Paulo: Editora Revista dos Tribunais, 1987.

———. *As ilusões da liberdade: A escola Nina Rodrigues e a antropologia no Brasil*. 2nd rev. ed. Bragança Paulista: Editora da Universidade São Francisco, 2001.

Costa, Emilia Viotti da. *The Brazilian Empire: Myths and Histories*. Chapel Hill: University of North Carolina Press, 2000.

Covin, David. "The Role of Culture in Brazil's Unified Black Movement, Bahia in 1992." *Journal of Black Studies* 27, no. 1 (1996): 39–55.

Cunha, Euclides da. *Rebellion in the Backlands*. Translated by Samuel Putnam. Chicago: University of Chicago Press, 1944.

Cunha, Olívia Maria Gomes da. *Intenção e gesto: Pessoa, cor e a produção cotidiana da (in)diferença no Rio de Janeiro, 1927–1942*. Rio de Janeiro: Arquivo Nacional, 2002.

———. "Sua alma em sua palma: Identificando a 'raça' e inventando a nação." In

Repensando o Estado Novo, edited by Dulce Pandolfi, 257–88. Rio de Janeiro: Editora Fundação Getúlio Vargas, 1999.

Damásio, Virgílio. "Introducção." *Gazeta Médica da Bahia* 1, no. 1 (1866): 1–2.

Dantas, Beatriz Góis. *Vovó Nagô e papai branco: Usos e abusos de África no Brasil.* Rio de Janeiro: Graal, 1988.

Dávila, Jerry. *Diploma of Whiteness: Race and Social Policy in Brazil, 1917–1945.* Durham, N.C.: Duke University Press, 2003.

Dean, Warren. *Rio Claro: A Brazilian Plantation System, 1820–1920.* Stanford, Calif.: Stanford University Press, 1976.

"O decreto de 18 de janeiro de 1890 que reorganiza o serviço sanitário terrestre da república." *Gazeta Médica da Bahia* 21, no. 8 (1890): 341–49.

Du Bois, W. E. B. "Review of *The Myth of the Negro Past* by Melville J. Herskovits." *Annals of the American Academy of Political and Social Science* 222 (1942): 226–27.

Dunn, Christopher. "Afro-Bahian Carnival: A Stage for Protest." *Afro-Hispanic Review* 11, no. 1–3 (1992): 11–20.

———. "Black Rome and the Chocolate City: The Place of Race." *Callaloo* 30, no. 3 (2007): 847–61.

———. *Brutality Garden: Tropicália and the Emergence of a Brazilian Counterculture.* Chapel Hill: University of North Carolina Press, 2001.

Dzidzienyo, Anani. "Africa-Brazil: 'Ex Africa Semper Aliquid Novi'?" In *Black Brazil*, edited by Larry Crook and Randal Johnson, 105–42. Los Angeles: UCLA Latin American Center Publications, 1999.

Edelweiss, Frederico. "Tupís e Guaranís: Estudos de ethnonímia e linguística." *Publicações do Museu do Estado*, no. 7. Edited and with an introduction by José Valladares. Salvador: Secretaria de Educação e Saúde, 1947.

Empresa de Turismo da Bahia. *Bahiatursa, 30 anos, 1968–1998.* Salvador: Empresa de Turismo da Bahia, 1998.

Faria, Vilmar. "Divisão inter-regional do trabalho e pobreza urbana: O caso de Salvador." In *Bahia de todos os pobres*, edited by Guaraci Adeodato A. de Souza and Vilmar Faria, 23–40. Petrópolis: Vozes, 1980.

Fernandes, Florestan. *A integração do negro na sociedade de classes.* São Paulo: Dominus, 1965.

Ferreira, Francisco H. G., Phillippe G. Leite, and Julie A. Litchfield. "The Rise and Fall of Brazilian Inequality, 1981–2004." World Bank Report WPS3867, <http://go.worldbank.org/SCWKYFRTX0>. 15 November 2008.

Ferreira Filho, Alberto Heráclito. *Quem pariu e bateu, que balance! Mundos femininos, maternidade e pobreza: Salvador, 1890–1940.* Salvador: Centro de Estudos Baianos, 2003.

França, Maria José do Espírito Santo. "Candomblé and Community." In *Black Brazil: Culture, Identity, and Social Mobilization*, edited by Larry Crook and Randal Johnson, 53–60. Los Angeles: UCLA Latin American Center Publications, 1999.

Frazier, E. Franklin. "Brazil Has No Race Problem." *Common Sense* 11 (1942): 363–65.

In *African-American Reflections on Brazil's Racial Paradise*, edited by David J.
Hellwig, 121–30. Philadelphia: Temple University Press, 1992.

———. "The Negro Family in Bahia, Brazil." *American Sociological Review* 7, no. 4
(1942): 465–78.

———. *The Negro Family in the United States*. Chicago: University of Chicago Press,
1939.

———. "Rejoinder." *American Sociological Review* 8, no. 4 (1943): 402–4.

———. "Review of *The American Negro* by Melville J. Herskovits." *American Journal of
Sociology* 33, no. 6 (1928): 1010–12.

———. "Review of *Negroes in Brazil* by Donald Pierson." *Annals of the American
Academy of Political and Social Science* 227 (1943): 188–89.

———. "Some Aspects of Race Relations in Brazil." *Phylon* 3 (1942): 287–95.

Freyre, Gilberto. "Deformações de corpo dos negros fugidos." In *Novos estudos afro-
brasileiros*, edited by Congresso Afro-Brasileiro (Recife), 245–50. Rio de Janeiro:
Civilização Brasileira, 1937.

———. *O escravo nos anúncios de jornais brasileiros do século XIX*. São Paulo:
Companhia Editora Nacional; Recife: Instituto Joaquim Nabuco de Pesquisas
Sociais, 1979.

———. *The Masters and the Slaves [Casa-grande e senzala]: A Study in the Development
of Brazilian Civilization*. Translated by Samuel Putnam. 2nd English-language rev.
ed. New York: Knopf, 1966.

———. "Nina Rodrigues recordado por um discípulo." In *Perfil de Euclides e
outros perfis*, edited by Gilberto Freyre, 191–96. Rio de Janeiro: Record, 1987.

———. "O que foi o 1. Congresso Afro-Brasileiro do Recife." In *Novos estudos afro-
brasileiros*, edited by Congresso Afro-Brasileiro (Recife), 348–52. Rio de Janeiro:
Civilização Brasileira, 1937.

Fry, Peter. "Feijoada e *soul food*: Notas sobre a manipulação de símbolos étnicos e na-
cionais." In *Para Inglês Ver*, edited by Peter Fry, 47–53. Rio de Janeiro: Zahar, 1982.

———. "Politics, Nationality, and the Meanings of 'Race' in Brazil." *Daedalus* 129, no.
2 (2000): 83–118.

Fry, Peter, Sérgio Carrara, and Ana Luiza Martins-Costa. "Negros e brancos no
Carnaval da Velha República." In *Escravidão e invenção da liberdade: Estudos sobre
o negro no Brasil*, edited by João José Reis, 232–63. São Paulo: Brasiliense, 1988.

Fundação Museu Carlos Costa Pinto and Pinacoteca do Estado de São Paulo. *O que
é que a Bahia tem: Ourivesaria do Museu Carlos Costa Pinto—Salvador: Exposição
da Pinacoteca do Estado de São Paulo, 3 de junho a 23 de julho de 2006*. São Paulo:
Pinacoteca do Estado de São Paulo, 2006.

Gershenhorn, Jerry. *Melville J. Herskovits and the Racial Politics of Knowledge*. Lincoln:
University of Nebraska Press, 2004.

Goldstein, Donna M. *Laughter out of Place: Race, Class, Violence, and Sexuality in a Rio
Shantytown*. Berkeley: University of California Press, 2003.

Gomes, Tiago de Melo. "Para além da casa da Tia Ciata: Outras experiências no uni-
verso cultural carioca, 1830–1930." *Afro-Asia* 29/30 (2003): 175–98.

Gonçalves, José Reginaldo Santos. *A retórica da perda: Os discursos do patrimônio cultural no Brasil*. Rio de Janeiro: Editora UFRJ-IPHAN, 1996.

Gonzalez, Lelia. "The Unified Black Movement: A New Stage in Black Political Mobilization." In *Race, Class, and Power in Brazil*, edited by Pierre-Michel Fontaine, 120–34. Los Angeles: Center for Afro-American Studies, 1986.

Gould, Stephen Jay. *The Mismeasure of Man*. Rev. ed. New York: W. W. Norton, 1996.

Graden, Dale T. *From Slavery to Freedom in Brazil: Bahia, 1835–1900*. Albuquerque: University of New Mexico Press, 2006.

Graham, Richard, Thomas E. Skidmore, Aline Helg, and Alan Knight. *The Idea of Race in Latin America, 1870–1940*. Austin: University of Texas Press, 1990.

Guimarães, Antônio Sérgio Alfredo. "Africanism and Racial Democracy: The Correspondence between Herskovits and Arthur Ramos (1935–1949)." *Estudios Interdisciplinários de América Latina y el Caribe* 19, no. 1 (2008).

———. "Baianos e paulistas: Duas 'escolas' de relações raciais?" *Tempo Social* 11, no. 1 (1999): 75–95.

———. "Classes sociais." In *O que ler na ciência social brasileira (1970–1995)*, edited by Sérgio Miceli, 13–57. São Paulo: Sumaré, 1999.

———. "Cor, classes e status nos estudos de Pierson, Azevedo e Harris na Bahia, 1940–1960." In *Raça, ciência e sociedade*, edited by Marcos Chor Maio and Ricardo Ventura Santos, 143–58. Rio de Janeiro: Editora FIOCRUZ, 1996.

———. "*As elites de cor* e os estudos de relações raciais." *Tempo Social* 8, no. 2 (1996): 67–82.

———. "The Misadventures of Nonracialism in Brazil." In *Beyond Racism: Race and Inequality in Brazil, South Africa, and the United States*, edited by Charles V. Hamilton, Lynn Huntley, Neville Alexander, Antônio Sérgio Alfredo Guimarães, and Wilmot James, 157–86. Boulder, Colo.: Lynne Rienner, 2001.

Guimarães, Archimedes Pereira. *Dois sertanejos baianos do século XX*. Salvador: Centro de Estudos Baianos, Universidade Federal da Bahia, 1982.

Harding, Jack. *I Like Brazil: A Close-Up of a Good Neighbor*. Indianapolis: Bobbs-Merrill, 1941.

Harding, Rachel E. *A Refuge in Thunder: Candomblé and Alternative Spaces of Blackness*. Bloomington: Indiana University Press, 2000.

Harris, Marvin. "Race Relations in Minas Velhas, a Community in the Mountain Region of Central Brazil." In *Race and Class in Rural Brazil*, edited by Charles Wagley. New York: UNESCO; Columbia University Press, 1963.

———. *Town and Country in Brazil*. New York: Columbia University Press, 1956.

Harrison, Shelby, William Ogburn, and Donald Young. "Foreword to 1941 edition." In Melville J. Herskovits, *The Myth of the Negro Past*, xxiii–xxv. Boston: Beacon Press, 1990.

Hasenbalg, Carlos. "Entre o mito e os fatos: Racismo e relações raciais no Brasil." In *Raça, ciência e sociedade*, edited by Marcos Chor Maio and Ricardo Ventura Santos, 235–49. Rio de Janeiro: Editora FIOCRUZ, 1996.

Hasenbalg, Carlos, and Nelson do Valle Silva. "Notes on Racial and Political Inequality in Brazil." In *Racial Politics in Contemporary Brazil*, edited by Michael Hanchard, 154–69. Durham, N.C.: Duke University Press, 1999.

Healey, Mark. "Os desencontros da tradição em *Cidade das mulheres*: Raça e gênero na etnografia de Ruth Landes." *Cadernos Pagu* 6/7 (1996): 153–200.

———. "'The Sweet Matriarchy of Bahia': Ruth Landes' Ethnography of Race and Gender." *Dispositio/n* 23, no. 50 (2000): 87–116.

Hellwig, David J. *African-American Reflections on Brazil's Racial Paradise*. Philadelphia: Temple University Press, 1992.

———. "E. Franklin Frazier's Brazil." *Western Journal of Black Studies* 15 (1991): 87–94.

Herskovits, Melville J. *Acculturation: The Study of Culture Contact*. New York: J. J. Augustin, 1938.

———. "African Gods and Catholic Saints in New World Negro Belief." *American Anthropologist* 39, no. 4, part 1 (1937): 635–43.

———. "A arte do bronze e do panno em Dahomé." In *Estudos afro-brasileiros*, edited by Congresso Afro-Brasileiro (Recife), 227–35. Rio de Janeiro: Ariel, 1935.

———. "Deuses africanos e santos católicos nas crenças do negro do Novo Mundo." In *O negro no Brasil: Trabalhos apresentados ao 2. Congresso Afro-Brasileiro*, edited by Congresso Afro-Brasileiro (Bahia), 19–32. Rio de Janeiro: Civilização Brasileira, 1940.

———. *The Myth of the Negro Past*. With an introduction by Sidney W. Mintz. Boston: Beacon Press, 1990.

———. "The Negro in Bahia, Brazil: A Problem in Method." *American Sociological Review* 8, no. 4 (1943): 394–402.

———. "The Negro in the New World: The Statement of a Problem." *American Anthropologist* 32, no. 1 (1930): 145–55.

———. "Pesquisas etnológicas na Bahia." *Publicações do Museu do Estado*, no. 3. Edited and with an introduction by José Valladares. Salvador: Secretaria de Educação e Saúde, 1943.

———. "Preface to the Beacon Press Edition." In *The Myth of the Negro Past*. Boston: Beacon, 1958.

———. "Procedencia dos negros do Novo Mundo." In *Estudos afro-brasileiros*, edited by Congresso Afro-Brasileiro (Recife), 195–98. Rio de Janeiro: Ariel, 1935.

———. "Review of *City of Women*, by Ruth Landes." *American Sociological Review* 50, no. 1 (1948): 123–25.

Hobsbawm, Eric, and Terence Ranger, eds. *The Invention of Tradition*. Cambridge: Cambridge University Press, 1983.

Hochman, Gilberto. *A era do saneamento: As bases da política de saúde pública no Brasil*. São Paulo: Editora Hucitec-ANPOCS, 1998.

Holanda, Guy de. *Recursos educativos dos museus brasileiros*. Rio de Janeiro: Centro Brasileiro de Pesquisas Educacionais; International Council of Museums, 1958.

Holloway, Thomas. *Immigrants on the Land: Coffee and Society in São Paulo, 1886–1934*. Chapel Hill: University of North Carolina Press, 1980.

Hutchinson, Harry W. "Race Relations in a Rural Community of the Bahian

Recôncavo." In *Race and Class in Rural Brazil*, edited by Charles Wagley, 16–46. New York: UNESCO; Columbia University Press, 1963.

———. *Village and Plantation Life in Northeastern Brazil*. Seattle: University of Washington Press, 1957.

Ickes, Scott. "'Adorned with the Mix of Faith and Profanity that Intoxicates the People': The Festival of the Senhor do Bonfim in Salvador, Bahia, Brazil, 1930–1954." *Bulletin of Latin American Research* 24, no. 2 (2005): 181–200.

———. "Salvador's Transformist Hegemony: Popular Festivals, Cultural Politics and Afro-Bahian Culture in Salvador, Bahia, Brazil, 1930–1952." Ph.D. diss., University of Maryland, 2003.

Instituto Brasileiro de Geografia e Estatística (IBGE). *Censo Demográfico 1991. Características gerais da população e instrução: resultados de amostra*. Rio de Janeiro: Fundação IBGE, 1996.

———. "Indicadores sociais." <http://www.ibge.gov.br/home/estatistica/populacao/condicaodevida/indicadoresminimos/sinteseindicsociais2007/default.shtml>. 3 January 2009.

———. *Síntese de indicadores sociais: uma análise das condições de vida da população brasileira, 2007*. Rio de Janeiro: IBGE, 2007.

Jackson, Walter. "Melville Herskovits and the Search for Afro-American Culture." In *Malinowski, Rivers, Benedict, and Others: Essays on Culture and Personality*, edited by George W. Stocking Jr., 95–126. Madison: University of Wisconsin Press, 1986.

"José do Prado Valladares." *Revista do Instituto Geográfico e Histórico da Bahia* 82 (1958–60): 270–71.

Klein, Herbert S. *The Atlantic Slave Trade*. Cambridge: Cambridge University Press, 1999.

Kraay, Hendrik, ed. *Afro-Brazilian Culture and Politics: Bahia, 1790s to 1990s*. London: M. E. Sharpe, 1998.

Landes, Ruth. *City of Women*. Albuquerque: University of New Mexico Press, 1994.

———. "A Cult Matriarchate and Male Homosexuality." *Journal of Abnormal and Social Psychology* 53, no. 3 (1940): 386–97.

———. "Fetish Worship in Brazil." *Journal of American Folklore* 53, no. 210 (1940): 261–70.

———. "A Woman Anthropologist in Brazil." In *Women in the Field: Anthropological Experiences*, edited by Peggy Golde, 119–43. Berkeley: University of California Press, 1986.

Lara, Cecília de. *Nova Cruzada: Contribuição para o estudo do pré-modernismo*. São Paulo: Instituto de Estúdos Brasileiros, 1971.

Leal, Maria das Graças de Andrade. *A arte de ter um ofício: Liceu de Artes e Ofícios da Bahia, 1872–1996*. Salvador: Fundação Odebrecht; Liceu de Artes e Ofícios da Bahia, 1996.

———. "Manuel Querino entre letras e lutas-Bahia, 1851–1923." Ph.D. diss., Pontifícia Universidade Católica de São Paulo, PUC-SP, 2004.

Levine, Robert M. "The First Afro-Brazilian Congress: Opportunities for the Study of Race in the Brazilian Northeast." *Race* 15, no. 2 (1973): 185–95.

————. *Vale of Tears: Revisiting the Canudos Massacre in Northeastern Brazil, 1893–1897*. Berkeley: University of California Press, 1988.

Lima, Ari. "Blacks as Study Objects and Intellectuals in Brazilian Academia." *Latin American Perspectives* 33, no. 4 (2006): 82–105.

Lima, Silva. "Terceiro Congresso Brazileiro de Medicina e Cirurgia: Discurso inaugural do presidente, Dr. Silva Lima." *Gazeta Médica da Bahia* 22, no. 4 (1890): 145–59.

Lima, Vivaldo da Costa. "O candomblé da Bahia na década de 30." In *Cartas de Edison Carneiro a Artur Ramos, de 4 de janeiro de 1936 a 6 de dezembro de 1938*, edited by Edison Carneiro, 37–73. São Paulo: Corrupio, 1987.

————. "Os obás de Xangô." *Afro-Asia* 2–3 (1966): 5–36.

Lima, Nísia Trindade, and Gilberto Hochman. "Condenado pela raça, absolvido pela medicina: O Brasil descoberto pelo movimento sanitarista da Primeira República." In *Raça, ciência e sociedade*, edited by Marcos Chor Maio and Ricardo Ventura Santos, 23–40. Rio de Janeiro: Editora FIOCRUZ, 1996.

Lisboa, Elysio de Carvalho. "O Museu da Bahia." *O Estado da Bahia*, 22 March 1941.

Lund, Joshua, and Malcolm McNee, eds. *Gilberto Freyre e os estudos latino-americanos*. Pittsburgh: Instituto Internacional de Literatura Iberoamericana, 2006.

"A luta anti-tuberculosa e a prophilaxia individual." *Gazeta Médica da Bahia* 50, no. 4 (1918): i–xiii.

Lühning, Angela. "Acabe com este santo, Pedrito vem aí: Mito e realidade da perseguição ao candomblé entre 1920 e 1941." *Revista USP* 28 (1996): 194–220.

————. "Pierre Fatumbi Verger e sua obra." *Afro-Asia* 21–22 (1998–99): 315–64.

Machado, Helio. "Prefácio." In Carlos Ott, *Evolução histórica da cidade do Salvador*. Vol. 5 of Ott, *Formação e evolução étnica da cidade do Salvador*, xv–xvi. Salvador: Prefeitura Municipal do Salvador, 1955.

Magalhães, Basílio de. *O folclore no Brasil, com uma coletânea de 81 contos populares, organizadas pelo dr. João da Silva Campos*. Rio de Janeiro: Imprensa Nacional, 1939.

Magalhães, Juracy. *Minhas memórias provisórias: Depoimento prestado ao CPDOC*. Rio de Janeiro: Civilização Brasileira, 1982.

Mahoney, Mary Ann. "The World Cacao Made: Society, Politics, and History in Southern Bahia, Brazil, 1822–1919." Ph.D. diss., Yale University, 1996.

Maio, Marcos Chor. "A história do projeto UNESCO: Estudos raciais e ciências sociais no Brasil." Ph.D. diss., Instituto Universitário de Pesquisas do Rio de Janeiro, 1997.

————. "A medicina de Nina Rodrigues: Análise de uma trajetória científica." *Cadernos de Saúde Pública* 11, no. 2 (1995): 226–37.

————. "O projeto UNESCO e a agenda das ciências sociais no Brasil dos anos 40 e 50." *Revista Brasileira de Ciências Sociais* 14, no. 41 (1999): 141–58.

————. "Tempo controverso: Gilberto Freyre e o projeto UNESCO." *Tempo Social* 11, no. 1 (1999): 111–36.

————. "UNESCO and the Study of Race Relations in Brazil: Regional or National Issue?" *Latin American Research Review* 36, no. 2 (2001): 118–36.

Maio, Marcos Chor, and Ricardo Ventura Santos, eds. *Raça, ciência e sociedade*. Rio de Janeiro: Editora FIOCRUZ, 1996.

Martins, Wilson. *The Modernist Idea*. Translated by Jack E. Tomlins. Westport, Conn.: Greenwood, 1970. Reprint, 1979.

Massi, Fernanda. "Franceses e norte americanos nas ciências sociais brasileiras (1930–1960)." In *História das ciências sociais no Brasil*, edited by Sergio Miceli, 410–60. São Paulo: Editora Revista dos Tribunais, 1989.

Matory, J. Lorand. *Black Atlantic Religion: Tradition, Transnationalism and Matriarchy in the Afro-Brazilian Candomblé*. Princeton, N.J.: Princeton University Press, 2005.

———. "The English Professors of Brazil: On the Diasporic Roots of the Yorubá Nation." *Comparative Studies in Society and History* 41, no. 1 (1999): 72–103.

Mattoso, Katia M. de Queirós. *Bahia, século XIX: Uma província no império*. Rio de Janeiro: Nova Fronteira, 1992.

McCann, Bryan. *Hello, Hello Brazil: Popular Music in the Making of Modern Brazil*. Durham, N.C.: Duke University Press, 2004.

McNeely, Ian F. *"Medicine on a Grand Scale": Rudolf Virchow, Liberalism, and the Public Health*. London: Wellcome Trust Centre for the History of Medicine at UCL, 2002.

Meade, Teresa. *"Civilizing" Rio: Reform and Resistance in a Brazilian City, 1889–1930*. University Park: Pennsylvania State University Press, 1997.

Mello, Agenor Bandeira de, and Silvio Batalha, eds. *Cartilha histórica da Bahia: A República e seus governadores*. 5th ed. Salvador: Empresa Gráfica da Bahia, 1990.

Merrick, Thomas W., and Douglas H. Graham. *Population and Economic Development in Brazil, 1800 to the Present*. Baltimore: Johns Hopkins University Press, 1979.

Métraux, Alfred. "UNESCO and the Racial Problem." *International Social Science Bulletin* 2, no. 3 (1950): 384–90.

Miceli, Sergio, ed. *História das ciências sociais no Brasil*. Vol. 1. São Paulo: Editora Revista dos Tribunais, 1989.

Mielche, Hakon. *From Santos to Bahia*. Translated by M. A. Michael. London: William Hodge, 1948.

Mintz, Sidney W., and Richard Price. *The Birth of African-American Culture: An Anthropological Perspective*. Boston: Beacon, 1992.

Monarcha, Carlos, ed. *Anísio Teixeira: A obra de uma vida*. Rio de Janeiro: DP&A, 2001.

Moreira, Juliano. "Rudolf Virchow (traços geraes de sua vida)." *Gazeta Médica da Bahia* 33, no. 4 (1901): 149–67.

Moreira, Juliano, and Henrique Autran. "Silva Lima e a *Gazeta Médica da Bahia* (1866–1916)." *Gazeta Médica da Bahia* 49, no. 8–9 (1918): 384–97.

Moreira, Widow Juliano. "Juliano Moreira e o problema do negro e do mestiço no Brasil." In *Novos estudos afro-brasileiros*, edited by Congresso Afro-Brasileiro (Recife), 146–50. Rio de Janeiro: Civilização Brasileira, 1937.

Moura, Roberto. *Tia Ciata e a Pequena Africa no Rio de Janeiro*. Rio de Janeiro: FUNARTE, 1983.

Myrdal, Gunnar. *An American Dilemma: The Negro Problem and Modern Democracy*. New York: Harper, 1944.

Nascimento, Abdias do. *Brazil: Mixture or Massacre? Essays in the Genocide of a Black People*. Dover, Mass.: Majority, 1989.

————, ed. *O negro revoltado*. Rio de Janeiro: Nova Fronteira, 1982.

Nava, Carmen, and Ludwig Lauerhass, eds. *Brazil in the Making: Facets of National Identity*. Lanham, Md.: Rowman and Littlefield, 2006.

Needell, Jeffrey D. "The *Revolta contra Vacina* of 1904: The Revolt against 'Modernization' in *Belle-Epoque* Rio de Janeiro." *Hispanic American Historical Review* 67, no. 2 (1987): 233–69.

Nina Rodrigues, Raimundo. *Os africanos no Brasil*. 8th ed. Brasília: Editora Universidade de Brasília, 2004.

————. *O alienado no direito civil brasileiro: Apontamentos medíco-legaes ao projeto de código civil*. São Paulo: Companhia Editora Nacional, 1939.

————. *O animismo fetichista dos negros bahianos*. Edited by Arthur Ramos. Rio de Janeiro: Civilização Brasileira, 1935.

————. "Anthropologia: Collecção anthropologica." *Gazeta Médica da Bahia* 22, no. 4 (1890): 160–64.

————. "Anthropologia pathologica: Os mestiços brazileiros." *Gazeta Médica da Bahia* 21, no. 11 (1890).

————. "Assistencia medico-legal aos alienados no Estado da Bahia." *Revista dos Cursos da Faculdade de Medicina da Bahia* ano 3, no. 3 (1904): 163–470.

————. "Contribuição para o estudo de lepra no Estado do Maranhão." *Gazeta Médica da Bahia* 20–21 (1889–1890): vol. 20: 105–13, 205–11, 301–14, 58–68, 404–9; vol. 21: 121–32, 225–34, 55–65, 445–55.

————. "O craneo do salteador Lucas e o de um indio assassino." *Gazeta Médica da Bahia* 24, no. 9 (1892).

————. *As raças humanas e a responsabilidade penal no Brasil*. 3rd ed. São Paulo: Companhia Editora Nacional, 1938.

————. "A reforma dos exames medico-legais no Brazil (appello ao Congresso de Unificação das Leis Processuais." *Revista dos Cursos da Faculdade da Medicina da Bahia* 3, no. 3 (1904): 9–53.

Novaes, Tássia. "Bahia Azul enterrou US$ 300 mi em Salvador." *A Tarde On Line*, 23 March 2007. <http://www.atarde.com.br/cidades/noticia.jsf?id=739048>. 30 June 2009.

Nunes, Antonietta de Aguiar. "Política educacional na Bahia por ocasião da implantação da República: Dois projetos em conflito, 1889–1895." *Revista Estudos Acadêmicos da Faculdade Ruy Barbosa* 2, no. 1 (2000): 31–38.

————. "A reforma da educação baiana em 1881: O Regulamento Bulcão." *Gestão em Ação* 2, no. 2 (1999): 71–84.

Oliveira, Lúcia Lippi, Mônica Pimenta Velloso, and Angela Maria Castro Gomes, eds. *Estado Novo: Ideologia e poder*. Rio de Janeiro: Zahar, 1982.

Oliveira, Waldir Freitas. "As pesquisas na Bahia sobre os afro-brasileiros." *Estudos Avançados* 18, no. 50 (2004): 127–34.

————. "Os estudos africanistas na Bahia dos anos 30." In *Cartas de Edison Carneiro a Artur Ramos, de 4 de janeiro de 1936 a 6 de dezembro de 1938*, edited by Edison Carneiro, 21–37. São Paulo: Corrupio, 1987.

Ott, Carlos. "Vestígios de cultura indígena no sertão da Bahia." *Publicações do Museu do Estado*, no. 5. Edited and with an introduction by José Valladares. Salvador: Secretaria de Educação e Saúde, 1945.

Pallares-Burke, Maria Lúcia G. *Gilberto Freyre: Um vitoriano dos trópicos*. São Paulo: UNESP, 2005.

Pandolfi, Dulce, ed. *Repensando o Estado Novo*. Rio de Janeiro: Editora Fundação Getúlio Vargas, 1999.

Pang, Eul-Soo. *Bahia in the First Brazilian Republic: Coronelismo and Oligarchies, 1889–1934*. Gainesville: University Presses of Florida, 1979.

Parés, Luis Nicolau. "The Birth of the Yoruba Hegemony in Post-abolition Candomblé." *Journal de la Société des Américanistes* 91, no. 1 (2005): 139–59.

———. *A formação do Candomblé: História e ritual da nação jeje na Bahia*. Campinas: Editora de Unicamp, 2006.

———. "The 'Nagôization' Process in Bahian Candomblé." In *The Yoruba Diaspora in the Atlantic World*, edited by Toyin Falola and Matt D. Childs, 185–208. Bloomington: Indiana University Press, 2004.

———. "Shango in Afro-Brazilian Religion: 'Aristocracy' and 'Syncretic' Interactions." *Religioni e Società* 54 (2006): 20–39.

Peard, Julyan G. *Race, Place, and Medicine: The Idea of the Tropics in Nineteenth-Century Brazilian Medicine*. Durham, N.C.: Duke University Press, 1999.

Pereira, Antônio Pacífico. "Hygiene das escolas." *Gazeta Médica da Bahia* 10 (1878): 193–201, 241–52, 289–95, 337–47, 433–49.

Pereira, Manuel Vitorino. "Ato de 10 de janeiro de 1890, criando o serviço de saúde escolar." In *Idéias políticas de Manuel Vitorino*, 85–99. Brasília: Senado Federal, 1981.

———. "Ato de 31 de dezembro de 1889, reformando a instrução primária e secundaria." In *Idéias políticas de Manuel Vitorino*, 77–84. Brasília: Senado Federal, 1981.

———. *Idéias políticas de Manuel Vitorino*. 2 vols. Brasília: Senado Federal, 1981.

———. "Regulamento de hygiene escholar." *Gazeta Médica da Bahia* 21 (1890): 301–17.

Perry, Keisha-Khan. "The Roots of Black Resistance: Race, Gender, and the Struggle for Urban Land Rights in Salvador, Bahia, Brazil." *Social Identities* 10, no. 6 (2004): 811–31.

Pierson, Donald. *Negroes in Brazil: A Study of Race Contact at Bahia*. Chicago: University of Chicago Press, 1942.

———. "A raça e a classe na Bahia." In *O negro no Brasil: Trabalhos apresentados ao 2. Congresso Afro-Brasileiro*, edited by Congresso Afro-Brasileiro (Bahia), 163–65. Rio de Janeiro: Civilização Brasileira, 1940.

Pinho, Osmundo S. de Araujo. "A Bahia no fundamental: Notas para uma interpretação do discurso ideológico da baianidade." *Revista Brasileira de Ciências Sociais* 13, no. 36 (1998): 109–20.

———. "Espaço, poder e relações raciais: O caso de centro histórico de Salvador." *Afro-Asia* 21–22 (1998): 257–74.

Pinho, Patricia de Santana. "African-American Roots Tourism in Brazil." *Latin American Perspectives* 35, no. 3 (2008): 70–86.

———. *Reinvenções da África na Bahia*. São Paulo: Annablume, 2004.

"Professor Nina Rodrigues." *Gazeta Médica da Bahia* 38, no. 2 (1906): 57–67.

"Quarto Congresso Brasileiro de Medicina e Cirurgia." *Gazeta Médica da Bahia* 31, no. 1 (1899): 43–46.

Ramos, Arthur. "Introdução a edição brasileira." In *Brancos e pretos na Bahia*, by Donald Pierson, 23–25. São Paulo: Companhia Editora Nacional, 1945.

———. *The Negro in Brazil*. Translated by Richard Patee. Philadelphia: Porcupine, 1980. Reprint, 1980.

———. "Nina Rodrigues e os estudos negro-brasileiros." In *O negro no Brasil: Trabalhos apresentados ao 2. Congresso Afro-Brasileiro*, edited by Congresso Afro-Brasileiro (Bahia), 337–39. Rio de Janeiro: Civilização Brasileira, 1940.

———. *O negro brasileiro: Ethnographia, religiosa e pyschanalyse*. Rio de Janeiro: Civilização Brasileira, 1934.

———. "Prefácio." In *Novos estudos afro-brasileiros*, edited by Congresso Afro-Brasileiro (Recife), 11–14. Rio de Janeiro: Civilização Brasileira, 1937.

Redfield, Robert, Ralph Linton, and Melville J. Herskovits. "A Memorandum for the Study of Acculturation." *Man* 35 (1935): 145–48.

Reis, João José. "Batuque: African Drumming and Dance between Repression and Concession, Bahia, 1808–1855." *Bulletin of Latin American Research* 24, no. 2 (2005): 201–14.

———. "Candomblé in Nineteenth-Century Bahia: Priests, Followers, Clients." *Slavery & Abolition* 22, no. 1 (2001): 116–34.

———. *Death Is a Festival: Funeral Rites and Rebellion in Nineteenth-Century Brazil*. Chapel Hill: University of North Carolina Press, 2003.

———. "Introdução." In *Escravidão e invenção da liberdade: Estudos sobre o negro no Brasil*, edited by João José Reis, 9–16. São Paulo: Brasiliense, 1988.

———. *Slave Rebellion in Brazil: The Muslim Uprising of 1835 in Bahia*. Baltimore: Johns Hopkins University Press, 1993.

Risério, Antônio. *Avant-garde na Bahia*. São Paulo: Instituto Lina Bo e P. M. Bardi, 1995.

———. "Bahia com 'H': Uma leitura de cultura baiana." In *Escravidão e invenção da liberdade: Estudos sobre o negro no Brasil*, edited by João José Reis, 143–66. São Paulo: Brasiliense, 1988.

———. *Carnaval Ijexá*. Salvador: Corrupio, 1981.

———. *Caymmi: Uma utopia de lugar*. São Paulo: Perspectiva, 1993.

Robock, Stefan H. *Brazil's Developing Northeast: A Study of Regional Planning and Foreign Aid*. New York: Brookings Institution, 1963.

Rocha, Carlos Eduardo da. *Roteiro de Pelourinho*. Salvador: Oficina do Livro, 1994.

Rodrigues, João Jorge Santos. "Olodum and the Black Struggle in Brazil." In *Black Brazil: Culture, Identity, and Social Mobilization*, edited by Larry Crook and Randal Johnson, 43–52. Los Angeles: UCLA Latin American Center Publications, 1999.

Rodriguez, Julia. *Civilizing Argentina: Science, Medicine, and the Modern State*. Chapel Hill: University of North Carolina Press, 2006.

Romo, Anadelia A. "Race and Reform in Bahia, Brazil: Primary Education, 1888–1964." Ph.D. diss., Harvard University, 2004.

———. "Rethinking Race and Culture in Brazil's First Afro-Brazilian Congress of 1934." *Journal of Latin American Studies* 39, no. 1 (2007): 31–54.

Ruggiero, Kristin. *Modernity in the Flesh: Medicine, Law, and Society in Turn-of-the-Century Argentina*. Stanford, Calif.: Stanford University Press, 2004.

Sampaio, Consuelo Novais. *Os partidos políticos da Bahia na Primeira República: Uma política de acomodação*. Salvador: Universidade Federal da Bahia, 1978.

———. *Poder e representação: O Legislativo da Bahia na Segunda República, 1930–1937*. Salvador: Assembléia Legislativa da Bahia, 1992.

Sampaio, Nelson de Sousa. "Meio século de política baiana." *Revista Brasileira de Estudos Políticos* 20 (1966): 105–24.

Sansi-Roca, Roger. *Fetishes and Monuments: Afro-Brazilian Art and Culture in the Twentieth Century*. Oxford: Berghahn, 2007.

———. "The Hidden Life of Stones: Historicity, Materiality, and the Value of Candomblé Objects in Bahia." *Journal of Material Culture* 10, no. 2 (2005): 139–56.

Sansone, Livio. *Blackness without Ethnicity*. New York: Palgrave Macmillan, 2003.

———. "Um campo saturado de tensões: O estudo das relações raciais e das culturas negras no Brasil." *Estudos Afro-Asiáticos* 24, no. 1 (2002): 5–14.

———. "Desigualdades duráveis, relações raciais e modernidades no Recôncavo: O caso de S. Francisco do Conde." *Revista USP* 68 (2006): 234–51.

Santos, Deoscóredes M. dos. *Axé Opô Afonjá: Notícia histórica de um terreiro de santo da Bahia*. Rio de Janeiro: Instituto Brasileiro de Estudos Afro-Asiáticos, 1962.

Santos, Jocélio Teles dos. "A Mixed Race Nation: Afro-Brazilians and Cultural Policy in Bahia, 1970–1990." In *Afro-Brazilian Culture and Politics: Bahia, 1790s to 1990s*, edited by Hendrik Kraay, 117–33. Armonk, N.Y.: M. E. Sharpe, 1998.

———. *O poder da cultura e a cultura no poder: A disputa simbólica da herança cultural negra no Brasil*. Salvador: EDUFBA, 2005.

Santos, Mário Augusto da Silva. *A república do povo: Sobrevivência e tensão—Salvador, 1890–1930*. Salvador: EDUFBA, 2001.

Schwarcz, Lilia Moritz. *O espetáculo das raças: Cientistas, instituições e questão racial no Brasil, 1870–1930*. São Paulo: Companhia das Letras, 1993.

———. *The Spectacle of the Races: Scientists, Institutions, and the Race Question in Brazil, 1870–1930*. Translated by Leland Guyer. New York: Hill and Wang, 1999.

Schwartz, Stuart B. *Sugar Plantations in the Formation of Brazilian Society: Bahia, 1550–1835*. Cambridge: Cambridge University Press, 1985.

"Scientific Notes and News." *Science* 15, no. 368 (1902): 115–20.

Seigel, Micol. "Beyond Compare: Historical Method after the Transnational Turn." *Radical History Review* 91 (2005): 62–90.

———. *Uneven Encounters: Making Race and Nation in Brazil and the United States*. Durham, N.C.: Duke University Press, 2009.

Seminário de Antropologia, Faculdade de Filosofia da Universidade da Bahia. *O ensino da antropologia na Bahia*. Salvador: Imprensa Oficial da Bahia, 1959.

Seyferth, Giralda. "A antropologia e a teoria do branqueamento da raça no Brasil: A tese de João Batista de Lacerda." *Revista do Museu Paulista* 30 (1985): 81–98.

Shaw, Lisa. *The Social History of the Brazilian Samba*. Aldershot, U.K.: Ashgate, 1999.

Sheriff, Robin. *Dreaming Equality: Color, Race, and Racism in Urban Brazil*. New Brunswick, N.J.: Rutgers University Press, 2001.

Silva, Jônatas C. da. "História de lutas negras: Memórias do surgimento do movimento negro na Bahia." In *Escravidão e invenção da liberdade: Estudos sobre o negro no Brasil*, edited by João José Reis, 275–88. São Paulo: Brasiliense, 1988.

Silva, Nelson do Valle, and Carlos Hasenbalg. "Tendências da desigualdade educacional no Brasil." *Dados* 43, no. 3 (2000): 423–45.

Silva, Paulo Santos. "A força da tradição: A luta pela redemocratização na Bahia em 1945." M.A. thesis, Universidade Federal da Bahia, 1991.

———. *Ancoras de tradição: Luta política, intelectuais e construção do discurso histórico na Bahia, 1930–1949*. Salvador: EDUFBA, 2000.

Silva Campos, João da. "Procissões tradicionais da Bahia." *Publicações do Museu do Estado*, no. 1. Edited and with an introduction by José Valladares. Salvador: Secretaria de Educação e Saúde, 1941.

———. "Tempo antigo: Crônicas d'antanho, marcos do passado, histórias do Recôncavo." *Publicações do Museu do Estado*, no. 2. Ed. José Valladares. Salvador: Secretaria de Educação e Saúde, 1942.

Skidmore, Thomas E. *Black into White: Race and Nationality in Brazilian Thought*. 2nd ed. Durham, N.C.: Duke University Press, 1993.

———. *Politics in Brazil, 1930–1964: An Experiment in Democracy*. Oxford: Oxford University Press, 1967.

———. "Raízes de Gilberto Freyre." *Journal of Latin American Studies* 34, no. 1 (2002): 1–20.

Smith, Robert C. "José Antônio do Prado Valladares, 1917–1959." *Hispanic American Historical Review* 60, no. 3 (1960): 435–38.

Smolka, Ana Luiza Bustamante, and Maria Cristina Menezes, eds. *Anísio Teixeira, 1900–2000: Provocações em educação*. Campinas: Autores Associados, 2000.

Souza, Guaraci Adeodato A. de. "Urbanização e fluxos migratórios para Salvador." In *Bahia de todos os pobres*, edited by Guaraci Adeodato A. de Souza and Vilmar Faria, 103–28. Petrópolis: Vozes, 1980.

Stepan, Nancy. "Eugenics in Brazil, 1917–1940." In *The Wellborn Science: Eugenics in Germany, France, and Brazil*, edited by Mark Adams, 110–52. New York: Oxford University Press, 1990.

———. *"The Hour of Eugenics": Race, Gender, and Nation in Latin America*. Ithaca, N.Y.: Cornell University Press, 1991.

Stocking, George W., ed. *Objects and Others: Essays on Museums and Material Culture*. Madison: University of Wisconsin Press, 1985.

———. *Race, Culture, and Evolution: Essays in the History of Anthropology*. Chicago: University of Chicago Press, 1982.

———. *The Shaping of American Anthropology, 1883–1911: A Franz Boas Reader.* New York: Basic, 1974.

Superintendência de Estudos Econômicos e Sociais da Bahia (SEI). "Bahia em números: Indicadores demográficos." <http://wi.sei.ba.gov.br>. 20 April 2009.

Tavares, Luis Henrique Dias. *Duas reformas da educação na Bahia, 1895–1925.* Salvador: MEC-INEP, 1968.

———. *História da Bahia.* 10th rev. ed. São Paulo: Editora UNESP, 2001.

Teixeira, Anísio. "Centro Educacional Carneiro Ribeiro." *Revista Brasileira de Estudos Pedagógicos* 31, no. 73 (1959): 78–84.

———. *Educação e cultura no projeto de constituição da Bahia.* Bahia: Imprensa Oficial, 1947.

———. *Educação não é privilégio.* Rio de Janeiro: José Olympio, 1957.

———. *Educação, saúde e assistência no Estado da Bahia em 1948.* Salvador, 1949. <http://www.prossiga.br/anisioteixeira/eng/artigos/educacao10.html>. 1 May 2004.

Teixeira, Luiz Antônio. "Da raça à doença em 'Casa-grande e senzala.'" *História, Ciências, Saúde* 4, no. 2 (1997): 231–43.

Telles, Edward E. *Race in Another America: The Significance of Skin Color in Brazil.* Princeton, N.J.: Princeton University Press, 2004.

"Terceiro Congresso Brasileiro de Medicina e Cirurgia." *Gazeta Médica da Bahia* 21, no. 10 (1890): 437–45.

Topinard, Paul. "Observations upon the Methods and Processes of Anthropometry." *Journal of the Anthropological Institute of Great Britain and Ireland* 10 (1881): 212–24.

Torres, Heloisa Alberto. *Museums of Brazil.* Rio de Janeiro: Ministry of Foreign Affairs, Cultural Division, 1953.

Torres, Octávio. *Esboço histórico dos acontecimentos mais importantes da vida da Faculdade de Medicina da Bahia, 1808–1946.* Salvador: Vitória, 1947.

Turner, Lorenzo. "Some Contacts of Brazilian Ex-slaves with Nigeria, West Africa." *Journal of Negro History* 27 (1942): 55–67.

Twine, France Winddance. *Racism in a Racial Democracy: The Maintenance of White Supremacy in Brazil.* New Brunswick, N.J.: Rutgers University Press, 1997.

Valladares, José. *Artes maiores e menores: Seleção de crônicas de arte, 1951–1956.* Salvador: Universidade da Bahia, 1957.

———. "Bahia and Its Museum." *Bulletin of the Pan American Union* 82, no. 8 (1948): 449–58. Also published under the same title in *Brazil* 22, no. 10 (1948): 2–5.

———. "Bahia e seu museu." *Boletim da União Pan-Americana* 50, no. 7 (1948): 333–42.

———. *Bêabá da Bahia: Guia turístico.* Salvador: Progresso, 1951.

———. *Dominicais: Seleção de crônicas de arte, 1945–1950.* Salvador: Artes Gráficas, 1951.

———. *Guia do visitante: Valido julho de 1946 a junho de 1947.* Salvador: Oficinas Tipográficas do Mosteiro de São Bento, 1946.

———. "Introdução." In "Procissões tradicionais da Bahia," by João da Silva Campos. *Publicações do Museu do Estado*, no. 1. Salvador: Secretaria de Educação e Saúde (1941): v–vi.

———. "Museus para o povo: Um estudo sobre museus americanos." *Publicações do Museu do Estado*, no. 6. Salvador: Secretaria de Educação e Saúde, 1946.

———. "Nota." In "Casos e coisas da Bahia," by Antônio Vianna. *Publicações do Museu do Estado*, no. 10. Salvador: Secretaria de Educação e Saúde (1950): 11–12.

———. "Nota da direção do Museu." In "Vestígios de cultura indígena no sertão da Bahia," by Carlos Ott. *Publicações do Museu do Estado*, no. 5. Salvador: Secretaria de Educação e Saúde, 1945: v–vi.

———. "Nota da direção do Museu." In "Tupís e guaranís: Estudos de ethnonímia e linguística," by Frederico Edelweiss. *Publicações do Museu do Estado*, no. 7. Salvador: Secretaria de Educação e Saúde (1947): n.p.

———. "Nota do tradutor." In "Pesquisas etnológicas na Bahia," by Melville J. Herskovits. *Publicações do Museu do Estado*, no. 3. Salvador: Secretaria de Educação e Saúde (1943): i–iii.

———. "Resumo histórico e organização atual do Museu da Bahia." *A Noticia*, 14 July 1939, 3, 8.

———. Review of *City of Women* by Ruth Landes. *Journal of American Folklore* 60, no. 238 (1947): 443–45.

———. *O torço da baiana*. Salvador: K. Paul Hebeisen, 1952.

Vargas, Getúlio. "A instrução profissional e a educação." In *A nova política do Brasil*, vol. 2, 113–24. Rio de Janeiro: José Olympio, 1938–41.

Vianna, Hermano. *The Mystery of Samba: Popular Music and National Identity in Brazil.* Translated by John Charles Chasteen. Chapel Hill: University of North Carolina Press, 1999.

Wagley, Charles. *Amazon Town: A Study of Man in the Tropics*. New York: Macmillan, 1953.

———. "From Caste to Class in North Brazil." In *Race and Class in Rural Brazil*, edited by Charles Wagley, 142–56. New York: UNESCO; Columbia University Press, 1963.

———, ed. *Race and Class in Rural Brazil.* 2nd ed. New York: UNESCO; Columbia University Press, 1963.

Wagley, Charles, and Thales de Azevedo. "Sôbre métodos de campo no estudo de comunidade." *Revista do Museu Paulista* 5 (1951): 227–38.

Wagley, Charles, Thales de Azevedo, and Luiz A. Costa Pinto. "Uma pesquisa sobre a vida social no estado da Bahia." *Publicações do Museu do Estado*, no. 11. Ed. José Valladares. Salvador: Secretaria de Educação e Saúde, 1950.

Weinstein, Barbara. *For Social Peace in Brazil: Industrialists and the Remaking of the Working Class in São Paulo, 1920–1964.* Chapel Hill: University of North Carolina Press, 1996.

———. "Racializing Regional Difference: São Paulo versus Brazil, 1932." In *Race and Nation in Modern Latin America*, edited by Nancy P. Appelbaum, Anne S. Macpherson, and Karin Alejandra Rosenblatt, 237–62. Chapel Hill: University of North Carolina Press, 2003.

Williams, Daryle. *Culture Wars in Brazil: The First Vargas Regime, 1930–1945.* Durham, N.C.: Duke University Press, 2001.

Winslow, Charles-Edward Armory. *The Conquest of Epidemic Disease*. Princeton, N.J.: Princeton University Press, 1944.

Yelvington, Kevin A. "The Anthropology of Afro-Latin America and the Caribbean: Diasporic Dimensions." *Annual Review of Anthropology* 30 (2001): 227–60.

———. "The Invention of Africa in Latin America and the Caribbean: Political Discourse and Anthropological Praxis, 1920–1940." In *Afro-Atlantic Dialogues: Anthropology in the Diaspora*, edited by Kevin A. Yelvington, 35–82. Santa Fe, N.M.: School of American Research Press, 2006.

INDEX